Imperfections but Gifted and Chosen

SONIA ANDERSON

Fulton Books, Inc.
Meadville, PA

Published by Fulton Books 2021

Photographer: Kalea Ayanna, LLC

ISBN 978-1-63710-518-4 (paperback)
ISBN 978-1-63710-519-1 (digital)

Printed in the United States of America

To the one great love of my life. Thank you for time, patience, sacrifice, and love. You are forever my eternal soulmate.

Part 1

Chapter 1

Some would probably say that life, at times, can be considered unpredictable. For Savannah, this argument would be described as designed by fate. There may be events in your life that you have experienced and choose to forget. In her case, Savannah remembers moments when she was only four years old. These thoughts or memories would come frequently, and then there are times years would pass before she would dream of these memories.

As a child, she would be described as quiet and somewhat shy around other people. Although these were some of the characteristics that described her, they did not completely define who she was or going to become. She lived in a small two-bedroom house where she shared a bedroom with her little sister and baby brother. One late night, she was awakened by the sound of a toy piano playing that was on a shelf in her room. As she looked up toward the shelf, there lay a doll beside this piano. Savannah climbed out of bed and went to her parents' room where she stood by her father's side of the bed and asked if she could get into bed with them.

She remembers that her father grumbled words that she did not understand at the time. As she stood there in the dark room, she could feel a presence there in the room with her. The next morning, her parents were discussing what they thought happened that night. The next thing she knew, her mom took her piano away, and she never saw it again.

Time has passed, and the family had gone through many challenges. It was years later when she learned what had taken place that night when she went into her parents' room. Her mom told her that she and Miles had a priest come to the house and pray over it because there was a spiritual attachment to the piano. Her dad told her that he remembers a noticeably short woman had come into their bedroom that night. He stated that as Savannah climbed into the bed, this entity sat on him and he asked, "What did she want?"

This is where they learned that the piano belonged to someone that had been deceased. From that day forward, Savannah had been experiencing unusual incidents throughout her childhood into her adult life. She grew up in a household with her mother and two siblings, Miles Jr. and Sapphire. Although her parents, Miles and Olivia, were married for several years, their relationship was not the best. Savannah's parents were separated for much of her life. She remembers that her dad would come home for a few months and then he was gone again. She never understood why daddy had to leave all the time and only returned years later.

At this point, she began to question herself as to why her father would never stay with them. Savannah remembers in some detail her young childhood from the age of four. For the most part, she was a happy child but still had some insecurities and questions. She did not understand that her family's lives will change on one early Sunday afternoon. The sun was shining, and the house was quiet as she and her siblings were down for a nap. There was a knock at the door, and she heard her father's voice.

With excitement, she jumped out of bed and headed to her parents' bedroom only to hear them arguing. The bedroom door was cracked just enough that her tiny little face could peek inside. She witnessed something very devastating for any four-year-old to see and hear. Her mother was lying across the bed, sitting up, with her hand trying to shield her face. Savannah's father was arguing with her, and he had a gun in his hand, pointing it at her mother. She was begging him not to hurt her, and she pleaded for her life.

There was a loud sound, and her father dropped the gun in shock and ran to her mother. Savannah stood there as if she were paralyzed and could not move. Her father grabbed a towel and wrapped it around her mother's hand where the bullet had entered.

8

At this point, her parents did not realize that she was there at the door. Savannah's father ran out of the door across the street to the gas station to call the ambulance for her mother. She remembers her mother walking to the living room and looking out of the large picture window as her dad was across the street.

Savannah had a little red rocking chair that sat in front of the window. One of the things she could think to ask her mother was why she was bleeding on her little red rocking chair. Her mother was very calm and assured her that everything was going to be okay. Weeks later, things were not all right as her mom had promised. Her dad was gone once again, and it was years before she saw him again. Meanwhile, life continued as predicted, and she still had issues with her father's absence and the pain he inflicted on her mother. Now at the age of nine, her dad was back in their lives once again.

Although she struggled with these issues, she loved her father very much and was so forgiving as she witnessed from her mother. The family was happy again because Dad was home, and what made things extra special, they moved into a new house. This house was in the same neighborhood as her grandparents. The house belonged to her grandfather's best friend that had just lost his wife of many years. Everything was back to normal once again, but she still had feelings of anxiousness and fear that it was not going to last. She was faced with more disappointment and insecurities as her life had to go through another familiar adjustment. By the time she was twelve years old, things started to become normal again with school and friends. She was doing so well in school and had quite a little social life. Her mother would give her slumber parties and cookouts in which she invited her classmates.

Life was good again, and then her father was back in the picture once more. This was very emotional and difficult for her because she knew that dad was not going to stay. He would always promise that he was home for good, and then one to two months later, he was gone again until it all fell apart, which resulted in her mother having a nervous breakdown. Miles had asked Olivia for a divorce, and as one could imagine, her fears, once again, came true and this devasted her. She had to grow up amazingly fast and make decisions that left her with the responsibility of tending to her mother and younger siblings. The family was in turmoil, and her mom could not function. She remembered the ladies from the church would take shifts coming by the house to sit with her mom and to check on the children. Savannah remembered the pastor and members of the church praying for her mother.

Meanwhile, Savannah took on the responsibility of cooking meals, doing laundry, and making sure her brother and sister were looked after. The nights were the worst because her mom would cry a lot and moaned with pain. She suffered a broken heart, and it was as if she had given up on life. Although things felt as if there was not going to be an end, one day, things began to change. Her mother's healing process had begun, and she was out of bed and eating, talking, and smiling again. The family was in a happy place again, and Savannah felt that she could breathe a little. As expected, there were still emotional scars, and she did not know how to handle them. Her mother never spoke about the trauma that she went through and was not able to assure her children that everything was going to be okay.

Olivia did not know how to express herself in a nurturing way to her children. Sometimes she would speak about Miles, but it was never in a positive light, and the children were always there as her audience. This is when Savannah decided that she was going to harden her heart so that she would never be hurt like her mother.

Chapter 2

Life had moved forward, and now Savannah was doing well in junior high school. She was an honor roll student, participated on the school track team, a cheerleader on the wrestling team, and had many friends. Things were feeling quite normal, and she had fun with her best friend in the world, Tamera Redding. The two of them did everything together from going to the mall on Saturdays, listening to music, dancing, playing in the neighborhood, and, of course, talking about boys. Their families would also do things together like cooking out and playing board games on the front porch in the summer months. Charles and Hannah Redding were genuinely nice neighbors.

Several of the kids in the neighborhood loved to come hang out on the front porch and listen to Mr. Redding tell stories about life. He kept them intrigued and captured our imaginations. They would have so many questions, and he was very generous and patient with all of them. Mrs. Redding was the mother figure and well respected. She would also give advice on life and share stories about her childhood. Joshua, their son, was the typical little brother that wanted to follow Tamera and Savannah everywhere that they went. The two got smart about it and would sneak out so that he would not see us leaving the house.

The girls were aware that Mr. Redding was sending Joshua to spy and to report back everything they may have been doing. Savannah's little sister, too, was always wanting to tag along with them, and as they did, Joshua would ditch her. One of the activities the girls participated in was Girl Scout at one of the neighborhood churches the Redding was members. Everyone was always excited about the cookie drives and the anticipation of what troop would win the grand prize. Miles and Joshua also were in the Cub and Boy Scouts too. Mrs. Redding was a den mother, along with one other neighbor, and Olivia also participated with the banquets.

One fall evening, there was a Boy Scout banquet which was at the church across the street from Savannah's house. It made perfect sense because that is where the weekly meetings took place. Her little brother was a Cub Scout, and she walked him across the street once a week. There were a lot of boys from the neighborhood that she went to school with and then some that she did not know. This is the moment when she laid eyes on the most beautiful boy that she had ever seen. Of course, she was shy and did not speak or talk to him because she would be embarrassed.

Later that night at the banquet, she learned that his name was Johnathan and that he was Miles's friend. She thought it was strange to see this guy way much older to be hanging out talking to this little ten years old. What she did not know was that the older Boy Scouts were mentoring the Cub Scouts. So they were building relationships and providing a strong bond between brothers. The banquet and awards ceremony were coming to an end, and the parents were talking and the kids running about. Savannah noticed Johnathan staring at her, smiling as he was talking to Miles. This made her extremely nervous as she did not know how to respond.

In the meantime, Tamera approached her and was talking about what a great time she was having as they were leaving the church building. The entire time she was going on about who her next boyfriend would be. Savannah was still captivated by her would-be admirer. When she wanted to go over and say hello, her mind was telling her this would not be a good idea. She kept giving herself reasons as to why it would be a mistake. She was shy and quiet and did not want to risk embarrassment. Besides, he showed interest first, and it was only fair that he came over to speak as she could see that was not happening that night. She and Tamera said their good-byes even though they just lived two houses down from each other.

Savannah entered the house, dashing up the stairs to her bedroom. All she could think of was writing her thoughts into her diary. Miles followed her upstairs, snickering and teasingly telling her that he had a secret.

Of course, she did not buy into his childlike antics and told him to get out of her room. Sunday had come and gone, and it was early Monday morning with the business of getting ready for school. Savannah was attending Westport Junior High School. Her brother and sister were in the kitchen eating breakfast after getting dressed for school. Mom was giving last-minute instructions as she was herding her sister and brother to get ready for their walk to school. Savannah left the house to walk down the street to meet Tamera where they both walked two blocks to catch the school bus. The bus stop was packed with kids from the neighborhood. The girls were huddled together, chatting about their weekend and the latest fashion. Of course, the guys were listening to a large boom box and talking about the usual boy things.

It was a typical Monday morning, and the school hallways were busy with students rushing to homeroom just before the last bell was to ring. You would hear the roar of young voices, along with the clashing and clanging of locker doors as they were slammed shut. There would occasionally be some short of discord or roughhousing from the jocks. Then it was also the would-be *slackers* that only came to school to skip classes just to hang out. And do not forget those groups of girls that would be considered mean girls. Yes, in 1980, those girls really existed. Savannah had a few girlfriends that she was awfully close to besides her best friend that was an upperclassman. Most of her friends were boys that hung out at her house on the weekends. She was an honor roll student, and her favorite subject was English. Everyone had that one teacher that was extremely strict about her classroom, and you did not attempt to misbehave. Mrs. Kasey was very stern and believed in prayer before each class period. Savannah loved her English class and looked forward to what words of wisdom that would be bestowed on her for the day. Mrs. Kasey was an inspiration and did care about her students. She always gave life lessons and shared stories from her childhood. She also would stay late after school to work with students that were having difficulties with the lessons. Being in junior high school had its challenges at times, but everything that has to do with growing up was a challenge.

The weekend has arrived again and not soon enough. Savannah loved spending time with her favorite aunt that was five years older at her grandmother's on the weekends. Her grandmother lived in the urban projects where everyone knew one another, and the kids played at the parks and community swimming pool. There she enjoyed the company of her aunt and her teenage friends. They sat up all night playing cards and board games and listened to music on the stereo. Savannah would learn the latest new dances from her aunt and her friends, which was so much fun. On Saturday afternoon, they would all catch the city bus and go downtown where they would eat at the Woolworth's lunch counter. They would also take in a movie at the Jefferson Theater where everyone would get a large bucket of butter popcorn and a Pepsi.

When the weekend came to an end, her mom would send for her to come home on Sunday. She would get back home just in time to hang out with some of her friends before it got dark. All the kids in the block would congregate on the corner under the streetlights. There would be kids on bikes and boom boxes blaring as everyone was laughing and talking about whatever the next hot topic was for the day. Savannah noticed in the crowd of boys a familiar face she had not seen in a while. Johnathan looked as she remembered the night at her brother's Boy Scout banquet. The two shared a long glance at each other as if no one else was around. She was still mesmerized by his smile and what she thought were beautiful eyes. He was tall and thin as most boys his age. They finally spoke to each other as the other kids in the block were engaged in their own separate conversations. Her brother was still running around giggling and making faces at her as he saw his older friend was talking to his big sister. It started to get late, and everyone had to go home because it was a school night. Of course, everyone would pick up where they left off the next morning at the bus stop.

Savannah could not sleep that night because she was thinking about Johnathan. She could not believe what was happening to her and why she was having these feelings. She had to remind herself that she vowed to never fall for any boy that would eventually betray and hurt her. The next day at school, classes went as usual and she hung out at lunch with her friends at the lunch table. The day seemed as if it would not move fast enough; all she wanted to do was get home in hopes of seeing Johnathan again. He was living with his grandmother at the time but was attending another middle school. She arrived home to take care of her daily chores and complete her homework. Later that evening, after her mom came home from work was when she and her siblings could go out to see friends or have company. There was a knock at the door, and her mom answered it, and by her surprise, it was Johnathan. He told her mother that he was there to see Miles. She welcomed him into the house and was talking to him for a moment how his day had been and how his grandmother was that lived in the house right behind theirs. Olivia was friends with his grandmother and visited with her from time to time. Savannah came down the stairs when she heard voices to see who their visitor may be. She was stunned and could not speak when she saw it was Johnathan. Needless to say, he became a permanent fixture in their household for months.

He was at their house every day and occasionally went with them to the grocery store and other routine places they traveled. Savannah became comfortable with him being around. Over time, the attraction had grown, and Johnathan built up the nerve to ask her to be his girlfriend. Although the anticipation had been building for months, her first response was no because she vowed to keep her promise to herself. This was not a deterrent because he was very consistent with his persistence and was never giving up. At first, she thought it was just a silly crush and not to take it seriously.

As time went on, she started to receive the attention of many boys. She did not understand what had prompted this attention. Most of the boys in the neighborhood were her friends, and she did not think of them in that way. So she did what she was good at—avoidance and dismissive. Her primary focus was school and her dream of joining the United States Air Force. She participated every week in the junior ROTC program at her school. This is where she met for the first time Sergeant Rhodes, Sergeant Spangler, and Major Easthom. These three individuals made an impression on her and were great role models. It was part of her plan to leave home after graduation and join the military where she would make a longtime career. This was supposed to be her fail-safe plan to have a fresh start and continue to live up to her vow to not trust a man with her heart.

She was still holding a lot of resentment because of her *daddy issues*, and this was the only way she could run from her broken family. She believed that her mother did her absolute best to raise her and her siblings, but there was also Olivia's broken heart and emotional baggage. Savannah wanted to believe in love and romance but did not trust it because there would always be a sacrifice. So on those weekends that she visited her grandmother, she began to read from her collection of novels. Romance novels were her favorite, and she would get so caught up in the fantasy of love, still in denial and fighting how she felt about Johnathan. She would never allow herself to act on those feelings and let him know how she really felt. Then things had changed for her one day.

There was another suitor in the picture, and she did not know how to react to the attention. It was on a crisp fall morning at school when there was a surprise fire drill, and the students and staff left the building as instructed. Everyone assembled in the rear of the building in the field where the football team met every day after school to practice. There was the sound of students chatting with their peers as they waited in the chilly morning air. The faculty was coordinating the groups of children to keep some sort of order. The sun was very bright, and you could see the air roll off your breath as you spoke. There were small groups of students huddled together to keep warm.

Finally, the bell rang, and the principal announced it was okay to return to the building. The faculty and students reentered the building with the anticipation of the warmth of the hallways and classrooms. The smaller groups became larger as everyone was moving at a slow pace as if a herd of cattle was being driven back into the building. Savannah was walking to her locker when she felt a tug on the belt of her coat from the back. She turned to find Donovan, an upperclassman, had grabbed her belt and was holding it as she walked. He called her name to get her attention, but all she could do is smile at him. The words *hello* never left her lips, and she was stunned that one of the most popular boys in the school was showing interest in her. At first, she thought maybe he was just kidding around because everyone knew her from the neighborhood, and she used to be best friends with his younger sister. Later that day, as she was going to her locker to change books before the next class period, Donovan showed up at her locker, and he asked if he could call her sometimes. Without thinking, she answered yes before realizing she had written her number down and said that he could call her. By the end of the school day, she walked to her bus with continued disbelief that she had done this.

What was I thinking? she thought as she boarded her school bus for the return home All she could think about was hoping he would lose her number and not call. As she walked home from the bus stop, that was all she could think about. Tamera was talking to her about her day and the latest gossip once she got home and began her daily routine before starting her homework. Her mom had come home after 5:00 p.m. to dinner that was prepared by Savannah. She nervously watched the phone, wishing it would not ring. Well, that hope ended when the phone did ring, and hoping it was not being the call she was dreading, she answered the phone with extreme hesitation after the third ring. Picking up the receiver, she said hello and the voice of Donovan was on the other end. Suddenly, her stomach felt sick, and she was so nervous she could hardly speak.

She responded and asked if he could hold until she went to take the call on the phone that was in her bedroom. She went upstairs to her bedroom and yelled down the stairs to let her mom know she picked up the other line. She could not believe how terrified she was to talk to him. He started the conversation, and she could only respond with short answers. Savannah could not believe that one of the most popular guys in school was calling to talk to her. There were all sorts of thoughts running through her mind. What was his angle, and what games was he playing with her? She knew there were other girls his age that was interested in him. *Why me?* she asked herself repeatedly. She could not stand it any longer and just wanted off the phone. So she made up a story that her mom was calling and could he hold for a moment.

She laid the receiver on her bed and went downstairs where her mom was making such a big deal out of her first phone call from a boy. Her mother approved of this boy because she knew his parents and was particularly good friends with his mother. In her mind, she was thinking that if she kept him on hold for a long period of time, he would just get a hint that she did not want to talk to him. Well, she thought at the time her plan would work. She went back to her room and picked up the phone and called his name, but he had hung up.

Great, her plan had worked, and she did not have to deal with that situation anymore. The next day, as she got off the school bus to enter the building of the school, she was praying that she would not have to see him. Well, she did not have that luck. She saw him down the hall by the lockers, talking with some of his friends. Savannah thought maybe if she walked past him with her head down, she did not have to give direct eye contact. She was exceptionally good at ignoring people as this was one of her defense mechanisms. The day went on as expected; she hustled between classes, stopping briefly to talk with friends, as they hurried to class before the tardy bell filled the hallways. She was just about to enter her English class as she saw Donovan at his locker, talking to one of the girls from her neighborhood. She was flirting with him, and Savannah did not like it. Why did she care? He looked over to see her watching him with this girl. He had this smile on his face that led Savannah to believe that he was enjoying the attention this girl was giving him.

At this point, she built up the wall she was famous for and dismissed what was happening at that moment. Later that day, when she returned home from school and went on with her daily routine, Mom was not home yet from work. She started dinner after completing her homework. Miles Jr., who was known as MJ, was in his room playing and Sapphire watching television. Five o'clock came and went and Mom was home. It was too cold to go outside that day. So she stayed in and read one of her Harlequin romance novels that her grandmother gave to her. On Saturday morning, there was a knock on the door. Mom went to answer, and there was Johnathan standing there with that beautiful smile. He came over to hang out for the day. Savannah had not seen him for a while and wondered what had been going on with him. He was staying with his maternal grandmother occasionally.

He lived with his dad, brother, and paternal grandmother due to his parents' divorce. She could very well relate to what he was going through because her parents were also separated. They began to spend a lot of time together, hanging out, watching movies, and talking about things that were not especially important. She and Johnathan became friends, and she was comfortable with that. He still insisted that he wanted to be her boyfriend, but she would not give the answer that he hoped for. She loved seeing him every day and always expected something exciting and new. Savannah still had many other young boys that were competing for her attention. It had become frequent that every time she would walk off her front porch and down the street that some guy was trying to talk to her. She ignored them to the point that she blocked out their voices. There had been times when a boy would walk with her to the neighborhood store in hopes of getting her phone number. Some of the guys that were intimidated by her would ask her best friend, Hal, to speak for them. She would always tell him no, and he would report the response back to the guy. This was one of the things that were a turnoff for her. She believed that if the boy were interested in her, he would come talk to her himself.

One thing about Savannah that most of the boys did not know was that they had to be aggressive in their approach. They had to have confidence within themselves and be very respectful to her. The days came and went as swiftly as time changes. She was becoming more attracted to Johnathan now and was extremely nervous around him whenever he came over to hang out. It was evident that she was falling for him, but her instinct warned her about the possibilities of getting hurt. One night, she, Johnathan, and her brother were outside hanging out and horsing around. He had grabbed her, tickling and wrestling her down on the porch. She screamed with both panic and laughter because she was very ticklish and did not want to wet her pants. She laughed so hard that she could barely breathe. Then it was as if everything had stopped; she remembered her little brother still horsing around with the two of them. They stared into each other's eyes, and she knew that something was different in his eyes.

Of course, she panicked and pushed him off her. Her heart was pounding with excitement and fear. She did not know what was happening at that moment. The mood had changed, and she was not sure what to do next. She was temporarily distracted when she looked up the street where she saw a guy riding a bike, heading toward her house. At the time she heard her neighbor Juanita call out the boy's name, Donovan, as he was turning the corner. He stopped and turned his bike around and went to talk with her and her friends. The only thing Savannah could think about was why Donovan was headed to her house.

She no longer had communications with him as she ignored him and did not take any more of his phone calls. Moments later, he was back on his bike and stopped at the end of her driveway. She was still talking with Johnathan on the front porch. Donovan asked her to come to him, but she ignored his request. Then he called her again in a more demanding tone. She looked up at Johnathan, and his facial expression was less than happy to know that another guy was there to see her. Savannah could not speak because she could see the hurt on his face. She did not want to talk to Donovan. Her eyes were still focused on Johnathan. She was trying to read his face, but in return, he told her that he did not care if she talked to him.

It was not the response that she had expected from Johnathan. She asked him if that was what he really wanted. He repeated that he did not care and for her to go talk to him. So out of hurt from his response, she said, "Okay, I will." Savannah did not want to talk to him, but she was stunned and hurt by Johnathan's response. She walked off the front porch to make him jealous. As she reached Donovan, she looked back once more to see if he was still there. He went into her house and slammed the door. She would have thought that he would just leave and go back home. Donovan asked her a few questions, trying to strike up a conversation, but she was not interested. Her mind was on Johnathan and how it must have felt for him to see her talking to another guy. In fact, she could not wait until it was over. Donovan did not hold her attention, and she really did not want to say two words to him. After about ten minutes of an extremely uncomfortable situation, she said good night and went into the house to find Johnathan still there.

When she entered the house, her mom was in the kitchen when the phone rang. It was Johnathan's grandmother calling for him to come home. You could tell that he was not ready to leave. There was so much he wanted to say to Savannah, but if only he could get her alone to have this discussion. She noticed that he did not have his glasses on and stated that he did not know where he has placed them in the house. Everyone started searching all over the house for his glasses. Savannah went upstairs to check her brother's room when Johnathan followed her.

As she turned to tell him that she did not see them, he was already in her space. They both looked at each other, and the words that needed to be spoken would not come. The moment in time had come and gone with disappointment that they did not say what was on each other's hearts and minds. She was hoping for another opportunity as they went downstairs to continue their search. Her mom had a large table at the foot of the stairs that collected a lot of things. Savannah started to search the table and noticed that his glasses were tucked away so that they would not easily be found. She told him that she found his glasses and went to hand them to him. She looked up into his eyes, and he stared down into hers.

She was handing the glasses to him but holding his hand at the same time. At that moment, she wanted to tell him that she wanted him and that she loved him. The words would not come as she was in a trance with the look of hurt and disappointment in his eyes. Why could she not tell him that she was in love with him? He walked out of the house, and her chest and throat felt as if they were going to explode because she felt that she would never see him again. For days, she waited in hopes that he would come over. There was no sign of him hanging out in the neighborhood. He was no longer staying at his grandmother's home. He had moved in with his mom. Then the days turned into weeks, months, and then years. She thought about him every day. She had to face the fact that she messed up and it was her fault. If only she could get the one chance to apologize and to tell him how she really felt about him.

Chapter 3

Time does not stand still as life continues to move forward with no mercy. It was the final semester of her final year in middle school. The excitement and anticipation for moving onto high school was in the air. She could feel that her classmates were anxious about passing those final exams and having those meetings with their guidance counselors. Most of her peers were focused on the idea of becoming high school freshmen. Then there was the other half that was nervous because they did not know what to expect. Finally, on graduation day, all her peers were dressed in white dresses and black suits with ties. You could see the proud parents, faculty, and staff smiling with expressions of overwhelming happiness.

After all the congratulatory speeches and farewells, her peers that were headed to different high schools said their goodbyes. This was the last summer that most of them would hang out because they were in different school districts. It was a particularly good summer break. She and her siblings visited her father and family members in Virginia Beach for two weeks. Savannah loved the beach and the smell of the ocean. She remembered how cold the water was when she first entered. After playing at the beach for half the day, her father and stepmother took them home to clean up for dinner. Her grandfather and uncles came over to the house where her dad grilled out as the kids played in the large backyard. She remembered the sounds of her dad's laughter as her grandfather told stories. Savannah loved her dad very much; she was considered a daddy's girl to most.

There was also her favorite uncle, Mick, that she adored and was so overly excited to see him. She was filled with joy and happiness because her birthday was the next day. Savannah already knew what she wanted for this special day. She did not want girlie clothes, shoes, or handbags at the least. All she could think of was the ten-speed tan boys' bike that she saw in the Montgomery Ward's Department store a few days ago. She did not have to put a lot of effort into asking her dad because he would give her the world. The next day, she and her stepmother and siblings were off to the store to purchase her new bike. Savannah could not wait to get the bike to the house so that she could ride throughout the neighborhood. Dad knew that Miles Jr. and Sapphire would want a brand-new bike as well, so they reaped the benefits from Savannah's birthday. When they got back home, Cousin Sydney was already at the house, waiting with her bike.

The girls were going bicycling, but they had to take Sapphire with them. Sydney took them over one of her friends' houses that lived nearby. There were quite a few girls and a couple boys all hanging out in the driveway. They were all friendly as Sydney introduced them to everyone. Savannah noticed that the boys were cute and weird at the same time. She thought that most boys their age were so immature and annoying at times. After hanging out for a while, the girls had to start their journey back home which was about two to three blocks away. They had beat the streetlights coming on for the evening. Her stepmother, Gina, asked if she had met any of the kids in the neighborhood. Sydney spoke for her, stating that she met Derrick and Donald, as she winked her eye. Gina laughed as Savannah had a look of terror on her face and embarrassment.

It was all in good fun, and they all started to laugh and joke about it. Dad had just gotten home and was out in the garage, tinkering with an engine he and Granddad were working on. They were talking about going finishing tomorrow night on the rocks, an area in Norfolk that they fished for years. This spot literally was on the bay, and at night, they would bring gas lanterns with all their fishing gear and coolers. Meanwhile, the girls were in the kitchen, planning a sleepover and ordering pizza. They stayed up all night talking about boys and watching horror movies until, one by one, they were falling asleep on the floor piled with pillows and blankets.

The sun was shining very brightly into the large kitchen window. Savannah woke by the smell of bacon, eggs, coffee, and other delightful aromas seeping out of the kitchen. Gina was busy at the stove cooking as Dad was sitting at the kitchen table, reading his paper and drinking a cup of coffee. She sat down at the table, still sleepy eyed, resting her forehead on her folded arms. Dad lowered the paper, looking over his eyeglasses, asking her, "Late night?" She moaned as he chuckled at her with his hilarious laughter. The breakfast was superb as always because Gina was an excellent cook. This was the last day of our summer visit with Dad and Gina.

So we were going on a family fishing trip that night on the bay with granddad and her uncles. Savannah was not ready to go back home just yet, but she did miss her mom. She had spoken to her later that day on the phone to tell her about all the fun things they did. It was time to pack our things up because we were leaving the next morning to head back home. Later that evening, they all piled into Dad's truck and headed to the bay. When they arrived, Granddad and her uncles had already set up on the rocks. You had to be incredibly careful walking on them because you did not want to slip and fall into the ocean bay water. Everyone was casting their reels into the dark water. Savannah was so fascinated with the excitement of catching a live fish.

Granddad called her over to him, and he showed her how to bait with live bloodworms. Yes, it was gross but thrilling to see how effortless it was for them to bait so quickly and catch fish as soon as their bait hit the water. There were large buckets and coolers filled with salt water. All night, they were catching and filling the coolers with live Atlantic croaker and spots. That was one of the best times ever, and she would never forget the stories and the laughter of her family that night on the rocks. The next morning, Dad was up packing the car. It was still dark, and the kids were still asleep. They all loaded into the car and were headed back to Roanoke. Although Savannah was a little sad to be leaving her dad and stepmom, she was also excited to see her mom and friends again.

There was still plenty of time to enjoy the rest of the summer with her best friend, Tamera. She knew that there was a lot of catching up, and Tamera was sure to give her all the details. Five hours later, they were back. Dad dropped Gina off to his mom's because he dared not to bring her to the house. Grown-up drama is the worst, especially when it involves one man and two women. They said their goodbyes to Dad, and he told them that he loved them. Savannah was sad to see him leave although this was the norm for her family. One would think that a person would become immune to the disappointment and grief. The one thing that she has endured and focused on was the time that she does get with him. She loved her dad so very much no matter what his faults may have been—a true father and daughter's love that could not be broken.

The absence of time and so many missed first events still did not change the fact that she loved him unconditionally. There was still a place in her heart that still had trouble with trust and the love for that special guy that may enter her life someday. She knew that there may be many that come and say that they are the one. Her primary focus entering high school with many expectations and set goals for her life. The one thing she did not want to do is focus on meeting that perfect guy. She did not want her parents' life because there is no such person that existed on this earth. In her mind, she will continue to stay focused on studying hard so that she can take care of herself. She wanted to do things that her mom was afraid of doing. Living life to the fullest with no regrets for not taking chances.

All that she can think about now is not walking in her parents' shoes. She wanted much more for her life. Savannah still was interested in traveling the world, and she knew that joining the United States Air Force, once she graduated, was her ticket. So at last there was a plan, and all she had to do was not get distracted by any means.

Chapter 4

School starts in two weeks, and all her girlfriends were excited about starting a new year. Tamera would be in the twelfth grade and upperclassman, senior, the elite as it is known as in high school. All she could talk about was the senior boys and the athletes. The special perks that come along with being a senior, and especially the very last year, was she would have to ride a school bus to school every day. Savannah had her fears because she did not know what to expect. She knew that she would see most of her friends from junior high school there. It was also a possibility that she may see friends that she grew up with in elementary. Would they remember her, or what if she did not recognize any of them? She was also nervous because Donovan would be there, but she got over that fear quickly.

He had moved on with Juanita, and they had a child together. The one person she did hope to see would be Johnathan because it had been several years since she saw him last. It was Saturday afternoon, and the girls went bicycling—one of their favorite things to do. They rode to one of the neighborhood playgrounds down the street from Tamera's cousin Nicole. The park was crowded that day with guys on the court, playing basketball. There were children laughing and playing on the swings and jungle gym.

Savannah and her girlfriends parked their bikes to go sit on the swings and catch up. They all had stories to share and could not wait for the first day of school. There was discussion about what outfits they would be wearing and how much fun they each had school-clothes shopping. Savannah told them about her two-week vacation at the beach and the people she met while visiting. They laughed and talked about some of the gossip that was floating around over the summer. It was always about who was dating who and how long. Nicole began to talk about her crush but was afraid to say anything to the guy. She had three older brothers, and everyone knew them in the neighborhood. Most guys would be intimidated by that fact. Her face lit up every time she mentioned his name. The problem she faced was the fact that he had already graduated from high school. He knew how she felt about him because she was friends with his younger sister. It did not matter to Nicole; she wanted to be with him.

Tamera told her to tell him how she feels about him. One of the things that we loved so much about Tamera was her go-get-them attitude. If one could describe her would be a feisty, opinionated, strongminded, carefree, but loving person. She was not afraid to speak her mind and let people know how she felt about things. It was starting to get dark, so the girls rode their bikes back to Nicole's house, and then they left, heading back home. It was still early when Savannah arrived home, exhausted from bicycling; she raided the refrigerator for leftovers. She went to her room where she hung out, listening to her stereo. She loved music, especially lying on the bed in the dark, listening to the quiet Storm Station.

The phone rang in her room, and she answered to hear the voice of Cameron. He was one of her friends that she hung out with in the neighborhood. They have known each other since kindergarten and had been friends ever since. She and Cameron always had a fun time talking about what was going on in the neighborhood with their other friends. The two were amazingly comfortable with each other and could talk about anything. Savannah was suspicious that Cameron was feeling something more, but she dismissed it. How could that be? They were the closest of friends and had so much fun goofing around with no high expectations. The next morning, Savannah had to get up and be ready for church. Mom did not drive or own a car at the time, so her aunt picked them up every Sunday. The closer they approached the church, one could hear angelic and soulful voices electrifying the air. Everyone emptied out of the car and walked up to the church steps and into the double doors. Like every Sunday, the church was filled to capacity to the point deacons placed folding chairs into the aisles to compensate for overflow.

If you have ever attended or was a member of an Apostolic Pentecostal church, this was the norm. They had their favorite seats on the pews, which they sat every week. The adults always sit one pew behind the children so that they could keep a close eye on them. As Savannah and her cousins all piled on one pew, some of their church friends accompanied them. The pastor, along with elders and ministers, were all seated on the pulpit. The choir was seated in the stand behind them and the musicians were on either side. The sound of the organ, baby grand piano, and drums made you feel as if your heart was going to beat out of your chest.

The choir was preparing to sing their first selection, and as the introduction began, the choir bellowed deep from the diaphragm. The soloist began to sing, and the choir swayed from side to side, clapping, and the tempo picked up. You could see people in the audience began to stand and clap, with some playing tambourines. Occasionally, some would begin to shout, dance, and praise the Lord in the Spirit. After about an hour of music, announcements, prayer, and shut-in request and offering, the pastor would begin his sermon for the morning. There was always a topic that was related to present-day issues and situations that many people were facing at the time. When service was over and the church was dismissed, everyone gathered in groups and fellowshipped. Savannah could not wait to get home and eat because they would be due to return to church for night service. Another week had passed, and she was in her daily routine. It was fall, so the days were warmer, and then it would turn cooler at night. She and her friends still would hang out on the front porch in the evenings after school. Everyone would huddle up once the wind picked up and the temperature dropped. At this point, Savannah could not stay outside any longer and said her goodbyes.

She went into the house upstairs to her room and lay across her bed. The music was playing on her stereo, and she was writing in her diary the events that took place for the day. She was thinking about Cameron, so she called him just to talk because she was bored. The two laughed and talked about when they were kids in elementary school. She could never forget your first-grade teacher, Mrs. Wilkerson. They talked for about an hour before they realized how late it had been. That night, as she was sleeping, she had memories flooding her by the way of dreams. Everything seemed so vivid, and it was difficult to distinguish between what was real and not real.

For some reason, she began to dream about Johnathan, and playing back in her mind was what she could have done differently. She could see Donovan and still hear his voice as she was focused on Johnathan. The dreams were coming more frequent now, and she felt the pain of hurting the first guy she ever fell in love with and did not tell him. The next day, she went to school with these dreams still hanging in the back of her mind. What did this mean? She kept asking herself as she tried to analyze and replay that night. It has been several years since that night, and she wanted to move forward with her life. She was still missing him and was wishing that someday she would see him again. Savannah learned that was not going to be as easy as she thought. She reverted to the promise she made when she was a little girl to never give in to love. It was very painful, and she still had some fear and resentment from her parents' life. But for some reason, life was not going to work out that way. Each week, she was getting unwanted attention from guys, and she did not understand it. Most of her friends were boys, and she did not understand the change. She had not changed the way that she dressed or carried herself.

Savannah had to figure out that sometimes a person is destined to walk the path that God has put you on. One day, she was walking on campus at school, and this guy approached her in the breezeway between Smith and Coulter halls. He was smiling like there was no tomorrow as he approached her. He told her how pretty she was as he grabbed her hand, introducing himself. Raymond was his name, and he could not tear himself from her. He was so captivated by her and could not stop smiling. She did remember seeing him around campus, and he rode her school bus. He asked if he could call her, and in response, she told him no. Raymond then proceeded to ask if she was dating anyone, and her answer was still no.

It was evident that he was not going to give up. Weeks have passed, and she was being approached by guys that did not attend her high school. Most of these guys were upperclassmen and well-known in their neighborhood and hers. Of course, there was still Raymond confessing his feelings for her. At first, the attention was annoying, then it became intriguing as she slowly began to like the attention. Although all attention was not welcomed, she was very selective to whom she entertained the idea of being pursued.

Chapter 5

There was one thing that was evident that no one knew about was her keen perception of people. She was what one would consider as a people watcher. Even when she was a small child, there was something about her ability to see what others choose not to see. Savannah was incredibly quiet and shy even around family members. Now she did have fun playing with her cousins on the weekends when she was young. She can remember the numerous huge birthday parties her mom gave her as a child. There was even a time when her mom gave her a slumber party and invited all her sixth-grade friends. For Savannah, that was one of the most exciting times that she could remember. Some of her girlfriends were the most popular girls in the sixth grade. When word got out that she was having a slumber party, she believed every boy in the surrounding neighborhood showed up at her house that Friday evening.

As the parents dropped the girls off at the house, their faces would light up with excitement. The girls all huddled on the front porch as the boys started arriving and circling the church parking a lot across the street. It looked as if it was a couple dozen boys riding bicycles all with their eyes focused on the girls that were on the front porch. Savannah knew most of the boys because they were her friends too. When Mom saw what was happening, she made all the young ladies come into the house. That night, the house was filled with giggles and laughter. There were girls camped out in the living room and dining room floors with sleeping bags. Mom also invited one of Sapphire's friends and a cousin so that she would not be left out.

They remained upstairs with Mom because it was Savannah's party and her friends. There was so much food and drink and music, which played up until midnight when Mom pulled the plug. Savannah remembered so vividly the good times she used to have when she was young. Even in the sixth grade, she had a crush on a boy that was her friend since kindergarten. At the end of the school year, Mom gave one last party, which was her sixth-grade graduation party. She invited all the kids in her class, including the boys. Mom gave a cookout, and her aunt Joyce chaperoned and her boyfriend, Tony, was the DJ. Savannah knew all the latest dances because her aunt had taught her. On every slow song, Trent would come grab her hand and pull her to him to dance. She knew that he liked her because she had a crush on him too.

The two danced all night, except when one of her other guy friends would ask her to dance on all the faster songs. Savannah had the first party in the neighborhood. She and her family were new to the neighborhood back then. After that night, other older kids took suit and started having cookout parties. I guess this was the first time that she had ever let a boy that was a friend get that close in her personal space. The alarm clock went blaring at 6:30 a.m., and she woke up realizing she had been dreaming about some special times in her childhood.

It was 7:15 a.m. Just like clockwork, she was knocking on Patrice's door like every morning before school. She went upstairs to her bedroom and talked while Patrice got ready for school. They walked to the bus stop together every morning. Later that evening, after homework had been done, she went back to Patrice's house to hang out. Her brother and his best friend, Chris, would be horsing around and doing guy things. One of their other friends that lived in the house behind them with his grandmother would come hang out as well. Colby was one of the neighborhood boys that was labeled as a *bad* boy to some. Savannah could see that his actions were just a smoke screen to whatever was going on with him. They all used to laugh and talk about everything that was going on in school and the neighborhood. He, too, was also known as a womanizer and did not have respect for girls. The rumors about him were not pleasing or appealing to Savannah. She always kept her distance from him, especially when he began to show interest in her. She was determined that she was not going to be his next victim.

One day, they all were sitting on Patrice's front porch laughing and talking. Savannah was sitting on the stoop of the front porch, and Colby was leaned against the banister. She turned her head to look over her shoulder because she felt like someone was staring at her. Colby had his eyes focused dead point on her. He was looking at her differently as he wrinkled his nose to her. In response, she rolled her eyes and turned away from him. Then after that, each day he would always come over whenever she was there. He was starting to flirt with her, and as usual, she ignored his attempts.

Savannah could always treat a person like they were not in the room or at the same time and space as her. What she did not realize was that this made him more intrigued, and he pursued her more. As time went by, he was always there whenever she came to visit with Patrice. If she knew him, this was never a look that she had ever received. It was getting late, so she told everyone good night, and Patrice and her sister walked her halfway up the block to her house. Colby also walked with them, but he was still giving her this look. All night Savannah thought about this and tried to play back if she had given him any reason to think that she was interested in him. Maybe she was reading more into it than it really was at the time. She knew that she was not the type of girl that he usually came after. She was quiet, smart, sophisticated, and was well-liked.

There was never any time she was found to place herself in any compromising situation. Savannah knew that she should not give any more thought to this crazy notion. Little did she knew that the next day at school there was a new suitor. This person just appeared out of nowhere as she was on her way to class. As she was passing through the library in the direction of her gym class, she heard a person call out her name. She turned to see this guy smiling at her. Savannah did not know who he was and why he was calling her name. She had never seen him before and looked at him with an irritating expression. In the locker room, now dressing out for class, she dismissed him out of her head as quickly as he had appeared.

The last-period bell rang, dismissing school for the day, and she was headed to the bus to grab a good seat. Of course, she knew that if no one was sitting beside her, Raymond would be sure to sit there. She could have told him that she did not want him to sit there. The one thing about Savannah was she never treated anyone badly or spoke negatively to a person. She was truly one of the nicer girls that one could meet. She was flattered that Raymond was so taken by her. He was a nice guy from what she observed, but he was not her type.

But how could she know that if she did not give him the opportunity to prove himself? He spoke well and with respect whenever he saw her. She could see that he would just melt whenever he had the opportunity to sit with her. He knew where to run into her every day at school as they passed and headed to class. He would gently grab her hand as she was trying to pass and ask if he could call her. She would smile and tell him no as she was pulling away from him. The one thing she could say about Raymond was he was persistent but respectful in his pursuit of her. Now with all the attention, Savannah began to think hard about how she wanted to handle this situation. She had several guys coming at her all the same time. Most girls would be in heaven to have that many guys pursuing her. There was one thing that kept entering her mind, and she questioned, "What is their game?" She could not and would not allow some guy to use her for one thing only.

Savannah knew her personal worth, and she was not going to allow anyone to destroy the one thing that separated her from the rest. Yes, she was a virgin, and everyone knew it. For many boys in high school, their primary mission was to conquer their quest. Although she knew what her primary mission was in life, it was beginning to become a challenge. What scared her was the fact that her heart was getting in the way. Now that she was getting this attention, she felt that it was her duty to get a handle on it quickly. Well, that was the plan until Colby began to press more.

He decided that since she would not give him the attention, he was demanding he would take things into his own hands. Sitting in her last class for the day, which was biology, Colby popped in and took her algebra book and walked out of the class. She knew he wanted her to follow him out of class, but she did not fall for that trick. Besides, they rode the same bus home every day, and she knew that she could get her book then. When Savannah boarded the school bus, she took her seat, waiting for Colby to get on the bus. Once he got on the bus, he walked past her without looking and sat in the back. The ride home was the same—everyone talking and the boys in the back laughing and joking around. It came to her stop, and everyone got off and walked in the direction of their homes. She was walking with three of the other kids in the neighborhood on her way home.

Colby was walking in front of them, and he was moving quickly that she would have to speed up to catch him. She was not going to chase him to get her book back. So she thought that she would wait until his grandmother got home to collect her textbook. The other kids turned to the street to go into their houses, and that left her alone walking toward her street. By the time she had reached the end of his street, passing his house, she heard him call out to her. He had stuck his head out of the front door. She knew in her gut this was not going to be a good idea. She remembered the rumors that people spoke about him getting girls to come into his house.

There was a part of her that wanted to listen to herself and another that was strangely curious. Why was she going to his house when she knew that his grandmother was not at home? When she reached the door, he was standing there and opened it. He asked her to come in so that he could return her book. She was not going to play that game, so she turned to walk off the porch. He said wait and opened the door again. She stepped in as he went to the kitchen and returned with her book. She stayed close to the door so that she could leave quickly.

As he walked toward her, he had that same look in his eyes that she had seen before. She knew that this could not be good. Savannah started to back up the closer he got. She backed into the door, which closed behind her. There they were close enough to feel each other's breath. She felt frozen and could not move. All she could think about was how she was going to get out of this. She asked the question, "What?" as he moved closer. Her eyebrow lifted with curiosity as she was intrigued by the flirtation. There were no words as he leaned in closer to her. She was very still as she felt the coolness of his lips touching hers. Yes, he kissed her with the gentlest touch. It was not what she had expected from him. She always thought he would be that guy that was very abrasive and demanding physically. Before she could think, she kissed him back as if it were familiar. She did not know how long the kiss lasted, but she held the back of his head and invited him to kiss her more. She stepped back, and all she could think about was getting out of there. Colby leaned in again as she kissed him once more. He grabbed her hand and pulled her to him and said, "Come on," as he was trying to lead her to his bedroom.

Savannah braced herself and pulled in the opposite direction, telling him no in a very exact tone, and he let her hand go. His reaction came as a surprise to her. She had always heard the rumors of him forcing girls to do things. Savannah could not believe that he stopped and did not force the issue. She turned from him and walked out the door and headed home. This was her very first kiss with a person she would have not chosen to be her first kiss. When she had the opportunity to have that first kiss, she wanted Johnathan to be the one. All she could think about was what she just did. How was it that she allowed him to kiss her and surprisingly she was very receptive? He was good kisser; she had to give him that credit.

Then it dawned on her that she had been attracted to Colby all this time. The questions just came rushing, and it was too fast for her to figure them out. The kiss was more than she could have imagined. It was so sweet and gentle, something that she would expect from two people that were in love. But here was the tricky part of it all: she was not in love with him, and he surely did not love her. She did not know if he had real feelings for her or if she was on his list of girls to conquer. The next day was Saturday, and her mom was at work, and she was doing her weekend chores as usual. Her sister and brother were upstairs in their rooms, and she was in the living room cleaning.

It was about 10:00 a.m., and there was a knock at the door. When she opened the door, it was Colby standing there, staring into her eyes. Before she could ask him why he was there, he had entered the house, greeting her with a good-morning kiss. She could not respond fast enough to ask him what he was doing. She once again kissed him back without thinking. It seemed so natural, like it was meant to be. He was about to say something to her when Miles Jr. and Sapphire came running down the stairs. Savannah told them to go back upstairs. Colby kissed her again and told her that he would see her later and then he left. The question that kept eating at her was, was this really happening? She knew deep down that this could not be happening. How was she going to get out of this, and had she let it go too far already?

For the next few days, she avoided any contact with Colby, hoping he would just forget about her. Well, as she figured, it did not work. Everywhere she went, he was there. She spent a lot of time with her friend Patrice, and he would always show up. They never spoke a word of what happened between the two of them. In fact, she never let him get her alone again to talk about anything. In her mind, she thought if she did not talk about it, then she did not have to face it. One day, they were all on the porch, talking with Mrs. Walker, and Colby decided to stand next to Savannah as she was leaning up against the banister. She had her hands behind her back as she was listening to Mrs. Walker talk. Colby stood close enough beside her that she could feel the heat from his body.

The funny thing about it was she did not move away from him. She stood still and looked on while Mrs. Walker was telling her story. He reached behind her with his hands so that no one could see as he grabbed her hand gently and held it. She discreetly withdrew his hand without notice and walked to the other side of the porch. She could tell that he was looking at her and with purpose. This time, his eyes were not playful or teasing. There was something about his actions that was different, and this scared her. Savannah and Patrice went into the house and were sitting at the kitchen table while her mom was cooking. They were just talking and catching up on things, mostly current events. She dared not to discuss her current events with her friend or anyone else. Then she looked up, and he was there standing in the doorway of the kitchen. He said hello to everyone as he walked over toward Savannah as her heart pounded.

She could not understand why he had such an effect on her. He stood behind her at the kitchen counter as he was talking to Mrs. Walker. She stated that she had to run across the street to check on one of the elderly neighbors and she would be back. Meanwhile, Patrice and Savannah continued their conversation while Colby still stood behind Savannah's chair. Patrice looked at her, and then Colby and asked what was going on between the two of them. Savannah responded with a shrug and stated that there was nothing going on. She stated that she did not know what Patrice was talking about.

Patrice looked up at Colby, and whatever expression he had given her, she did not believe Savannah. She made a statement to them both, "Y'all must think I'm stupid." Savannah continued to brush it off as nothing and no big deal. The one thing that Savannah could admit to herself was the fact that she felt something for Colby. She would never tell him or anyone else that secret. She could not trust him with her heart. In her mind, they both were just playing a cat-and-mouse game. In fact, that was a game that was not going to have a winner. Savannah vowed that she would not let herself be vulnerable to any guy. That vow included Colby no matter what she was feeling at the time. It was a new day, and that meant she had to be focused on more important things than what happened between her and Colby.

Chapter 6

It had been a couple weeks since Savannah went to visit with Patrice in fear that Colby would be there. She decided to spend time with her other friends for a while. They had already graduated from high school, so she did not get to see them as much. Tamera was working a full-time job now, and she spent the remainder of the time with her boyfriend. Savannah was so happy to catch up with Tamera again. They talked all night and laughed about the good times they used to have. Tamera was engaged now and was excited about getting married. She had her whole life planned out according to her. The two of them had moved in together.

Savannah knew that things were changing rapidly, but she was happy for her best friend. She understood that she had to move on with her adult life. The end of sophomore year was approaching; it was mid-spring. This meant school would be out for the summer in a couple months. She was sitting in class when Kristina approached her and started to talk about her close friend Bryson. It turned out that he was the guy that had been speaking to her on the way to gym class. Kristina spoke highly of him and asked Savannah if she was going to talk to her friend that was like a brother to her. She talked about him being such a good guy and that he was interested in getting to know her. Savannah did not want to have anything to do with him and told Kristina that she was not interested.

She thought that would be the end of it, but she was wrong. He was appearing out of nowhere, but he was never too persistent. She did not see him every day, only occasionally. So here she had at least four guys coming at her all at once, and she did not know what direction to go. Savannah created a list and added them to it, from top to bottom, in the order of who approached her first. She only had three on the list in which she was giving some consideration to whom she may allow to date her. It was not in stone, and she had plenty of time to decide. There was one of them that could be a strong contender, but the verdict was still pending. She was not going to rush into any quick decision. She was having the time of her life with this attention.

For each guy, there was something that she liked very much about them. Cameron had been her friend since kindergarten, and she was wonderfully comfortable with him. He was her friend, and he treated her so well. He was always nice to her, and he made her laugh. The problem with that relationship was that they were friends, and if it did not work, their friendship would be lost. Raymond was someone new she had just met at school. He was nice to her as well. She did not know anything about him and was afraid to venture out to get to know him. He was very persistent and was honest about his intentions toward her. She was impressed with his mannerism and soft-spoken words. This was not enough to make her turn in his direction.

There was Colby; she knew him from the neighborhood, and they all hung out with the other kids there. Savannah only knew about his reputation and the rumors that came along with it. She did not really know the true person. Who was to say that was the true him? He was considered a *bad* boy, and she did not want to be involved with anyone labeled with that status. Now this boy named Bryson had been thrown into her confusion. She was not interested in this guy and did not care if he was friends with one of the most popular girls in school. After a while, he started to show up more frequently. He would approach her with his gentle soft-spoken voice and tell her that she was pretty. He also wanted to call her, and she would tell him no too.

Then one day, out of the blue, he appeared in her biology class where the class was full to its capacity. If anyone really knew Savannah, she did not like to be the center of attention. Two of her friends, Bradford and Peyton, were sitting across the room from her when Bryson walked up to her. All eyes were on her, and she did not like it. He asked this time in front of everyone if she was going to talk to him. She could have died at that moment. She turned her head away from him and told him no in that exact tone she was known for.

Meanwhile, Bradford and Peyton were enjoying the pressure that Bryson was putting on me. After he left the class, the guys teasingly asked if she was going to give him a chance. Savannah was at her boiling point at this moment and rolled her eyes at them both. This only fueled them more to tease her about this invasion of privacy. Kristina was also in the same class, sitting behind her, and then she began to ask why she did not want to talk to her brother. Savannah just ignored her and focused on the biology teacher's lecture for the day.

When class ended and she was walking to her bus, all she could think about was Bryson. Who was he, and why was he so interested in her? She got home and put her books down on the kitchen table to prepare for homework. Mom had left chicken in the sink for her to start dinner. Savannah was an incredibly good cook, and she enjoyed doing this because it made her feel good about doing something for others. She started her homework while watching some of her after-school programs. She could not focus on either because she was so occupied with Bryson. Yes, he has suddenly boosted her curiosity. She knew nothing about him, but she dared to go around asking people about him. All she had to do was talk to Kristina about him. That was not going to happen because she kept her personal life private. She had not discussed with her best friends that these guys were pursuing her. Savannah decided that the next time Bryson asked for her phone number, she would give it to him. She wanted to know more about him, and it had to be on her terms. One could say that was one of the things about her—everything had to be on her terms.

A few days went by and she had not seen or heard from Bryson. She had talked with Cameron after school as usual and they talked about everything. Savannah found herself flirting with him and had to catch herself. He was flirting back, and this was not the norm for the two of them. She knew that they both were entering dangerous territory. They said their good nights and stated they would see each other tomorrow. Later that night, she was listening to her stereo like always, and she was thinking about Bryson. She was hoping that tomorrow she would see him in the hallways at school. She still had another dilemma to deal with, and she knew it was not going away so easy. Colby was still floating around in her thoughts as well. She could not stop thinking about him either. What was she going to do? She told herself to stop obsessing and go to sleep.

The next day of school could not arrive fast enough. She got off the bus, went to her homeroom hall to her locker, got her books, and headed to walk the halls with her girlfriends. She still did not see him, but she saw Colby hanging with his friends. She turned her head from him with a flirty smile as she walked past them. Savannah knew this drove him crazy and made him want her more. Remember, she wanted to be in control of everything, and it all had to be on her terms. Cameron was in the hall with their mutual guy friends, hanging out as well. They spoke to one another like friends do as she and the girls were laughing and talking to one another. The day went on, and still no sign of Bryson. She was just about to give up when the last bell rang, and she was headed to her bus. She heard someone call out her name behind her, and she turned to see that it was Bryson. He walked with her across the field toward the school buses, and he asked if he could call her. She told him yes and gave her phone number to him and said, "You better call."

It was Friday night, and she was sitting at home, watching television. Mom was downstairs doing laundry, and her sister and brother were not at home, so she had a little peace and quiet. The phone seemed to be ringing all night with the first caller asking to speak to her. When she stated it was her on the phone, the caller hung up. She recognized that voice; it was Thomas. There was no way he could disguise that deep voice. She knew that she did not give Thomas her phone number. The phone rang once more, and she answered, and another voice asked to speak to her. She did not recognize the guy on the other side. She asked if he was Bryson, and the caller stated, "Evidently you were expecting someone else." She asked who the caller was, and he replied, "Kevin." She apologized for mistaking him for Bryson. The problem was she did not know he was going to call her that night. They were working on an English literature assignment that they were paired up on by their teacher. The embarrassing thing about it was he seemed to have had an attitude about it.

Savannah did not recall talking to him in a way that would lead him to believe that she was interested in him. The phone rang again just seconds after she hung up with Kevin. She was a little hesitant to ask who the caller was this time. It was the call she was waiting for all evening. She took the call up in her bedroom. She and Bryson had talked for hours, and it seemed as if they had known each other for an exceptionally long time. He asked her a lot of questions about herself and what her interests were. The big question finally came as he asked if she was talking to anyone. Her response was quick and intentional. She told him that she was not talking to anyone. She kept to that answer because she felt that she was not in a serious relationship with anyone. Savannah was still very much in denial. She knew that she was not telling the truth. There was still the issue of Colby, and he was not letting go.

At this point, her interest had waivered somewhere else, and he was not going to be an issue. She was dead wrong about that analogy. Colby was not giving up on her. He tried everything in his power to get her alone. This was not working for her. He did not know how to communicate with her. The one thing she could agree with was that they had a strong physical attraction. For the short time this all had been going on, he never really talked to her. She found this unacceptable and led her to believe that he only wanted her for one reason only. The other guys that pursued her talked to her. Maybe he did not know how to have a real conversation with a girl that he was interested in.

Savannah may have been the first girl that took him to a place that he was not familiar. She did not know what he was thinking and did not want to wait for him to decide if he wanted a real relationship with her. He knew like every other guy that Savannah was true dating material. She was no one's pass-around girl and some would consider as the girl that every guy wanted to date. The catch to that idea was she did not allow just anyone to talk to her. She was very well respected, and everyone knew her as being this very smart girl that got along with everybody.

Things were becoming more interesting by the minute. She had to decide, and it was not as easy as she thought it would be. Savannah went back to thinking about considering Cameron because he was a genuinely good guy. She put him to the test one day when everyone was hanging out at the school in the neighborhood. Savannah was on the tennis court, talking to some friends. He was on the basketball court with his friends. Everybody was out on the playground that evening. She told her friends that she would be back she had to run to the house and use the bathroom.

As she was walking from the field, she heard a ticking sound approaching her from behind. She turned, and it was Cameron on his bike following her home. It became weird to her because he was not talking to her. He was just smiling and following her like a little puppy. It was way out of her comfort zone because they talk all the time on the phone. She got home, went in the house, and then came back onto the porch to leave. She noticed that he was giving her a different look, and from experience, she knew what it meant. Savannah decided to put him to the test to see if he really wanted to take it there.

She flirted with him and gave the opportunity for him to say whatever was on his mind. She waited and gave more hints that it was okay and nothing. Maybe he was nervous and was trying to build up his confidence. Savannah grew impatient and rose from the stoop and started walking back to the playground. When they arrived, her best friend, Hal, approached her and asked if she was dating Cameron now. She told him no as she was walking back onto the tennis courts. Savannah did not realize how insensitive she was being toward Cameron. She thought about it and decided that he will continue to stay in the friend zone.

It would be a distraction if they were to start dating and it did not work out. They had to be aggressive with their pursuit of her. This was what she was used to, guys being confident and respectfully aggressive when they wanted to talk to her. Cameron was removed from her list of contenders in this race to her heart. Now this left Raymond, Colby, and Bryson. She also removed Raymond from the list because she was not really attracted to him. She was overly flattered, but it was not enough. Yes, he was aggressive in his pursuit, but not aggressive enough. The chemistry was just not there, and it could not be forced. The last two on the list were Colby and Bryson, and, the chemistry was off the charts with the two of them.

Chapter 7

Another week had passed, and Savannah continued to talk to Bryson on the phone. He asked if he could come to see her on Friday night. She could not wait to spend time with him. Friday came, and she decided not to go hang out with Patrice, as she usually did on Fridays. The real reason she ditched was because she did not want to deal with Colby. Savannah had shifted her attention to Bryson, and all she wanted was to spend time with him. She had waited until 8:00 p.m. for him to show up, and he had not. Savannah decided to lie down and take a nap. She woke up to her mother yelling up the stairs that some boy was at the door to see her. Savannah slowly got off her bed and went to the bathroom to wash her face. She came downstairs still very sleepy and cut the porch light off because it was blinding.

There he was dressed in tan pants, Members Only jacket, white shirt, and tan hat. She did not forget the shoes; they were tan Stacy Adams. In that split moment, she took notice of everything he had on his body. Although she was sleepy and could not adjust her eyes, she managed to observe everything about him that night. This was the moment that she realized how good-looking he was. She had never paid any attention to it before, but tonight she was mesmerized. He stepped up onto the porch and circled to the right side of her. As she lay her head on the stone pillar on the porch, trying to fully awaken, he grabbed her gently, pulling her close to him.

She had placed her hands onto his chest. Bryson held her with care as he was enchanted by her as well. Savannah's head was lowered as she still tried to wake up from her nap. She could smell the cologne he was wearing, which was both masculine and soft. Savannah lifted her head to look into his eyes when his lips met hers. She was taken by surprise because she did not see it coming. He backed away to see if it was okay. Savannah was stunned and lifted her eyebrow in approval, and he leaned in again and kissed her. She kissed him back with intensity and passion, holding the back of his head to bring him closer. He moaned with acceptance as he kissed down her neck, then she felt a sharp but electrifying pain. Bryson had bitten her on the neck, drawing her deeper into his body. She exposed her neck even more, inviting him to have her, but it suddenly felt wrong. Savannah was thinking about Colby; she still had unfinished business with him. She felt that it was not fair to him to be making out with another guy. He was her first kiss, and it did mean something after all. She still did not trust him with her heart although something was happening that was causing her to start feeling something for him.

This was her reasoning at the time, but it was brief as she dismissed him out of her thoughts. She went into the house to use the bathroom, leaving Bryson on the porch for a moment. When she reached the bathroom, she investigated her neck in the mirror and noticed that he had left *hickeys* on both sides of her neck. Savannah had never let a guy get that close to bite her. She was still thinking about Colby and how he would react if he had seen these marks on her neck. It was complicated because they were not dating and there were no commitments on either side of the situation. She got herself together and went back outside to Bryson. It was as if she could not help herself, and the chemistry between them was electrifying. She knew it was wrong to tell Bryson that she was not seeing anyone else.

All she could think about was having the opportunity to choose which guy that was better for her. For the rest of the night, they spoke little to no words as the two of them enjoyed each other's company. He said his good night after the final kiss. Savannah went in the house, walking on cloud nine. Now she had a tough decision to make, but not tonight. Monday morning came, and she walked the halls, heading to her first-period health class. When she opened the doors, she saw Colby and his best friend, Brandon, standing up against the lockers. He had been waiting to see her that morning.

Brandon alerted him that she had just walked in the door. Colby did not have a class over their first period, so she knew something was not right. He had not seen her over the weekend and for a good reason.

Savannah thought to herself that she was in trouble, but he did not know anything about what had taken place over the weekend. As she walked past the two of them, Colby looked at her with both passion and frustration. Savannah could see in his eyes that he was becoming serious about this nonexistent relationship. Brandon had a smirk on his face, as if to say she was in trouble, although he was giving his best friend the props for catching a girl that no other could. After all, it was not long ago that he was pursuing her. At this point, she knew that Colby had told his best friend about the two of them. She gave Colby a flirty smile as she walked past him to her class. All she could think about was there was no way he knew about Bryson.

When she entered her class, no one was there, so she put her books on the desk. She turned around and Colby was there in her face. He grabbed her by the arm and pulled her briskly out of the classroom and into the hall out the side door. He put her up against the door as it closed behind them. He was so close that she could feel his breath. Savannah noticed that he had taken extra care in how he dressed that morning. He smelled so good from whatever men's cologne he had put on. She could not look him in the eyes because she did not want to show her guilt. Remember she had those two hickeys on her neck, so she made sure that her collar and sweater was buttoned high. Colby never said a word, then he was always like that with her. Everything with him was physical, and that was one of the things that kept her wanting to give in to him. He leaned in for a kiss, but she turned her head away. He looked at her with puzzlement because he was used to her responding back and kissing him when he demanded. It was different this time; he tried a second time, and she rejected him. He was about to ask her something, and she was afraid it would be about the sudden change. She was stuck and could not think of anything else but to tell him that it was over, and she walked away.

Now she'd finally done it—no more worries about making a choice between Colby and Bryson. Well, that was what she thought. Later that day, after school, she went to visit with Patrice. As soon as she walked in the house and sat down, there he was Colby. It was almost like he was timing her every move. She really did not want to talk to him. She thought it was clear when she told him earlier today that it was over between them. Savannah did not talk to him, she ignored him while everyone was talking. She could feel his eyes on her, and she did not want to look at him. It was one of her weaknesses whenever she was near him, but she had to fight it.

They were not in a real relationship, and she no longer wanted to explore that possibility. If only he would talk to her and express what his true intension were with her. She was never going to initiate the conversation because he was pursuing her. Savannah felt that she did not owe anyone an explanation for her actions because it was always her choice. She was getting ready to leave for the night, and Colby was still hanging around. She wished that he would just open his mouth and tell her how he felt. This would be his last chance to tell her how he felt about her. Savannah could have given him an explanation as to why she said they were done. That would have been the right thing to do. She needed to know if he was for real, but she did not bank on that happening. Savannah waited until Colby had left the room to go talk with Patrice's brother. It was her chance to leave without him seeing her. She tipped out of the door and was walking briskly toward her house in hopes that he would not know that she was gone. She heard footsteps moving quickly behind her. Savannah turned, and he was on her again, grabbing her by the arm to stop her. She asked him what he wanted, and with no answer as usual, he leaned down to kiss her without permission. This time, the kiss was different; it was filled with anger and resentment. She did not kiss him back as she pulled away from him and walked away.

At that moment, she decided that whatever she and Colby was doing had run its course. It was over, and his reactions helped her make a clearer decision that night. Something inside of her was jumping for joy that it was not going to drag on forever. But the other side of her was a little disappointed because he did not try hard enough. She was really wanting to give him the benefit of the doubt. She will never know how he really felt about her. Savannah was left with a lot of questions as to why he could not be himself when he was around her. At one point, she thought she saw a small glimpse of him—the vulnerable side of him. Maybe if she was a little more patient with him, she could have scratched the surface of his heart. Of course, she did not want to be that "I can change him" cliché.

That never works, and most women set themselves up believing that they can change a person. Sometimes they get what they asked for, and then sometimes they would not. Who was to say that she did touch his heart and he did not know how to deal with it? She remembered the expression of happiness on his face when he came to see her the Saturday morning after that first kiss. Now that she thought about it, he was genuinely happy and could have thought of her becoming his girlfriend. He probably thought about nothing or anyone else but her and that kiss all night. After all, she was a catch, and quite a few guys were pursuing her. There was still a big part of her that did not trust him. She continued to ask herself, "How could you start to have feelings for a person and do not trust him?"

Chapter 8

It had been two weeks since she heard from Bryson. Savannah had made up her mind that she wanted to be with him. She called his house, and he was not there, so she left a message with his mother. There was no way for her to know if he returned her calls because she was never home. It was another weekend, and she had not heard anything. She had decided that she was going to spend time hanging out with her other friends. Savannah did also spend some time in the Lincoln Terrace housing projects. When Sunday night came, she decided that, on Monday morning, she was going after Bryson. This was what she had thought about all night, trying to play it in her head how she was going to approach him.

Two weeks had passed, and she did not know whether he had moved on. He could have been thinking the same thing about her. The time did give her what she needed to break things off with Colby. She arrived at school and went to her locker and homeroom to drop off her books. She had asked one of her girlfriends if she wanted to walk the halls. They headed out of the building toward Camper Hall where she hoped to find Bryson. Savanah never told her friend what the purpose for going to Camper Hall that morning. As they were getting closer to the hall and just before she reached the door, she thought, *What if he has moved on?* Savannah did not care as she was there now. No turning back or regrets. She opened the door, with eyes totally focused.

There he was standing up against the locker with his best friend, a lot of girls all around him. It did not matter to Savannah who was there. His best friend, Roman, saw her first, and he left, and as he passed her, he spoke. She was so focused on Bryson and her mission that she hardly even noticed if all that he had said was her name. Bryson looked up, and his eyes were in a trance as she approached. He was smiling, and they both never took their eyes off each other. Savannah did not care who was standing there; she moved up between him and all the girls that were standing there talking to him. She placed her hand upon his chest, saying hello. The girls were giving her a look, as if asking what was she doing there and with Bryson. It never mattered to her as she told Bryson to come with her. He followed, still mesmerized by her and the bold action that she took.

People were staring and pointing as he walked with her to her homeroom class. They could not believe their eyes, and the news of this union was all over the campus by the end of the day. No one could believe that someone that was quiet and shy was officially dating that guy. He was one of the most popular guys in the school. Everyone knew and loved Bryson. It was official; she came to claim her man and had let everyone know it. She and Bryson were off the dating market, but not everyone received that news. That week in school was remarkably interesting. The same guys from Savannah's neighborhood that told Bryson that she did not talk to boys were wiping the egg off their faces.

She and Bryson were walking down the hall one morning, and the fellows were standing by the lockers talking. When the two of them came down the hall, all eyes were on them. She could see out of her side vision that Bryson was practically popping his collar at the guys. He was almost gloating with a smile that said, "You all said I would never get her." Cameron was one of the boys that were standing out there that day. Savannah looked over at him, and he had such a look of hurt and heartbreak. She remembered that look so quite well as that was the very same look that Johnathan, Donovan, Raymond, and Colby shared. She was very selfish and inconsiderate of their feelings. These boys had pursued her, and at least three of them did have feelings for her. She could not say the same for the other two guys. Throughout the day, many people approached her to confirm what they had already heard. Most of the guys that knew

Bryson gave him his *props*, which was a congratulations. Some of his friends were in the same class with Savannah, and they asked her because they did not trust the word of mouth. That day, when she got onto the school bus, she looked to see if Raymond was on the bus yet. He had not boarded yet, so she took the seat next to one of her friends. When he finally boarded, he saw that his usual seat next to her was taken. He went to the back of the bus where most of the guys sat. The bus was making its way out of the parking lot and onto their destination.

Once they were on the way, two of the guys that both she and Bryson knew came from the back to where she was sitting. Like most of the other people that had been asking her questions about her and Bryson, they asked who she was dating, and she told them and once the two were satisfied with her answer, they went to the back of the bus to confirm and report what she had told them. Well, Raymond was one of the nonbelievers that day. He was so sure that he was making progress with Savannah. He really pursued her and was not giving up. At that moment, she knew that Raymond would be heartbroken.

It was also evident that Colby did not believe that it was true. He continued to pursue each time she came to visit with Patrice. From that day forward, Raymond never spoke another word to Savannah, just like Cameron, Donovan, Johnathan, and soon, Colby. Bryson and Savannah talked on the phone every night before going to bed. They talked about both their childhood and families. He told her about the first time he had ever laid eyes on her. When Bryson was about nine years old, he used to pass her house on the way to his grandparents. He described how he remembered the way she looked. He also told her that he used to say then that someday he was going to marry her. Savannah teasingly laughed it off as she was not even close to thinking about marriage. In fact, she had different plans for her life, and falling in love and getting married was surely not one of them. Even at fifteen years of age, she still had daddy and trust issues. It still amazed her that she was currently in a relationship with this guy. All she wanted to do was enjoy every experience possible that the average high school student encounters. She was not thinking about a long-term relationship.

Savannah vowed that once she graduated high school, she would be leaving town. Her dream was to join the United States Air Force so that she could travel and make a difference. It was her ticket to be in control of her life and heart. Bryson even then talked about marrying her someday. He had fallen in love with her in such a short time. Although Savannah liked him a lot, she was not in love with him. She was just going through the motions to keep from hurting him. For the longest time, she would never tell him that she loved him whenever he told her. Savanah found this to be going entirely too fast. They had been in the relationship for two weeks now.

One night, things changed for the two in a very intimate way. It was something about the way they kissed each other that broke all rules. They were sitting in the living room on the love seat, and the laws of nature overruled them. She took him by his hand and led him into the family room where it was dark. Her mom was upstairs in her bedroom that night. So they were careful not the make any sudden noises that would alert her to what was about to happen. Savannah did not care; all she wanted was Bryson at that moment. He continued to ask her if she was okay about what was going to happen. He wanted to make sure it was okay because he knew she was a virgin. Savannah did not want him to ask her any more questions. She was overrun with emotion and desire for him. The moment came when she invited him to have the most precious gift a young girl holds. He was so sweet and gentle with her, but she wanted more and now. This was the night that she lost her virginity to Bryson. She had made the choice a long time ago that it would be to someone that she trusted. Savannah was not going to give herself to just anyone or everybody. Whoever the first was going to be the last. This was so important that she did not want to make a mistake in choosing the guy she wanted to date. After it was over, she panicked when he said the words, "You could get pregnant." She lost all sense of control and reality at this point. That was the last thing she thought about while they were having sex.

She went upstairs to the bathroom, passing her mother's room. She closed the bathroom door and started running the water in both the sink and bathtub. Mom knocked at the door because of her suspicions. She asked, "Are you and that boy doing something?" Savannah had never lied to her mother and was not going to start now. She answered her mother with a yes. Well, you would have thought all hell had broken loose. Mom told her to tell Bryson to leave her house and to never return. Savannah was grounded for about a week and could not hang out with friends, with no phone or television. This was considered as harsh punishment at the time. Her mother did not have to physically punish her. Savannah was still feeling the discomfort for a few days from her first sexual encounter. She was only able to talk and see Bryson at school. Occasionally, late at night, she would wait until her mom went to sleep before she called him.

One week had passed and she could not wait to see Bryson again. She left, walking to his house one afternoon. When she arrived and knocked on the door, his mother answered. She let her in the house, and Bryson introduced the two. His mother was very pretty and sweet to Savannah. Later, Bryson took her upstairs to the family room to watch television, listen to music, and hang out. The two had been dating for about a month, and he was having strong feelings. She was still thinking about Johnathan, Cameron, and Colby from time to time. Savannah did not kid herself to think that any of them was thinking about her. She had done them wrong with her nonverbal and very vague actions. She had started to miss hanging out with Patrice.

One day, she decided to go visit, and they just picked up where they had left off as friends. The school year was about to end, and it was hot one afternoon, so they decided to walk to Highs Ice-Cream Parlor. She did not know that Colby was going to join them. The two of them never said a word to each other. She could tell that he still could not keep his eyes off her. They all started walking through the neighborhood on the way to the store. Patrice and Savannah were walking in front, and her sister, along with her little friend, was behind them. Colby was walking behind them, as well with Patrice's two-year-old son, riding on his neck. Savannah knew in her guts that he was watching her from behind. She ignored it and continued to laugh and talk with Patrice.

Although she had moved on with Bryson, he still did something to her whenever they were close to each other. The curiosity got the best of her, so she turned to see, and it was not what she had expected. Their eyes met, and she could see that he was extremely hurt. One of his defense mechanisms kicked in as she read the words he silently spoke to her. It was not good at all; he called her the B word. She giggled it off like it did not mean anything to her. But the truth was it really did sting, and it was hurtful. She never in her life had anyone call her that word. So she shook it off and gave him a quick smirk as she turned back to her conversation with Patrice. She tried to stay focused on what Patrice was talking about, but it was difficult to cover how she was feeling at that moment. Savannah had become particularly good at covering how she felt about things. Colby had surprised her, and it hurt. The question to herself was, why did she care about what he thought and even said to her? Savannah was like that with Bryson as well, and he was her boyfriend. She did not ever tell him how she really felt about the relationship. All she continued to believe was that this was temporary.

Savannah kept telling herself that she was not looking for a long-term relationship. She did not believe that anyone could be happy forever. When she had gotten home that night, she was still thinking about Colby. Then she began to play back in her mind if she misread something the whole time they were involved. The questions came again; rather, she made a mistake when she did not give what they were doing a chance. But then she would think about the other what-ifs, that was not so good. It always brought her back to the trust issues. She was so confused because, rationally, if he did not have feelings for her, then he would not have reacted the way he did. Most guys give up when a girl rejects them. She believed that Colby saw something, too, that just maybe they could have had a chance. Why would he look at her the way he did every time they were together? Was he in love with her? She would never know. Later that night, she received a call from Bryson. She had not seen or talked to him all day. He told her that he had his cousin's car and did come by her house looking for her. The two of them talked all night, and he confessed that he was so in love with her. Savannah still would not tell him that she loved him. She knew that she had feelings for him and just maybe she was falling in love. Bryson continued to talk about them and their relationship. She asked him about his day, and he had been hanging out in the park with his cousin and their friends.

Finally, summer had come, and school was out. Everyone was making plans for end-of-the-year parties. Savannah and Bryson did not have any plans. He did invite her to his family cookout where she would meet the rest of his family. He had planned to work during the summer at Billy's and Shoney's. The two of them went to the movies, mall, and out to eat every weekend. At this point, they were spending each day together. Savannah was happy being with him and enjoyed his company. One day, she had started to miss some of her friends and wanted to see them. The friend that she missed the most was Tamera.

So she called her one afternoon, and she came over to see Savannah. She did not have anything to do because her boyfriend was at work. It was perfect timing because Savannah did not have any plans with Bryson. She had not heard from him all day, so she figured he was out with his best friend. They were just about to leave her house when the phone rang. It was Bryson on the phone. He asked what she was about to do. She told him that she was just about to leave the house. She told him that she and Tamera were catching up and going to the park. Then he began to say that he wanted to see her. She told him that she would see him later. He still insisted for her to stay home. She continued to say that she was leaving.

At this point, Bryson was becoming angry and said that he needed to get his jacket. Savannah told him that she would leave it downstairs and he could come pick it up. Her mom was at home, and she would give it to him. This was not acceptable to Bryson. She had become irritated herself and told him she had to go. He tried everything to keep her engaged in the conversation, but she was done. Savannah hung up the phone in his ear. She and Tamera left the house, walking to the park down the street from their block. They talked about each other's love life and how they missed hanging out with each other. Everyone was out in the park that evening, and one of the guys that they knew came over to talk with them for a while. He left and went back across the street to his house. The two were sitting on the swing and pushing themselves back and forth as they laughed and talked. Then the atmosphere changed suddenly, and Tamera jumped off the swing. Savannah asked her what was wrong, and she told her Bryson was coming and he looked like he was mad. She got up and turned to see him walking fast through the park with his eyes focused on her and his nostrils flaring. Tamera told her she would see her later and started to run. Savannah braced herself as he drew closer to her.

As he was walking, he kicked one of the one-hundred-year-old oak trees as he approached. He did not speak a word as he grabbed Savannah by her throat and started choking her. She was grappling at his hands to turn her loose as he was backing her up down the street. They ended up in the middle of the street, and she could hear some of the guys in the park yelling for him to let Savannah go. Bryson could not be reasoned with at this point. There was a car coming up the street and the horn blaring. It was his aunt as she slammed the brakes and jumped out of the car. She was swearing and told him to take his hands off Savannah. She told them both to get in the car. Savannah did not see why she had to get in the car. She just lived two blocks up the street and surely could find her way home.

While they all were in the car, his aunt was swearing and fussing at Bryson. She told him that he better not ever in his life put his hand on her or any other girl if he had breath in his body. Savannah was silent and did not dare to speak up and ask if she would let her off at home. His aunt drove them to her house where she went into the house to call Bryson's mother. They both sat on her front porch steps, and he was grabbing at his foot. He took his shoe off and found that he had caused damage to his toe from kicking the tree. Bryson's cousin Richard was home on leave from the Navy and was in front, washing his car. The whole time they were on the steps, Richard was looking at Bryson as he had given him a lecture as well. Savannah tried to tell Bryson that she was sorry for making him so angry. She reached for his hand, and he was not receptive.

He was the one that owed her an apology for attacking her. Bryson tried to get up off the steps and had a little trouble. He needed medical attention and could not walk home. Richard offered to give them a ride two blocks up to his house. When dropped off at his house, Bryson's mother was giving him another lecture on his behavior. This was the very first time that Savannah was introduced to this side of Bryson. She was clueless to this other side of him, and it frightened her. She still went with him to the urgent care center to get treated and returned with him back to his house. Bryson still did not say much to her, and this should have been her clue to leave and never come back. She loved him and was concerned about his injury. Later that evening, she was still at his house, and he started to come around as he also apologized. When Bryson dropped her off at home, she had a lot to think about that night. What other things about him she did not know? Savannah was up all night, and this was the first time she ever encountered this type of anger toward her. She was having memories from her childhood when she had heard her parents arguing and the result. She was reminded why it was important that she not be in a serious relationship. She did not want to be hurt emotionally, but now she had to worry about protecting herself physically. Although she loved him, there were questions as to whether she should continue with this relationship. She decided that it was time to break up with him, but she did not know how. A week had passed, and she did not have the courage to break it off with him. The two spent a lot of time together and were inseparable. Savannah continued with the normal routine in hopes that things would stay good. She was always wondering what would set him off again. She already knew that he was jealous. One night, she was at his house and they were listening to music and watching television.

The phone rang and he answered, and there was another girl on the other end. Savannah was a little jealous too. She did not like him talking to other girls. The difference with that would be she never said anything to him about how she felt. He talked to whoever was on the phone for a moment before disconnecting. This was her chance; she told him that it was over, and she stormed out of the room and out the front door. She had reached the end of the block, and he had caught up to her. He grabbed for her, and she jerked from him, telling him that it was over. She was breaking up with him and did not want to see him anymore. Well, that did not work out as planned. One thing she did find out quickly was he did not like to be embarrassed. This time, he used his fists to punch a telephone pole. It scared her more because she remembered his temper before. He followed her home, and the two did not speak one word to each other. It was dark coming across the bike trail at night, and she hurried so that she could pass over the field to the streetlights.

When she got home, she sat on her porch but still did not say anything to him. Bryson approached her in the gentle way he always did whenever he thought she was going to leave him. He was apologizing once again, telling her that he was in love with her and could not lose her. Savannah did not want to hear this apology because their relationship was in trouble. The two of them had some individual issues that could no longer be ignored. She realized that it would not be easy to end this relationship. She feared that things would become unhealthy, and this would not be beneficial. A year had passed, and they were still together with no other incidents. She did love him, but a part of her was still questioning if she should stay with him. She did not want to end up like her parents.

Savannah would sometimes think about the what-ifs in her life. She still had plans to join the United States Air Force, and that would be her escape from everything. There were times that the two were happy, but sometimes good things must come to an end. Bryson had never put his hands on her again, and all things were good again. He realized that she wanted to leave him, so he did everything possible to keep her happy. Focusing on the remainder of the summer was their priority. Bryson had a summer job, so the two only could spend time with each other on his days off. While he was working, she spent time visiting with her grandmother. Savannah also loved going to her aunt's house and hanging out with her cousins on the weekend. They still went to church on Sundays and hung out after service.

Savannah's mother was working two jobs at the time. So there were some Sundays that they did not go to church. She had to stay home to babysit her younger sister and brother. It was tough sometimes not being able to hang out with neighborhood friends. But she found productive things to do around the house to pass time. One of her mother's rules was not to leave the house while she was not home. Her mom also did not want anyone in the house in her absence. In her alone time, Savannah would read mystery and romance novels. This was one of her hobbies that she loved to do besides writing. She also loved to bake and search for exceptionally good recipes in her mom's old cookbooks. Savannah remembered how nervous but excited she was to make her first pan of yeast rolls. She had to pass Granddaddy's seal of approval, of course. Granddaddy made the best *light rolls*, which he called them on every Sunday morning with fried chicken for breakfast. Even now she still remembers the aroma that flooded the kitchen every Sunday morning. These were the best times for Savannah to focus on and the things she dreamed about.

Chapter 9

It was well into the summer now, and Savannah decided that she wanted to study for her learner's permit. She would be a junior when school started up in the fall and she wanted to drive. Mom did not own a car, but her grandfather had a car and van parked in his driveway. She already knew how to drive because, at the age of twelve years old, she told her dad that she wanted to drive. One day, when Dad was going to pick Mom up from work, he let her get behind the wheel of his Oldsmobile. Savannah had been watching people drive for years and figured that she could learn from watching. It turned out that she was an incredibly good driver, so Granddaddy told her that she had to get her permit.

She studied the driver's book, and Bryson took her over to the DMV on a Saturday to take the test. She passed with flying colors and could not wait to show her grandfather. Everyone that learned how to drive went on a road test with Granddaddy. He was strict with the rules of driving. You would get the lecture that he was driving before the first license plate was in production. Her grandfather was born in 1906, and he had seen a lot in one's lifetime. He often told stories about his childhood growing up on a farm. He remembered going to bed before dark and getting up before the first light. Granddaddy talked about the hustle and bustle of city dirt roads traveled by horse and wagons.

There was also the mention of automobiles and the railroad system in town. So with the history he had to share about transportation, his approval was warranted. She had fun driving the fifteen-passenger van that he owned. So whenever he had to go to the grocery store, she would volunteer to drive him. She drove anytime she had the opportunity. Bryson would drive his mom's red LTD to work and when they spent time together. She would go pick him up at night after work, so she got lots of practice. The weekends seemed to become shorter due to Bryson's work schedules with two part-time jobs. Savannah missed him a lot but knew that working on the weekends helped to finance their dates. They would always go to the movies every other Friday night that he was not working.

On Saturdays, they would go visit with his grandparents, Pop and Grans. His grandfather would always get such a kick out of teasing Savannah about other girls and Bryson. She would giggle with laughter as Pops went on with his great big smile and winking his eye. Savannah loved sitting on the front porch, talking with his grandparents. Bryson's grandmother, of course, thought the sun did not rise without her *baby*. Yes, he was spoiled rotten by his grandparents, and they were not ashamed to let anyone know it. There were also stories about his football years and how great he was in doing what he loved. Then Aunt Pearl would stop by and sit for a while, catching up on the church gossip with her sister.

She and Pop would always have such an interesting discussion which would lead to an argument. They would always have some sort of debate or discussion where the two disagreed. It was always interesting to see and hear how the elders interacted with one another. Most teenagers would find it boring or had no interest in learning about life from the older generation, let alone sit long enough to get anything out of it. They would also be entertained by his aunt Jennie, who was the most opinionated and bold with an obvious high level of confidence. She was not afraid to tell you where she stood on things. Sometimes she would come across as a little intimidating for someone that did not know her. Under all that, she was extremely sweet and loving, but do not get on her *bad* side.

Then there was his younger aunt, Sarah; she was so sweet and outgoing. Both Bryson and Savannah loved her so much. The two would always hang out at her house on some weekends. The family would always take their vacation every summer at the family homestead. This was the home that Grans and her sister were raised when they were kids. They would travel to Waverly, Virginia, every summer to spend a week at their homeplace. Bryson's mom and dad, along with him and his little brother, would all go. He talked about going fishing and swimming with his cousins that still lived in Waverly. He also remembered when his grandfather would take the men out on his big fishing boat in Norfolk on the bay. Bryson spoke about catching fish and having such a good time with his family. He also recalls a time when a storm was coming in and they could not make it back on time. Pop had anchored and tied to one of the bridges crossing the bay as the storm approached.

Bryson said that the water was fierce, and the wind was blowing the boat where it rocked and bounced up and down in the water. He had never been so scared in his life. Everyone had hankered down below in the boat as the storm raged. Bryson became seasick and swore that he would never get on another boat. His memories brought back some of the recollections that Savannah had with her grandfather and family fishing in Norfolk. The two of them continued to have so much in common about their childhood. He could not go on the family vacation because he worked two part-time jobs this summer.

Of course, another reason he did not want to go this time was because he had a new girlfriend. In two weeks, the family was preparing for the big vacation back home where they visited their other family that lived there. Some of the things that the men enjoyed and were anxious to do was go fishing over in the Norfolk-Virginia Beach area. Bryson's mom enjoyed fishing also, but she loved her shopping too. While they were gone, Bryson had some chores of his own to do. His grandfather owned some farmland and other property out of the city. On this land, he had pigs that needed to be tended while he was on vacation. Savannah decided that she wanted to tag along with Bryson one morning to take Pop's truck to the local grocery store to pick up discarded produce. She wondered what this had to do with feeding the animals. He explained that this was part of the food supply to the pigs. They drove like what seemed to be forever, and then they were there. Once he was done with feeding the livestock, they headed back to the city.

The next day, he had to work, so Savannah stayed at home and read some and watched movies all day. She decided to go down to Patrice's house to visit with her. The two girls had not seen or talked to each other for what seemed to be such a long time. Savannah missed her girl time with some of her friends. Once again, she was feeling a sense of losing some of her ability to balance relationships. It felt good to be out in the neighborhood, hanging out with friends. She had a sense of freedom and did not feel that she had to check in or be accountable for her actions. She did love Bryson and spending time with him. It has been a year now since they have been in a relationship. Savannah began to think more about slowing things down to the point of asking for some free time. She already knew that if she was to bring the subject up again about breaking up, Bryson would not be agreeable to that suggestion and things would not go well.

The more she thought about it, the more she felt it was time to have some separation. After all, they were just sixteen years old and had the rest of their lives to become so serious. She wanted to experience everything in life, including finishing high school and making a career in the Air Force. Savannah wanted to travel and see the world through her eyes and not others'. She did not think about dating other people, but she knew that if she broke up with Bryson, it could be a strong possibility it would happen. She often thought about Johnathan while she was dating Bryson. She wondered if he was okay and how life was treating him. Savannah could not understand why she was not able to stop thinking and worrying about him. Even after all those years, she continued to play it back in her mind the last night that she saw him. Why was she still having these feelings for him? He had been long gone, and she continued to question if she had made one of the biggest mistakes in her life. She would never know if he was to be her first true love.

Savannah had to clear her head because she had to build up the nerve to have this conversation with Bryson. He was a good guy, and any girl would have loved to be in her place. None of that mattered to her because she was not attracted to him because of who he was.

She wanted to be sure that she was not cheating herself out of the life she had dreamed. Bryson came by after work that night, and the two sat on the front porch, talking about their day. He was off work the next day and wanted to spend some quality time with her. So she agreed that tomorrow would be good, and she would come to his house. All night as she was lying in bed, she could not stop thinking about how she was going to bring up this important conversation. Savannah never had any doubts about how she felt about Bryson.

It was going to be difficult to tell him that she loved him very much and still want some time off. Bryson was the type of guy that did not do well with rejection, and he had a temper to match. He was totally in love with her and did not want to lose her. One could say he had some insecurities about their relationship ending. He did not want to ever break up with Savannah. He had even told her that someday he planned to marry her. This was not in the plans for Savannah, and the longer she stayed with him, the harder it became to leave. Her reasons for wanting to leave him did not have anything to do with being treated badly. That was far from the truth as she could see. He never treated her badly and had always respected and loved her. It took a while for her to reciprocate the same feelings toward him. He fell deeply in love with her first, and at the time, she was not in love with him. She never told him that she loved him even when he told her all the time. The next day had come, and she walked to his house early that afternoon. He was waiting for her and opened the door after the first knock. She greeted him as she always did with a kiss when she entered. They went to the kitchen where he was fixing himself some lunch.

She sat at the table, watching him at the counter making his sandwich. After he finished making his lunch, the two went upstairs in the family room where they always spent time. The television was on, along with his stereo playing as they entered the room. Savannah took off her shoes and climbed onto one of the sofas while he sat on the floor at the table to eat his lunch. She picked potato chips off his plate as he was eating and watching television. Savannah always helped herself to whatever he was eating or drinking. After she helped him to finish his lunch, he took the dishes downstairs to the kitchen to clean and put up. She was still upstairs, watching television and thinking to herself when it would be a good time to bring up the topic.

Her heart was beating fast, and she was extremely nervous and still could not get the nerve to speak about it. She was still a little shy and did not always express how she truly felt about things. During their entire relationship, she had this problem and never spoke up about things even when she did not agree with Bryson. There were times that she did not like when he would go off with his best friend, Kristina. Savannah did have some insecurities about their close friendship as well because she did not really know her. She did not care for quite a few habits of Bryson's, but she kept quiet and never spoke about it. Bryson had come back upstairs to spend some quality time with her. He missed loving on her and kissing her as he was so used to their physical relationship.

Savannah could not connect with him physically that day because her emotions were all over the place. He knew something was not quite right that day with her. He pulled her close to him and tried to be tender and loving, but she could not give him that affection. Then she just blurted out that she could not do it any longer. He looked at her and asked what she was talking about. She repeated that she could no longer do this and wanted out. She told him that she wanted to break up with him. He did not respond well to what he was hearing. He wanted her to explain why she wanted to break up, but she could not give him the answer that she had been practicing in her mind. She was dealing with fear and confusion as his temper began to rise.

He grabbed her by the arm as she was turning to leave. She started to cry and told him that she wanted to leave. He kept standing in front of her, blocking her from leaving. She made it around him and ran downstairs to leave out the front door. She could not get it unlocked, so she went to the side door to try it. He was already downstairs, but he went in the other direction. She did not know where he had gone. She was still trying to get the side door unlocked when she heard him behind her. When she turned around, she was shocked and terrified at what she saw. Bryson was standing in the living room with a small silver gun with a pearl-white handle.

At this point, she screamed in tears and fell to her knees because she thought he was about to hurt her. She could not stop crying as she lay on the floor pleading for him not to hurt her. At that point, she became hysterical, and those memories of her father shooting her mom came flooding back into her memory. Bryson had never seen this part of her being so vulnerable and helpless. He started to cry and dropped to his knees in front of her and lay on top of her, weeping uncontrollably. He still had the gun in his hand as she looked away from him. He told her that he was sorry and that he could not lose her, not now. Savannah was shaking with no control of her own body. All she could think about was saying something that would distract him. She wanted out of that house and away from him.

He removed the gun from his hand and pushed it away on the floor. She lifted both arms and embraced him to comfort him and told him that she loved him. This was her chance to defuse the situation and improve her chances of survival. She would have said anything at this point to keep herself safe. If she had any doubts before, this incident was the proof that she needed to cut ties with him. She did not know that he had some personal issues going on with him as well. What was it? She was too afraid to ask. As usual, after a fight they had sex, but this was not a fight; it was something more life-threatening to them. Even though she gave in to sex, she was crying silently as he was making love to her.

Later, he walked her home, and there was no conversation. It was the longest and quietest walk home she had ever had. She could not find the words and did not care to make conversation. What do you say when your life was in danger? She wanted to tell her mom so badly what had happened when she got home that evening. She knew it would have been bad for Bryson, and he would probably not see the light of day again. She did not want to get him into trouble. What he thought was love was emotional and physical control. He told her time after time that he was so very much in love with her. She was afraid and never spoke about breaking up with him ever again. Now she was in this relationship with this guy that she did love, but it was not healthy whenever he got mad. Savannah found herself living a lie. She could not be honest with him without fear. She knew she had become a casualty of love and emotional instability. The questions began to pile on top of one another as she thought about her life. It had not even begun, and she is faced with such difficult decisions. These were adult changes, and no teenager should ever be faced with such an emotional challenge. Savannah felt that there was something deeper going on with Bryson.

She could not stop thinking about the words he kept saying to her, "I can't lose you, not now." What did he mean? She dared not to ask him, but it was haunting her. She needed for him to be completely honest with her as well. Before they started to date, she never asked anyone about him or his past. She only heard about his popularity and football stardom after they started dating. Those things did not matter to her because she was never interested in a person because of popularity. Savannah did want to date a normal person with no attachments or pressures. She always treated everyone the same and did not matter if they were popular or not. She already knew that he was well respected and liked by everyone.

So what was he hiding from her? She never felt that she could not trust him because she did. She had fallen in love with him. That would explain why she did not tell anyone about the incident that took place at his parents' house. Between the two of them, there were issues that needed to be brought to the surface. For now, they will never bring up the incident and decided to move forward. It was better not to open that Pandora's box because it was apparent that neither of them was equipped to handle what was in it. It was the first day back to school, and they were returning as eleventh graders. She and Bryson were walking the hallways again, and she went back to being the girlfriend of Mr. Popularity. One of the things that she had learned to be good at was not showing her true emotions.

Chapter 10

The new school year had started on a high note with the excitement of becoming rising seniors. Savannah was preparing for what will be next after graduation. She was still active with her participation in the junior ROTC program at school. This was one of what she thought was the best opportunities for her to pursue the career she had dreamed. One evening after school, she was sitting in the den, watching television with Bryson, and she started up the discussion about her future. Savannah was so excited to tell her mom that Sergeant Spangler was helping her with the process of getting processed for the Air Force. Mom was not happy about her talking about leaving after graduation.

She objected to the idea and told Savannah that she was not going to join anyone's military and that she will be attending college. This was not what Savannah wanted to hear, and it was heartbreaking to listen to Mom protest her dream. Bryson was not actually jumping to her defense. He knew that she dreamed about leaving to join the military. Savannah believed that he secretly did not want her to leave as well. This would mean that he may never see her again and the relationship would come to an end. It was probably the fear of losing her because she always would talk about leaving and never coming back home.

One of the things that she was focused on included leaving her past behind and starting a new life. She was under the thumb of her mother's control and disapproval of many things that involved independence. She had never heard Mom speak about her brother and sister going off to college. In fact, she had never received encouraging words of wisdom; it was more of lecture and scare tactics, teaching them to be afraid of living. Her mother had never been on an airplane or boat because she feared many things. In their house, stories of superstitious beliefs were part of the norm for many years. Savannah decided that she was not going to be a casualty of her mother's fears and wounds. It was too late because she felt that she was already damaged goods, especially when it involved telling someone how she felt about them. It was still difficult for her to say the words "I love you."

Although she loved Bryson, it was particularly challenging for her sometimes in expressing her feelings to him. Even when she did not agree with him on things, she would always be submissive to what he wanted. There was one thing about Bryson he had a way with words and could be very persuasive. He knew exactly how to maneuver your feelings and heart. Savannah was still very defensive and protective of herself even though they have shared the most intimate moments in their relationship. It was evident she was in deeper and could not break ties from this relationship to save herself. She was on an emotional roller coaster within herself. Some would view them as the perfect couple because they both were well-liked and respected. She did not have any doubt that there may have been a few that would have loved to be in her place.

There should have been no complaints about the relationship because they could agree that they loved each other. She had to focus on the present at this time, and to accomplish that task, she had to live one day at a time. It was not going to be easy to block out memories of her parents' past relationship, all of what she did witness. These memories certainly had played a part in her desire not to stay in a long-term relationship. It also proved that she had a lot of emotional damage as well. For the meantime, Bryson was doing everything in his power to make and keep her happy. It was working and life seemed good, and the two of them were even more inseparable. After Mom had stated her case and there was no compromising to what she meant, this left Savannah feeling outnumbered. All she could think about was when she turned eighteen years of age, the choice would be hers. She knew that her mother's opinion would not change her mind about the dream of emotional and physical freedom. It was the middle of fall, and the temperatures grew colder each morning and warm by midday. With these changes, you would notice the change in the color of the leaves on the trees. This time of season was beautiful because the valley was surrounded by many peaks and mountains. These mountains were known as the Blue Ridge and Appalachians, which could be traveled from Virginia, North Carolina, West Virginia, and Tennessee. Bryson and Savannah had visited one of the smaller mountains within the city known as Mill Mountain.

If you wanted to see a perfect view of the valley and visit the local zoo, this is where you would want to come. It was also exciting to drive the Blue Ridge Parkway during the fall as well. Most teenagers would not consider appreciating the beauty of the changes of the seasons. Savannah surely was not your typical adolescent as she was much more mature than other girls her age. She did have a sense of awareness to things that most people would not be receptive to knowing. Savannah remembered incidents that she had experienced when she was younger. She always had felt that there was another presence around her that could not be seen or explained. She recalled sitting in her English class one morning and felt something hovering around her with a very coldness that lifted the hair on her neck.

There was another situation when she was at home one afternoon, lying on her bed, reading a book with her back to the bedroom door. She was in the house alone as usual because Mom had not arrived home from work. Savannah remembered feeling that presence again as she heard someone or something enter her bedroom. The floor creaked under the pressure of what was coming into the room. She already knew that this was an old house, and it was expected to hear settling from time to time. The strange thing about it was she was not afraid or spooked. The sun was shining very bright that evening, and the room was filled with the rays of sun through the curtains. She knew that she was not making things up in her head when she heard a woman's voice ask, "Is she asleep?" The voice was noticeably clear and distinct, and you could not make a mistake with identifying that it was a woman.

At that moment, she tried to turn over to face in the direction of the woman's voice, but she could not because she felt a touch on her back that would not allow her to turn. The touch was exceptionally light but effective in her not being able to move her body. Although the entire event was brief, it seemed like everything was happening in slow motion. Savannah was fully awake and very responsive in her actions. She had always had these encounters, and if not by touch, they would come in visions via dreams. It became the norm for her, and she shared these events with her mom. Well, she did not know then that Mom was telling people within the family about her experiences as if she was there. But you had to remember that this was a house where superstitions played a large role in Mom's beliefs. At the time, Savannah had no clue as to how significant these events would be to her someday.

Chapter 11

There was something different that day, and she could not exactly put her finger on it. Savannah thought maybe she had a stomach bug, but there was no way to know unless she had a doctor's visit. She was having some back pain, and it was exceedingly difficult for her to urinate without discomfort. Her symptoms consisted of fatigue, feeling the urge to urinate on an empty bladder, and she was feverish and nauseous. Savannah did not know what was wrong, but she knew that something was not right. She told Bryson that she believed that it was a bladder infection but wanted to make sure of it. The next day after school, she had him to take her to the doctor that her mom used for outpatient acute visits.

They arrived at the doctor's office and checked in so that she could be seen. Her medical information was already on file because this was where Mom took them on regular visits as well. She and her siblings did not have a pediatrician when they were coming up. Mom could not afford to pay to see one, so they always went to the clinic. The nurse called Savannah back and took her vitals and asked the typical medical questions. Savannah told her that she believed it was a bladder infection and gave a detailed explanation of her symptoms. The nurse gave her a container to fill with specimen to be tested after the doctor came in to examine her. Later that evening, she was at home hanging out with Bryson when the phone rang.

She answered it on the first ring because she did not want her mom to receive the call. As she expected, it was the clinic calling to tell her about the bladder infection. What she thought was confirmed, but there was more news that came along with that which was not expected. The nurse told her that she, indeed, had a bladder infection, but she was also pregnant. Everything in the room seemed to spin uncontrollably as she was listening to the instructions that the nurse was delivering. All she could hear was the statement "You are pregnant" and nothing else. Savannah was experiencing every fear all at once and felt that she could not breathe. The nurse was still on the phone, asking her what pharmacy she wanted to use to pick up her prescription for the antibiotic. Once the call was disconnected, she was filled with emotions that she had never experienced in her life. She went downstairs and told Bryson to follow her. He knew that something was wrong with her because she did not look well at all. She took him upstairs to her room, out of the hearing distance of her mom.

Savannah was confused and terrified all at once and did not know how to tell him. Bryson was very attentive and sweet as he hugged her and asked what was wrong. So she began to tell him that not only did she have a bladder infection, but she was also pregnant. This was the moment she was not wanting to face. The question she continued to ask herself, "Can it get any worse?" He could freak out and abandon her to face this all alone. One of the most terrifying fears she had always vowed to not happen to her had come to pass. As she was building up the courage to break the news, she was replaying the delivery of the phone call. She did not want to be another statistic, and she certainly did not want to give up her lifelong dream. Savannah told him that she was pregnant. She was bracing herself with the response that she was expecting. She was wrong about that assumption because Bryson's reaction was the opposite.

He was elated and filled with emotion and love. Savannah was confused and scared out of her mind. She quickly collected her emotions and told him that she could not keep this child. It was not in her plans and that they had to quickly plan a strategy that would not involve their parents. They knew that going to their moms would be out of the question. Bryson had his mother's car, so they told Mom that they were going to grab something to eat. As they drove off, the two came to a decision to ask his auntie for help. The first stop was at the pharmacy to pick up her antibiotic and then on to pick up some food. She was too upset to eat as her appetite had left. She knew that starving herself was out of the question. The medication had to be taken with food, and yes, she was carrying a living being. They finally arrived, and Auntie was happy to see them as she loved it when they could come visit with her on the weekends. She was that one adult they could share everything without fear.

Of course, they were not exempted from a lecture about their consequences. Savannah told her that she wanted an abortion but was scared and did not know where to go. She had heard about a clinic that performed the procedure, but there was a cost that came along with it. The two of them certainly did not have the money and were not going to their moms. Bryson's aunt suggested that she would help if they came up with half of the cost. He would have to work some extra overtime, but they were running out of time because she was already in the first trimester. The next evening, they were at Savannah's, sitting at the table, talking. She was preparing dinner before Mom got home and climbed into a chair to reach the canned goods in the top cabinet. Savannah told him that she was afraid to go through with the procedure. She stated that she would rather have a miscarriage instead of having such an invasive surgery. She felt that Bryson was not comfortable with the topic of terminating a child. He wanted to be there to support her and would do anything to make her happy.

It was about 10:00 p.m. Everyone was in the den, watching a movie. Savannah and Bryson were sitting on the love seat, and her mom was in the kitchen. She had to use the bathroom, so as she was getting up, there was a sneeze, and she felt a little pain in her abdomen. Savannah did not make anything out of it and continued upstairs to use the bathroom. As she was urinating, something did not feel right as she emptied her bladder. She thought maybe she was passing something related to her bladder infection. What happened next was unbelievable and horrifying for anyone to imagine. Savannah wiped and found herself holding a baby in her hand. She panicked and threw the baby in the toilet and flushed. Her heart was pounding rapidly as if she were going to pass out. She went downstairs and called Bryson into the living room to tell him that she needed to get to the emergency room as soon as possible. He immediately called his auntie to come pick them up. The entire time that she was experiencing this trauma, she did not trust her mother enough to tell her.

Savannah, currently in her relationship with Bryson, depended solely on him for comfort and support. Although her mom was no more than five feet away, she did not share this horrifying event. She was only sixteen years old and was willing to face this trauma with the one she grew to trust the most. Savannah had heard her mother mention often to one of her girlfriends that her daughter confided in Bryson too much. Mom believed that he was influencing her to do things that were not in her character. She would say things that were very hurtful at times to make Savanah break ties with him. It never worked because she was in love with him, and he was her world. Now they both are faced with this most traumatic situation in their young lives. They heard a car horn blow, and Mom asked who was in front of the house blowing.

Bryson spoke up and said it was his aunt coming to take them to pick up some food. The two of them grabbed a jacket and went out the front door and got into the car. Savannah rode in the back where she was filled with emotion and extreme fear. She did not know what to expect as they were getting closer to the hospital. Once the car pulled into the emergency room entrance, they got out and went to check themselves in. Auntie went to park the car and came in to make sure that they were all right. Savannah was called back, and a doctor asked her questions related to her visit. She told the doctor that she just had a miscarriage. He examined her and stated that there was no way that he could confirm that she had miscarried. She was upset because he looked at her as if she were not telling the truth. Savannah gave him a detailed description of what took place that evening and that she flushed the baby on her hand. He left the room and was gone for what seemed to be an eternity. When the doctor returned, he stated that there was no evidence and sent her home.

It was extremely late when Bryson and his aunt dropped her off. She went upstairs and climbed into bed about 2:00 a.m. The memory of what she witnessed would not leave as she tried to close her eyes. Hours had passed and Bryson called to check on her and to see if there was anything that he could do. She finally started feeling tired and wanted to go to sleep. The phone rang about 6:00 a.m. She answered it quickly to keep from waking her mother. On the other side was a doctor from the hospital. He identified himself as the on-call physician and had reviewed her case with the intern that was on duty the night before. It turned out that the intern had misdiagnosed. He ordered her to get to back to the hospital as soon as possible. It was profoundly serious, and you could hear the urgency in his tone of voice. She immediately got off the phone and called Bryson to come pick her up. It was about 6:30 a.m. when he showed up, and she tiptoed quietly out of the house.

When they arrived back at the emergency room, she was immediately taken back to an examining room. The OB doctor examined her and stated that she had to have an emergency D&C right away. Savannah was a minor, so he could not perform this operation without the consent of a parent. Bryson had called his aunt to return to the hospital. Savannah had to call her mother and break the news to her, but she was afraid. The nurse called her mom, who was already at work that morning. As one could imagine, it was not a pretty picture when Mom received the news. Mom had given verbal permission for Savannah to have the procedure. When it was all over, she had awakened from the anesthesia to find Bryson standing by her bed, holding her hand. His aunt was sitting in a chair by the door, and of course, her mom was in the room. Bryson leaned in to kiss her, and the two told each other that they loved each other.

Meanwhile, her mother was furious and was not pleased to see the unbreakable bond they had for each other. She was incredibly angry and said things that were hurtful. Auntie tried to smooth the situation by saying positive things, but her mother was not hearing it. She had to get back to work. Savannah was both afraid and embarrassed to hear her mother speak like that in front of Bryson's aunt. This was a time that she needed love and support from her mother. She realized that this would never happen because her mother never showed signs of affection. It was always a lecture or some superstitious rambling about why she should not do something. All she could think about at that moment was the love that Bryson and his family showed her. She did not doubt that her mother loved her, but she had never heard her mother say the words. Savannah believed that was one of the reasons she trusted and gave Bryson all of her. She did not know what love was and had never told anyone that she loved them. She remembered that her dad told her that he loved her all the time although he was not in the picture and she saw less to none of him while growing up.

Savannah remembered that it took her a long time to tell Bryson she loved him. He fell in love with her first and spoke the words before she could bring herself to say them. The doctor came into the room to give his prognosis and speak about some of the things that he had found. Savannah was afraid to hear the news, but he assured her that it was not the end of the world. He stated that everything went well and that she had an unusual but common double uterus. She did not understand what he was saying and thought it was an abnormal deformity. He explained that her uterus just had a thing lining that divided it into two sections. Auntie asked about the pregnancy, and he stated that based on the information, it was indicated that she had miscarried twins.

Savannah had to stay overnight so that the anesthesia would wear off. The next day, Bryson came to pick her up and to take her home. She remembered it was a cool spring Saturday afternoon, and she did not want to go home to face her mother. When they arrived at the house, Mom was already at work. Her mother worked at the hotel on most Saturdays and Sundays. Savannah put the key in the door and let herself into the house. She walked into the kitchen to find a handwritten note on the kitchen table from her mom. It read, in not so many words, that she was grounded and not to leave the house. She had expected that her homecoming was not going to be a warm and loving welcome. Savannah always braced herself from her mother's harsh rantings.

Her mother was bitter at times, and she believed it stemmed from her parents' breakup. It was clear that her mom was not over her father and held a lot of unresolved feelings for him. Bryson was turning to leave, and Savannah told him that she was going with him. She did not want to face her mother or hear the lectures or disapproving comments. This should have been a moment where she trusted her heart with Mom, but she just could not bear it. Savannah had emotionally and physically gravitated to the affection and love of Bryson's family. His mom was a beautiful person, and she treated Savannah like the daughter she never had. When they arrived at his house, she went into the kitchen to greet his mom.

At this point, Bryson's mom knew nothing of what had happened in the past forty-eight hours. Mrs. Wilson was preparing for a party that she was hosting at the house with family and friends. Savannah went upstairs to join Bryson in the den where she found him watching a movie and listening to his music. She was exhausted and climbed onto one of the sofas and fell asleep. It must have been hours before she had been awakened by one of his aunts. Of course, Auntie was at the gathering and came upstairs to ask how she was feeling. She was the only one in the family that knew about the pregnancy and miscarriage at the time. It was our little secret, and they trusted her not to speak about it, at least not now.

By the end of the night, there was some suspicion that the *cat* was out of the bag. It was time for her to go home, and she was not ready to leave. When they pulled up to the house, she did not want to get out of the car. She sat there for what seemed to be an eternity, trying to convince herself to just do it. Bryson was very caring and patient with her and told her that everything was going to be all right. She finally built up the courage and said her good nights to him and went into the house. Savannah did not go into the kitchen to speak with her mother. She immediately ran up the stairs and climbed into her bed. She was praying that her mother would not follow her upstairs. She had hoped there would be no lecture because Mom remained downstairs in the den. Savannah pulled the covers over her head and fell asleep in hopes that she would not have to face her mother. For several days, there was no communication between her and her mother. At the time, she did not know if her mother was still furious with her or just did not know how to talk to her. Savannah believed it may have been a little of both.

Chapter 12

It had been less than six weeks since the miscarriage, and both Savannah and Bryson were still trying to move on. This was a time that she needed a tremendous amount of love and support from her family, friends, and loved ones. But that was going to be difficult because she did not want to share the experience with anyone. Her mother has already shared the news with family members. However, this did not make Savannah feel any better. She did not want to even talk about it with Bryson. For a while, she seemed to have shut down from everything and could not fully understand what she was going through. After all, she was incredibly young and was already faced with the challenges of being a teenager. The thought of becoming a mother was never part of her plan, and she did not know how to cope.

Bryson was incredibly supportive although she felt that it was hard on him as well. She believed that he was a little disappointed that the pregnancy did not survive. This was a very intimate but emotional journey for each of them. One of the counters to their loss was the ability to comfort each other. The doctor had already given specific discharge instructions that Savannah was not to be sexually active for at least six weeks. She continued to remind Bryson that they had to wait, but he was so very insistent. She would tell him no, and he would give some sort of rebuttal as to why he could not wait. One thing about Bryson was he very persuasive and knew exactly how to use his charm on her. He told Savannah that he would be incredibly careful and that everything would be all right.

A lesson they should have learned from the past would have been to use birth control. Bryson was not for the use of birth control, and he, of course, gave Savannah what was a nonexistent reason as to why he could not wear condoms. She was so gullible and never protested his reasoning as to why he preferred not to use them. Savannah, as usual, gave in to his charm and was intimate with him, knowing it was not going to have a good outcome. She remembered before she was discharged from the hospital, there were also instructions on seeing a gynecologist about birth control. Savannah's mother never made a follow-up appointment with a doctor to discuss birth control. She did not have any direction as to where and what to do after having a miscarriage. The ideal situation, as it presented itself, should have been receiving the support from her mom. Savannah could have taken the responsibility on herself to get birth control, but she needed her mom. Two weeks later, Savannah discovered that she was pregnant again.

Now she and Bryson had to deliver the news to their mothers. They decided to tell their moms the same day that they found out. There was no other way of getting out of building up the courage to tell Mom. Later that night, after mom had gotten home from work, Savannah had dinner prepared. She decided to tell her mother that she was pregnant again. All she remembered was her mother closing all the windows in the house to keep the neighbors from hearing the swearing and yelling. After it was over, Mom opened all the windows and then called Savannah's grandmother to tell her what was happening. While she was at home telling her mom, Bryson was giving his mother the news as well. A few hours later, the phone was ringing, and it was Bryson on the other end. He said that his mother was not happy, and in fact, she blamed him for the mistake. She also asked him how he could do such a thing to Savannah. His mom called his dad and made him get on the phone to receive his second lecture.

Bryson's dad was in the Army and was stationed in Maryland, so he did not see his dad every day. The smoke had cleared and now reality was upon them. Bryson and Savannah's life will change forever, and the dreams that she had for herself was no longer in the picture. There was the fear of trying to figure out what to do next.

The one thing that was not going to change was the love they had for each other. For a noticeably short time, she did have some concerns about becoming a single mother. Most girls that she knew never had the father of their children in the lives of their baby. She did not want to be that statistic of being a teenage unwed mother. The first thing her mother and aunt wanted her to do was to go downtown to the welfare department to file for financial support. She remembered her aunt saying that she needed to go get a check and to tell the authorities that she did not know who the father of her child was.

Well, with that suggestion, she did not want to take part of it. So as expected, she gave the news to Bryson, and it was not good. He said that no child of his would ever be on welfare and that he will take care of his child. He was raised in a family that taught him about hard work and doing the right thing. It was his responsibility, and he was told by his mother and father that the choices he made in life he would live with them. He also was taught by his grandparents the value of family and the importance of becoming a man. Savannah told her mom that she did not want the support and that Bryson worked two part-time jobs after school and on the weekends. Mom thought this was a huge mistake and did not believe that he would stick around. She did not have enough faith in them to be able to support and raise a child. Savannah dismissed the lecture and the many negative attempts to discolor Bryson and his ability to take care of his child.

Life had to go on, so did attending school and completing. She and Bryson decided that they were going to summer school to take an extra class before next fall. She was not showing quite yet the first couple weeks of summer school. The two of them did not make any announcements to their remarkably close friends. The summer semester was well on its way, and Savannah was beginning to show a little. She could no longer wear any of her normal-size clothes. They decided to go to the local department store to buy a couple maternity outfits for her to wear. It was more comfortable at the time to wear just sundresses because the fit was perfect but loose enough to keep her comfortable. The next day, they went to summer school, and she wore one of the maternity outfits. At first, she felt like every eye in the universe was on her. There were the stares and whispers in the classroom, but she did not let any of it deter her from continuing summer school. Savannah had developed a certain confidence and did not show any fear or embarrassment.

But only if anyone knew that she was afraid and did not know what to expect with this pregnancy or the expectations of high school. Her life had changed, and there was no taking it back or crying about it. She was well into the pregnancy, and Bryson proved time after time his commitment to her and the baby. Now she was having cravings and sleeping a lot. Bryson would stop by the house every night after work to bring her a whole strawberry pie and two steak biscuits. Whatever she needed, he was there, and it did not matter the hour.

The fall of 1984 had arrived, and the first day back to school was exciting as ever for most. It was their senior year, and she decided that she was going to attend regular school that year. There were plenty of young girls that were pregnant that were enrolled in a pregnant teen school. Savannah was not having any part of it. She was not ashamed and did not feel that she had to hide her situation. She and Bryson still walked the hallways, and when she got too big to walk, they found a little spot-on bench under a tree.

This was where they would sit every morning while the weather was nice until the first period bell rang. She went to school every day, and when she had OB-GYN appointments, she would catch public transportation. The closer it became to the due date, the more nervous but excited she felt. She and Bryson began shopping for the baby, and it was fun for them. They would go every week on his pay dates to buy baby clothes, diapers, bottles, blankets, etc. Whatever they could think of to buy for the baby, Bryson bought it. The last thing they had to buy was a car seat to bring the baby home. Savannah's sister-in-law had given her a baby crib that she used with her niece. One side of Savannah's bedroom was a nursery at this point. The baby was growing, and there was quite much moving and stretching of this little one. She remembered the first kick which felt like a little flutter.

Savannah wanted a little boy, and Bryson wanted a little girl. He was already calling the baby Destiny as he would be touching Savannah's stomach. They did not want to know the sex of the baby and wanted it to be a surprise. Through the entire pregnancy, Savannah did not choose any girl names, and she was still undecisive about the name if it was a boy. Bryson was also thinking of some boy names as well, but he was determined to name the baby Destiny if it was a girl.

It was getting close to delivery as the baby was due in February. Bryson would take her to the mall to walk because that was something that women did prior to labor. It was part of the preparation of getting ready to welcome a new life into the world. Then she began to have a little discomfort from her back and abdomen as it dropped the closer it was to delivery time. One week before she was due, there were quite a few nonemergency visits to the ER. She would be sent home because it was not time for the baby to be delivered. This was her first pregnancy, and she did not know what to expect.

Then on Wednesday, February 27, 1985, it was time. She was in labor that night, and Bryson stayed with her throughout the night. The contractions were beginning to come now, and the pain was like nothing she had ever experienced. They were off to the hospital, and she had been admitted and taken back to the labor and delivery room. She was hooked up to the baby monitor and was explained that they were keeping an eye on how the baby was doing. The nurse also explained what will be happening when there were contractions as well. She remembered the nurse continued to come in the room to check how far she had dilated. You could already see the crown of the baby's head and the nurse commented on how much hair on the baby's head.

Savannah looked at the clock, and it was well after midnight, but she was nowhere near fully dilated. She tried to sleep, and every time she would get comfort, another contraction would come. She did very well with her breathing although she never took Lamaze classes. The nurse came back to check her again, and it was 11:30 p.m. on Thursday, February 28, 1985. She told Savannah that she was almost at ten centimeters and would be delivering soon. Bryson was there holding her hand and telling her that everything was going to be okay. She believed him and never doubted that it would not be okay. Another contraction came, and she could feel the pressure of the baby and wanted to push. The nurse checked this time, and she was fully dilated, and they were off to the delivery room. One other nurse took Bryson to a changing room where she had given him a pair of scrubs to put on over his clothes. The moment had arrived, and Savannah was ready to push. The doctor was at the end of the table, and Bryson was there, awaiting the arrival of his child. The nurse was behind her, supporting her back as she was sitting up and pushing as they instructed. All she could remember was this tremendous pressure, and then she was told to stop pushing. The baby's head was out, and the doctor was gently pulling the shoulders.

Then she was told to give one big push, and suddenly the pain stopped as she felt the baby come out. She lay back onto the table, and she was being congratulated that it was a boy. The doctor gave the baby a little tap on the bottom so that he would cry. He certainly had a healthy set of lungs on him, and he handed the baby over to Bryson. Savannah was extremely exhausted and could not muster up any strength to see what was going on with the baby. She saw Bryson carrying their son over to the warming lamp where the nurse weighed and cleaned him off. He was wrapped in a blanket and given back to Bryson.

As he was bringing the baby over, they were asked what the baby's name was. Bryson blurted out the baby's full name before Savannah could even respond. Mason Curtis Morgan was born Thursday, February 28, 1985, at 12:37 p.m., weighing six pounds, fifteen ounces. Later, Savannah was rolled into her room where she slept most of the day. Bryson was there when she woke and when the nurse brought the baby in to be fed. She did have a few visitors that came by the hospital to see her and the baby. Her mother did not come to the hospital to visit her or the baby. Savannah had to stay in the hospital overnight and would be released the following afternoon. It was customary that a patient and baby stay at least twenty-four to forty-eight hours after delivery to make sure the baby passed all test that was given. The doctor came into the room and gave his all-clear to be discharged the next morning. Savannah was filled with excitement and overwhelmed expectations. She was a new mother, and the journey was just beginning. All it took was one look at Mason, and she fell in love with him.

Bryson and his mom came to the hospital to pick them up and take them home. They pulled up to the house, and Bryson carried Mason into the house and took him upstairs and placed him in his crib. He could not stay because he had to be at work that day. While Mason was asleep, she made him a few bottles because she knew it would not be long before he will awake with hunger. Mom arrived home from work and could not wait to come upstairs to see her new grandbaby. She lifted him out of his crib and carried him to her bedroom. Savannah could see that her mother had fallen completely in love with Mason. It was time to feed him, and her mom decided she wanted to feed him. Savannah did not put up any objection; it meant more than she could say that her mom took to Mason so quickly. All the heartache and hurtful comments disappeared and were never spoken again from that day forward. Bryson stopped by to see his son the next day, bringing baby formula enough that would last for at least a month. Bryson was going to be a hands-on dad and did everything right.

Olivia did not have to do anything for them because Bryson had it covered. These actions proved to her that Bryson was the real deal. He did not care if she had approved or not; he was going to take care of his son. He continued to be very respectful to Olivia, and over time, their relationship developed into a very caring one. Six weeks was about to approach, and they needed a babysitter because Savannah was returning to school. They did not trust just anyone to care for their baby while they were at school. Savannah asked her grandmother if she would come to the house during the week and care for Mason while she was at school. Bryson paid her grandmother weekly and brought a monthly bus pass for her transportation to and from. Savannah took on a part-time job after school and on weekends, so her mother was happy to care for Mason on the evenings that she worked. Savannah was only away from Mason for a few hours three days a week. Her mom loved Mason so very much and picked him up every opportunity she was given.

As expected, she was spoiling him, along with her grandmother. Bryson's mom joined in the frenzy with her sisters and mother. Mason was the first great-grandchild and his mom's first grandchild. They were hoping for a little girl because there were only boys in the family. She was so appreciative of the love that was expelled upon her son. Savannah was determined that she was going to do everything possible to be the best mother to her son. One of the things she still needed to do was continue with her studies because she was graduating in June. The reality of her life was a full-time teen mom, high school student, as well as a part-time working mom. She was grateful for her grandmother helping them out so that she could finish school. She and Bryson were parents and knew that they had to make plans for their family after high school. He had decided after Mason's birth that he wanted to make a difference for his son.

He decided that he was going to join the United States Army right after high school. He also participated in the junior ROTC program, plus his father was currently serving in the Army. Bryson talked with dad about his plans, and he was given the support he needed. Spring was upon them, and everyone was making plans to attend the senior prom. Savannah did not want to miss out on a rite of passage, so she and Bryson made plans to attend. Everything was going well with school, and they both studied hard so that they would pass their final exams. There was so much going on in those few short months to include preparation for high school graduation.

In May, the two were all dressed up with a tuxedo and prom dress on their way to the prom. She did not want to be away from Mason long that night. After the prom was over, they went home to change clothes to go to an after-party, but it was not what they really wanted to do. Becoming parents do change a person, and their priority was to Mason. He was their life and especially important to them. Most high school seniors partied all night and did wild things. Bryson and Savannah were not eager to participate in those activities. They were more mature and took life very seriously. The weekend was over, and life had returned to their normal routine. It was the middle of the week when Savannah took Mason to visit with his Nana. She was so excited to see him and just loved and kissed him.

Bryson and Savannah hung out upstairs for a while, trying to have a little downtime. She was exhausted and feeling a little overwhelmed. Savannah was emotional that night and just wanted to pick a fight with him. There was no rhyme or reason for it, but she just lashed out at him. She knew that he would be leaving to go to basic training, which would leave her alone. For some reason, her old insecurities had gotten the best of her, and the thought of him not returning terrified her. So one of her defense mechanisms was to push him away. Well, it did not work because he was so used to her mood swings.

The ride home was incredibly quiet; she had tears falling from her face. Why was she so emotional right now? Fear was upon her, and she had no control of it. She kept thinking about his leaving, and she did not want him to. They went into the house, and she laid Mason down for bed. Bryson was still upstairs with Mason, and she was downstairs in the kitchen with her mom. He called for her to come back upstairs; she found him standing over Mason's crib. She did not understand why his facial expression was different. The first thing she thought was to prepare herself for some disappointing news. He started to kneel as if he was reaching under the baby's crib but removed an object. It was a jewelry box that had Fink's Jewelers printed on it. She was stunned, and her heart was pounding with excitement and fear. Was this really happening? He asked her to marry him as he slipped the ring onto her finger. She nervously said yes with a shakiness in her voice.

At that moment, all her fears and insecurities vanished. She went downstairs to show this beautiful piece of jewelry to her mother. Savannah was so nervous she still felt the jitters throughout the night. She was so very much in love with Bryson, and this was one of the most important nights of her life. He had already given her a beautiful healthy son, and now he was asking her to be his wife. Their life was just beginning, and they were excited about what all was about to come.

Chapter 13

It has been a year already, and Mason was turning one year old this February. Bryson has left for basic training in the United States Army. He will be completing his training by April, and his aunt Jennie was helping Savannah with wedding plans. It was more like Jennie doing all the planning and scheduling appointments. Savannah just tagged alone while everything was coming together. Her mother did not take part in the planning of the wedding. It was not because she did not want to help. Savannah did not include her mother in the planning. She knew that her mom could not afford to give her the wedding that she dreamed. She was incredibly grateful for Jennie's take-charge behavior because she did not have a clue as to where to begin.

It was already April, and the wedding was planned for June 7, and she was overwhelmed. Bryson's basic training graduation was coming up in a couple weeks. His family had already made plans for the trip to Missouri. They were driving down in his uncle's recreation vehicle and were taking a few family members. Savannah was excited with the anticipation of seeing Bryson again. She packed for herself and Mason for this journey to see his dad. It had been a while since he saw his dad, and he was growing like a weed.

The night before the big trip, she could not sleep at all because her mind was on Bryson. It had been about twelve weeks since she saw him last, and the only communication was letters and a few brief phone calls. The sun was rising and she was still awake, so Savannah got up to gather her bags and placed them at the front door. Bryson's mom called to let her know that they would be arriving about 7:00 a.m. to pick her and Mason up. The next stop was Pop and Gran's house to collect them, along with Aunt Pearl and his cousin's girl-friend, Michelle. The RV was filled with seven bodies and luggage. It was roomy with plenty of space for Mason to move about. The ladies were camped out at the table that was posted in front of the exceptionally long cushioned seat. On the other side of the camper, Savannah sat watching out the window with Mason talking non-stop with his baby chatter. They traveled from Virginia through West Virginia where the mountains reached heights that seemed to tower over the road. On both sides of the road, the mountains had cliffs and hollers that one could see hundreds feet down. Savannah looked down into the holler where there was a lake, and to her surprise, there was a naked man jumping into the water. She could not believe her eyes that this was possible so early in the morning. One hears about it and often sees these types of behaviors in the movies but not in reality. What more would she encounter on this trip?

They had stopped for breakfast and bathroom break, and the ladies all went into a local store to purchase goodies. After refresh-ing and stretching their legs, it was time to load up into the camper and drive several more hours. They had already traveled through Tennessee, and now they were in Missouri. The graduation was later that afternoon, and Bryson's dad was making good time. They finally arrived and checked into the hotel where everyone showered and got dressed. Michelle shared a room with Savannah and little Mason. Everyone else paired accordingly, leaving Aunt Pearl in a room to herself. We reached the base and found seats in an auditorium where many family and friends gathered in anticipation of seeing their loved ones.

Once the ceremony was over, everyone searched through the crowds to find their son, daughter, cousin, niece, or nephew who completed basic training. Bryson found his family and was greeted by his mom and grandmother. You could see the anticipation and love in his eyes when he laid them on her. It has been what seemed to have been a lifetime since he saw her last. Once he made his way through the hugs and kisses from the other family members, at last, he could touch her. He gave her a very gentle kiss on the lips, but she knew that he wanted more. It had only been about three months, but Mason still knew his dad. Savannah talked about him every day and showed him pictures of his dad. There was no surprise that he reached with both arms for his dad to pick him up. After all the emotions of being together again, the families were directed to the mess hall, also called the banquet hall or cafeteria, for lunch.

Everyone sat with their loved ones to eat and share that precious moment. All the graduates were granted a day pass to spend off the base with their families. Bryson was going to stay at the hotel with the family. His parents had paid for him a room to himself, but everyone knew that he would not be by himself for long. The mother of his child and fiancée was with them, and they had not seen each other in a while. They arrived back at the Best Western Hotel, and Michelle and Savannah went back to their room with Mason. A few minutes later, Bryson knocked at the door and came in and sat and talked with the two for a moment. Then they asked Michelle if she could keep an eye on Mason when he was asleep. She understood what they were asking her and immediately agreed with a smirk on her face. Michelle told them to go handle their business in a jokingly way.

Bryson took Savannah's hand and led her out the room and down the corridor to his room. The entry to all the rooms had exterior doors. He reached into his pocket for the key so that he could open the door. Savannah did not understand why she was so nervous. This was the man that she had a child with and was going to marry in two months. She did not know if it was the anticipation of being intimate with him again and not knowing what to expect. It had been what seemed to be a lifetime since he touched her. Savannah missed him so very much and could not wait another moment to feel the gentle touch of his hands on her body. He was very patient with her, as if it was the first time all over again. She felt the love and kindness in his heart and was more than sure that he was the man she wanted to spend an eternity.

The emotions were so high that it brought tears to their eyes because the two were so deeply in love with each other. It had been about an hour when Bryson walked her back to the room and watched a movie with them. Mason was still asleep from all the excitement that day. The next morning, everyone got up to get ready to check out of the hotel. Before taking Bryson back to the base, they stopped to have breakfast and say their goodbyes. He was coming home very soon in a matter of few weeks. He would be preparing for his first duty station before he and Savannah got married.

The family was headed back to Virginia, and Savannah was filled with emotions and did not say much on the trip back. She put up a smile under false pretense because she missed Bryson so much. The next morning, they had made it back home, and everyone was dropped off at Pop and Grans. Aunt Pearl was giving Michelle a ride back to her apartment because it was on her way home. Savannah waited patiently until Pop and Grans were settled into their home before Bryson's parents dropped her and the baby at home.

The few weeks had passed, and Bryson was finally coming home. His flight was due to arrive that night, so she and his mom and grandmother drove out to the airport to pick him up. Savannah's heart was pounding as they got closer to the airport and was getting out of the car. She could not wait to see him; all she could think about was loving him with everything she knew how. Finally, his plane had touched down, and he was departing the aircraft. His mother ran to him first and hugged and kissed him as if she were seeing him for the first time.

Of course, Grans had to get her precious hug and kiss as well. Savannah always waited patiently and respectfully until all the attention given to Bryson subsided. She knew it would be her turn and the wait would be well worth it. He was smiling from ear to ear and looked so handsome in his dressed uniform. It was something about a man in a uniform that sent chills down her spine. They were walking back to the car, and Bryson could not keep his hands off her. The two of them rode in the back seat of his mom's car as she was headed back to drop Grans by her house.

Once they arrived, he would not dare leave without spending some time with Pops. The time had moved so fast that it was way after 11:00 p.m., and Savannah had to get home to Mason. Bryson and his mom took her home, and they said good night. She went into the house to find Mason sleeping so peacefully in his crib. Her mother was still up that night and said he did well. Savannah was so tired and sleepy that she crashed onto her bed and fell asleep. The next morning, she was awakened by a gentle touch and found that Bryson had come to see her and Mason exceedingly early. She was still trying to open her eyes and focus. Bryson had already taken Mason out of his crib and took him downstairs to the kitchen to feed him breakfast. Savannah stumbled out of bed and went to the bathroom before she went downstairs to join them.

Her mom was just leaving to go to work and talked to Bryson for a moment while she waited on her bus. It was warm that morning with a little breeze blowing. Mason was sitting in his high chair and eating and laughing while his dad was playing with him. Savannah sat at the table after fixing herself a little breakfast. She was happy to see Bryson and Mason's little reunion; it seemed as if they picked up where they left off. He asked her about the wedding plans, and she told him that Jennie was making all the arrangements. Bryson really did not want a big wedding; he had suggested that they go to the justice of the peace. His concerns were about the cost and stated that he could not afford to pay for the wedding that his aunt was planning. Savannah, like any other bride-to-be, wanted the wedding cake and flowers. She never thought about who was going to pay for these things.

Bryson had made his stand and told her that they were going downtown. That was the last thing that she wanted to talk about, so she changed the subject. She could not believe they were having a strong disagreement over one of the most important days of their life. The next time she saw Jennie, Savannah knew that she had to tell her that the wedding she was planning was not going to happen. She did not want to be the one to tell Jennie no.

The timing had to be perfect for her to break the news to Jennie. Something else had taken precedence over this decision. Bryson had received his orders for his first tour of duty. He was to report within two weeks to serve four years in Germany. This was not the news that they were prepared for, and Savannah and Bryson could not bear to be apart for that long. She did not want to go to Germany, and he did not want to leave her behind. Bryson understood that he had no choice in the matter when he was called to duty. He and Savannah decided that she would stay here in the States. They went to look at some apartments that she and Mason would live until he returned. His grandmother had taken them to Grand Piano furniture store to purchase furniture for the apartment. It all seemed like a good idea at first, but the reality of it all scared Savannah.

Bryson's father was senior master sergeant in the Army, and he used his rank and years of experience to change Bryson's orders. His father was able to get him stationed in the States for the first two years. He was to report to Fort Hood, Texas, the largest infantry base in the country. Savannah was relieved but still was hesitant about leaving Virginia. She decided that she was still going to stay behind for a while. Aunt Jennie told her that it was her place to be with her husband. The wedding date was moved due to the change in his orders. They were married at his parents' house with a few close friends and family members. It was exceedingly small and intimate in front of the fireplace on Saturday, June 16, 1986.

Their life was just beginning as husband and wife. They spent their honeymoon night at the historical Hotel Roanoke where her mom worked. The honeymoon suite was beautiful, and the room service was very elegant. Savannah had never drunk alcohol before, so when the complimentary fruit tray and champagne arrived it was a little overwhelming. Bryson opened the bottle and poured a little into the champagne glasses on the beautiful table. They made a toast, and she sipped from the glass, just enough to taste. It was not one of her favorite things to experience, but it was very romantic. The night was magical and filled with love as Bryson made her fall in love with him all over again.

Chapter 14

It did not take her long to figure out that she could no longer live without Bryson. She had changed her mind after he was gone for two weeks. Savannah never took the apartment and had told his mom and grandmother to not have the furniture purchased or delivered. She was making plans to move to Texas to be with her husband. Savannah was packing everything that she could ship prior to her arrival. Bryson was also planning to live off base by leasing a one-bedroom apartment. He had already purchased bedroom furniture as well. She was already saying goodbye to her best friend, Tamara, and most of her family. The day had arrived for Savannah to take her first plane ride, traveling to Dallas/Fort Worth, Texas, and then onto a smaller plane to Killeen, Texas. Her mother went with her and Mason to the airport. Granddaddy's niece Betty helped load his van with some things that she decided to fly out with her.

Savannah remembered her mother always telling her and her siblings that when they turn eighteen years old, everyone was getting out of her house. She did not count on Savannah taking her threat literally until the day had come. Betty was helping her unload the van and carry some of her things to be checked-in baggage. Mason's playpen was also one of the items that she decided to carry out of necessity. Everything had been checked in, and she was now ready to board the plane with Mason. She said her goodbyes to her mom as she was boarding the plane. At that time, everyone had to walk outside and up in what seemed to be the longest stairwell to the plane. Savannah's mom came out onto the tarmac, and she decided to stay inside. She had a fear of planes and did not want to be that close to one. She had always had such superstitions about everything, including flying on a plane.

The plane was being pushed off so that it could begin its taxi down the runway. Savannah was sitting up front in the middle seat, with Mason sitting next to the window. She was a little nervous but, at the same time, very anxious and happy to be headed to her new life. The pilot came on the intercom system and announced that they were next in line to take off. The flight attendants made their rounds to make sure that everyone was buckled into their seats. The flight instructions were given as the plane was moving slowing up the runway. She was still watching outside the window in hopes of seeing her mom standing out by the fence. In those days, people could watch the planes take off and land all day.

There was an area alongside the airport that was fenced and people parked and watched the planes. As the plane began its take-off speed down the runway, she felt her body being pulled into the seat from the force of the plane's acceleration. She was still watching out the window, and as the plane passed, she saw her mother jumping up and down, crying and screaming as the plane lifted off the ground. All this was a shock to her because she had never witnessed her mom showing emotions of that level. Savannah always thought her mom meant what she said about the three of them moving out of her house. She used to hear such negative comments all the time.

So Savannah vowed that when she turned eighteen years old, she would move out and never return. She did not think it would be in the matter being married with a child. The flight seemed to have been forever, but this was her first time flying. They arrived in Dallas/Fort Worth, Texas, in which Bryson told her it was one of the largest international airports. She had to make her connecting flight, which was on the other side of the airport. She carried Mason and her carry-on bag to the train system, which took her across the airport. Savannah had never seen such a commotion of travelers and airport employees. It looked like a huge shopping mall with restaurants and a large variety of stores like JCPenney, Sears, and Roebuck.

She finally arrived in the concourse where her flight to Killeen would be boarding. It was a small plane that she literally sat two seats behind the pilot and copilot. Savannah was not thrilled about how cramped she felt and the turbulence that came along with the ride. Within forty-five to fifty-five minutes, she had finally arrived at the small airport in Killeen, Texas. Bryson was already waiting for her and Mason with his cousin Tony, who had come to pick her up. Savannah was so happy to see her husband and could not wait to greet him properly. After picking up her bags in the baggage claim, they exited the airport and were on the way to their new home. Bryson had gotten them an apartment in the same building as his cousin and his wife. This was Savannah's first time in Texas; as a child, she did not remember living anywhere outside of Virginia.

Her mom told her that they lived in New York when she was an infant, but Savannah did not count that as a true remembrance. As she entered the apartment, she took a moment to focus on the fact that she was really doing this. She and Bryson were starting their new life as a family. Savannah put her bags down and walked from room to room. It was only a one-bedroom apartment, with a kitchen, dining, living room, and bathroom off the master's bedroom. This was more than enough room for the three of them. They only had bedroom furniture at the time but would add to the apartment as Bryson paid off one room at a time. This was his way of paying cash for things and not acquiring a lot of debt. He had learned this from his grandparents and wanted to start on the right track.

They did not have a car at the time, so Tony's wife, Kristina, would take Savannah to the grocery store later that day. She laid Mason down for his nap, and she and Bryson reunited as a newly married couple would. She did not realize how tired she was after traveling all day and fell asleep as her head hit the pillow. When she woke up, it was time to take a trip to the grocery store. This would be her first time shopping for a household, and she thought it would be a little intimidating. She has her grocery list and coupons, ready to shop. When they arrived at the store, she had a plan of what she needed to do first. She grabbed her cart and proceeded with her list, but at some point, she got off track and thought only about cleaning supplies. How did this happen? When she went to pay for the groceries, she noted that there were more cleaning supplies than food. It was too late to put things back and readjust, but she did not want to be embarrassed. She never realized until she returned to the apartment that the military only got paid once a month at the time. Bryson told her that he would change his pay to twice a month so that she could manage the bills and shopping.

Luckily, they did not have any bills, only rent and electricity. A one-bedroom apartment in 1986 was about $285 a month. This would be her first lesson of life, and it was not taken for granted. The weekend came and went, and Bryson had to report to duty. His morning routine began with physical training (PT) each day before coming back home to shower and change into his uniform and off to work. Savannah loved to see him get dressed because she loved to see a man in uniform. It has been a month since she moved to Texas and already have learned how to get around on base. Although they did not have a car at the time, she would call a taxi to go to the grocery store and to the mall. She would sometimes put Mason in his stroller and take him for walks early in the morning. Savannah always wanted to get things done in the morning because the extreme temperatures were dangerous by midmorning. She had never experienced triple-digit temperatures until she moved to Texas.

The first Christmas there was spent by the poolside when Bryson and his cousin and their friends took a dip in the pool. Savannah did not know how to swim, and she had to keep an eye on Mason. Later that day, everyone met at Tony's and Kristina's where the women all prepared side dishes and the men supplied the beverages. Now for this group, there would always be the option of alcohol or nonalcoholic beverages. She got to meet some of the other Army wives and girlfriends. The men were gathered in the living room and watching whatever game that was on that day. The women would be at the dining room table where Kristina would be in the kitchen with her blender blaring, making margaritas and strawberry daiquiris. These gatherings took place quite often every weekend, whether it was a cookout or just everyone wanting to come together to hang out.

Sometimes she and Bryson would not go over because they needed to have some family time.

There was another couple that had a little girl, but she was just an infant. It was not always the best environment to have a child. There were always adult conversations and alcohol on the weekends. Bryson did have some of his own friends from work. One of his absolute rules was not to bring his friends home from work. He always stipulated that his home was for his wife and family. When he wanted to hang out with some of the guys from work, he would meet with them at their houses. Most of the time, it would be on lunch hour, and the guys would go over to Bob's home where he cooked Italian for them. Savannah did meet one of Bryson's friends, Tony and his wife, Sue. She did not speak English very well, but you could communicate with her if you would just pay close attention to detail. She and Savannah hit it off well, and they became friends. They had a little boy named Tony that was the same age as Mason. Both the children were toddlers at the time, and they had playdates whenever Bryson and Savannah would visit. Bryson was very particular as to who he introduced to his wife and family. He did not trust any man around Savannah because he was very territorial when it came to her. Life was good, and they were very much in love and happy.

Although they did not have a car the first year, it was not as much of a burden for them to go places. Savannah was comfortable with calling a taxicab to pick her and Mason up. This was their only form of transportation at the time to do grocery shopping. It was quite an adjustment to living the military life. There were always families moving in and out of the apartment complex due to military orders. She met some of the neighbors in the building upstairs and across the hall. Mr. Washington was one of the many people that she met, who was the maintenance man. He had a son with special needs named Lewis that always smiled and kept watch on all the activity that took place on the grounds. He loved wearing his cowboy boots and hat with long tube socks and shorts. Lewis kept us entertained with his witty conversations. There was never a time when you saw him without his boom box, listening to his country music.

Mr. Washington loved to talk about living in Texas and always confused Virginia from West Virginia whenever he would ask Savannah about her hometown. As time passed, she would meet some of Tony and Kristina's other friends from the base. She did meet a new couple, Matthew and Margie, from Richmond, Virginia, that moved in across the parking lot. He was stationed at Fort Hood and worked at Carl R. Darnell Army Medical Center. The two were genuinely nice and became good friends to Bryson and Savannah. Although they did not have any children, it did not take Margie exceedingly long to take to Mason. He was two years old and every bit active and kept you on your toes. Mason loved Margie and would get excited whenever he would see her. She would babysit Mason sometimes when Savannah would have a doctor's appointment.

For the short time she lived in Texas, there was only one other person she would trust to leave her son with. Kristina, of course, was family and kept him for Savannah once while she went to the grocery store. Mason was not feeling well, and she did not want to take him out. It was nice to have family living so close by because it could get lonely at times. Savannah was a housewife, and she grew not to enjoy it. She wanted her independence and some time to herself. Savannah decided to have a talk with Bryson about going back to school in the evenings when he got off work.

He was supportive of the idea and wanted her to be a part of something that made her happy. She also wanted to get a job working part-time, but they could not afford the day care, and she did not trust anyone. Margie and the other women had jobs and were at work all day. Savannah felt so left out when the girls would talk about work and coworkers on the weekend. She wanted to make her own money, so Kristina introduced her to one of her friends that needed a babysitter. Savannah did not decide right away because she wanted to talk to Bryson about it. After the two had a conversation, she called Kristina, and they set up a meet and greet with Troy and Patricia Johnson, parents to little Kayla. The husband was stationed on the base, and his wife worked at one of the local banks. Kayla was a beautiful little princess with a big personality. She as Mason were the only child and was accustomed to that one-on-one time.

The first week went well as the children learned social skills with playing, sharing, and simple communication. Each day was an adventure with two toddlers competing for attention. Savannah had set schedules for them daily to keep the kids on a routine. There was time set aside for play and developmental skills. She provided games with shapes, sizes, letters, and numbers. Then by noon, it was lunchtime and then nap time for Mason and Kayla. While the children were napping, it gave Savannah the opportunity to do a few chores within the apartment. In these moments, it was the perfect time to reflect on the most important things in life. She thought about family, friends, and loved ones that played an especially important role in their lives. It was a blessing to include new friends within the boundaries of what would be considered close-knit. Well, in the ideal world, it would have been received with welcome arms.

Chapter 15

Things began to change in the babysitting agreement that was made between Savannah and the Johnsons. Each week that went by, the payments were less and far between. She would talk with Patricia and ask about the babysitting money, but she would be told that Troy would be paying her. At the time, Savannah was somewhat passive and did not always speak up about things. She did not want to bring it up with Bryson due to the fact he did not care for Troy. He always thought Troy was a little arrogant and had some type of chip on his shoulder. She had no choice and decided to talk with Bryson who was not so happy about the situation and told her to not continue to keep their daughter. Bryson was not going to allow them to take advantage of Savannah's kindness. She had become attached to Kayla and enjoyed babysitting such a sweet little girl.

These were Tony and Kristina's friends, and she was doing this as a favor to them because they were family. Savannah decided to speak with Kristina about the Johnsons because she wanted to understand what the reasons would be for them not to pay. Bryson had already put his foot down and was not going to budge. It was either she confronted them or he would and that was not going to be a pretty picture. So she called Patricia and told her that she needed to speak with them about not paying the money. Monday morning came, and Patricia dropped the baby off before work. She gave Savannah some money, but it was the back payments. She noticed that Patricia's mood was different and not as friendly as before. Savannah could not understand why she would have an attitude with her when they were the ones not paying their babysitting debt. Savannah was appreciative that she did get some of the money, but fair is fair.

Later that evening, when they came to pick up Kayla, she could see that Troy had an attitude as well. Bryson had walked in just as they were about to get into discussion about what was agreed and the reasons for not holding up to their part of the agreement. Troy showed his arrogant self, and Bryson had to step in and ask him to show a little respect. It was as if we were the ones that had done them wrong. The two were both very defensive and were in complete denial that they were not honest and forthcoming. Savannah and Bryson realized that there was not going to be any remorse or apology.

Troy paid what was owed, and Savannah told them that as of that day, she would no longer be able to keep their child. Of course, this decision put them in a bind because they both had to work and did not have anyone else to keep their daughter. The short-term relationship ended in a matter of minutes, and Savannah was relieved that she no longer had to wrestle with the emotional bondage. Weeks had passed and her daily routine continued as usual. She wanted more although being a wife and mother was a large part of her life. Savannah needed to find time for herself and pursue some independence. She wanted to go back to college so that she could complete her associate's. All she wanted to do was contribute to the household and make a difference. Bryson was content with her being at home with Mason and welcoming him home every day, but he loved her enough to support her dreams. At the time, they did not have adequate transportation for her to get to and from campus.

So she decided to wait until they were able to purchase a car so she would not have to be traveling at night by taxi. After waiting over six months, Bryson spoke with his grandfather and told him he would be traveling back home to begin his car search. The plan was to send Savannah and Mason ahead of him so that she could visit with her mom and then he would join them within a week.

It was the middle of August, and they decided this would be the best time to take a little vacation back home. Savannah was prepared to purchase a bus ticket for her and Mason. It was a coincidence that Tony and Kristina were going to Virginia for his brother's wedding. To save them money, Tony offered to give Savannah a ride since they were making the same trip. It all worked out, and Bryson did not have to worry about his wife and child traveling alone on a Greyhound bus back east.

For the next few days, Savannah made sure that Bryson had enough food and clean laundry while she was gone. In that time, the group increased because Jeff, one of their hometown friends, was traveling back the same week. Margie was also from Virginia and wanted to make the trip also, and her husband was going to be on call and could not make the trip. So it was decided that she would ride with Jeff to help him drive back, and she was going to be dropped off at the Greyhound bus station in Roanoke and head to Richmond, her hometown. It all was planned accordingly, and everyone was prepared for the twenty-three-hour trip from Texas to Virginia. The next morning, everyone met at the apartment around 1:00 a.m. because it was cooler to travel through the state of Texas early morning. Some days, it would be close to ninety degrees before 8:00 a.m., and no one wanted to be traveling in the sweltering heat. They were on their way; Bryson said his goodbyes to his wife and son as the two cars drove off into the darkness.

The first few hours, there was adult conversation and then dead silence. Savannah drifted off to sleep with the sound of music lightly playing in the background. What seemed like a full night's rest was only about an hour or so because she was restless from the motion of the car. The temperature in the car changed frequently as Tony let the window down for the cool night breeze to keep him awake. The sun was beginning to rise, and they had stopped for breakfast and bathroom break. Everyone got out of the car to stretch their legs and to regain circulation from sitting and riding so long. They were in Little Rock, Arkansas, and had hundreds of miles to go before entering the state of Tennessee. Tony needed rest from driving all night, so he gave the wheel to Kristina to take them into the state of Tennessee. Margie did the same with Jeff to give him a break so that he could get some sleep.

Meanwhile, Savannah had to keep Mason entertained with toys and reading books to him. After all, traveling with a toddler is most interesting, and riding for such lengths could drive anyone a little bonkers. He finally fell asleep after eating his favorite snack, and all was well once again. She decided that it would be best for her to nap so that she could catch up on much-needed rest too. What seemed like days of driving was twenty-two hours of highway in front and behind them. It was a delight to see the Blue Ridge mountains again as they crossed from Bristol, Tennessee into Bristol, Virginia. They had a little over two hours left before arriving in Roanoke. Everyone was practically counting down the miles left as they drove past landmarks and many things that reminded them of returning home. It was getting dark, and they were a half hour out from the Hershberger exit. Savannah had not been home in a year and was anticipating seeing her mom again. First, they had to drop Margie off at the Greyhound bus terminal so that she could continue her trip back to Richmond. After saying their goodbyes to Margie, she was the next drop-off to her mom's.

As they pulled up to the house, her mom had the front porch light on already and every light on in the house. Tony helped with the bags as Savannah hugged Kristina, saying they would see one another in a week. Oliva heard the chatter and closing of doors and opened the front door to greet Savannah. Mason was already standing on the front porch, waiting to see his grandma. She grabbed him up and held on to him and filled his little chubby face with kisses. Mason giggled as his eyes were filled with joy because he had not seen her in such a long time. He had to tell her about his adventure traveling in the car in toddler translation. A two-year-old's conversation can be remarkably interesting when they are trying to express themselves. Tony and Kristina had driven off into the night, and they were entering the house. Savannah was happy to see her mom and was anxious to tell her about life in the big state of Texas. It was getting close to Mason's bedtime as he could hardly hold his little eyes open.

Savannah had got his bathwater ready and was trying to undress him to put him in the tub. He was already falling asleep, and it was a struggle to keep him sitting up in the water. She gave him a quick wash, drained the tub, and just wiped him down and put his pajamas on and laid him down to sleep. She was tired from the road trip as well and wanted to just sleep. Savannah called Bryson to let him know that they had made it and would be calling him in the morning. It was the weekend, and he would surely be home. He told her that he missed her and Mason already and could not wait to make the trip next week to Roanoke. Savannah lay across the bed that she slept in when she was a teenager in high school. It brought back old memories from when she and Bryson would be on the phone talking until dawn some nights.

As he continued to talk, she felt herself nodding off into dreamland. She could not hold her eyes open any longer and told him that she needed to go to bed and that she would call him in the morning. Savannah drifted off to sleep with the comfort of being home again.

Chapter 16

She woke up in a remarkably familiar place, with the same smells and sounds of life outside her window as the warm summer breeze blew the sheer curtains softly into her childhood room. It was nearly 9:00 a.m., and Mason was still asleep in the bed across from her. Savannah lay there for just a few minutes longer, remembering the times spent in this room. It seemed as though time had never stopped as she looked at the pictures that were still on the wall from her childhood. A lifetime of memories was at her disposal as she remembered her first encounter with the supernatural in that exact room. For most people, they would be frightened with that sort of experience outside of watching a scary movie on the television. Savannah had always been a unique little girl, and it had transpired into her teenage and early adult life.

She could also remember some not-so-happy times spent in that house when her dad left them for the last time. Savannah always felt that there was a higher purpose for the things and people she had encountered in life. There was a moment of complete déjà vu as she sat up on the side of the bed. Savannah stood up and walked across the warm hardwood floor that made a creaking sound as she approached the bedroom door. As she entered the bathroom, the antique window was already opened, letting the fresh morning breeze into the room. One would think that they were in a time capsule with the original claw-foot cast-iron bathtub. The hardwood floor that had been tiled with linoleum was a blast from the past. The sink was attached to the wall, which floated above the floor. There was also the antique toilet with the antique-inspired handle. She looked out of the window down into the yard where Mom had already hung the first load of laundry on the clothesline. She could hear lawnmowers roaring in several of the neighboring yards. These were the memories that came rushing back to her as she stood there mesmerized.

It all came to a screeching halt when she heard "Mama, where are you?" Mason was awake, and she knew he would be wanting to know where mama was. Savanna went back into the bedroom to find Mason with his big brown eyes, just smiling. She said good morning as he was climbing out of the bed onto the hardwood floor. He walked on his toes and wrapped his little arms around her legs as she reached down to pick him up. Mason buried his head in her chest as she kissed him good morning.

As they were walking down the stairs, she stopped to open the front door so that the morning light could come streaming into the living room. It was one of the routine things that her mom did when she was growing up to open the front door, keeping the storm door locked. They made their way into the kitchen where she seated Mason in a chair at the table. She began making his favorite, which was pancakes. Mason loved the tiny little round forms of pancakes that were perfect for his little mouth. He also would have a scoop of eggs and a strip of bacon. While he was eating his breakfast, Savannah joined him at the table to eat as well. She also dialed back home to see how Bryson was doing since they were gone. The two talked for a moment, and Mason wanted to talk to Daddy so that he could tell him about his little adventure.

After he was finished telling his dad all that he could get in one breath, Savannah took the phone from him so that she could have some mommy and daddy time on the phone. Bryson said that he would be in town by the end of the week and missed them so very much. She told him that she had planned to take Mason over to see his Nana today. Bryson told her that he would be calling his mom later that morning, so she would know that they were coming. Savannah's mom was also in the kitchen, keeping Mason company while she was on the phone with Bryson. After she ended the call with him, Savannah and her mom caught up on what had been happening while she was in Texas. Her sister was back with her little boy, who was only less than a year younger than Mason. Mom talked about the troubles that she was having with her sister and the lack of responsibility that was there. Savannah could not wait to see her nephew but, at that point, did not know when she was going to get the opportunity. After she and Mom talked a little more about what her plans were, she mentioned that they were going to buy a car while they were in town. Savannah's mom did not drive at the time, so she always rode with her best friend and neighbor down the street.

Most of the time, she was on the go with Granddaddy's niece that took her mom a lot of places as well. Savannah did have her driver's license, so she could always use granddaddy's car if she needed. Once breakfast was done, it was time to get their day started. She bathed Mason and got him dressed, and then she called her mother-in-law to catch up and to let her know they were coming up to visit. It was already past noon, and she was ready to go visit with her other family. Bryson's grandparents just lived several blocks away, but she decided that they would go visit with them the next day. She finally arrived at her mother-in-law's house, and they had the best time catching up with each other. She was like a mother to her, and they had a remarkably close relationship.

Nana could not wait to hug and kiss her Bunkie; that was what she called him—Nana's Bunkie. Mason just laughed and giggled as his Nana held him and gave him all the best kisses in the world. Soon after, there was a knock on the door, and a loud voice came roaring into the house. It was his aunt Jennie; she heard that they were at the house and could not wait to see them. Mason would always brace himself whenever he saw her; he knew the extra-long hugs and kisses were coming even if he did not want them. They all gathered in the kitchen where Nana was already cooking, filling the house with aromas that Savannah remembered from her teenage years. She spent a lot of time in this house when she was young, so it was her second home.

Mason was marching to his own beat as he made his rounds in the house, exploring. His Nana was filling him with goodies as he passed through the kitchen. Savannah felt at home and was happy to hear the laughter and interesting conversations she had missed. She also missed Bryson, who was still back in Texas, counting the hours before he would be with his family again. They have talked for hours at a time since she and Mason has been back home.

Meanwhile, the house was beginning to fill with more relatives and friends as Nana and Jennie continued preparing food for the gathering. One thing Savannah did miss was the family cookouts and the sound of laughter and music as it blared in the backyard. Bryson was due to come home in a couple days, and she could not wait to see him. His dad was home from Maryland, where he was stationed in the US Army. He was always moving from base to base as he traveled the country. Bryson's mom did not want that life of moving so much and not having a place to truly call home. That was not the life she wanted for her children, and it was best for them to grow up around family. The hour had come when everyone had arrived and greeted one another with love and laughter.

The house and the backyard were overflowing with people, and the barbecue grill sent billows of smoke into the air. The tables were filled with every food that you could imagine, along with large tin washtubs filled with ice and soft drinks buried in the bottom. For the adults, there was a minibar set up in the corner of the yard where one of Bryson's uncles bartended.

Savannah met more of the family that she did not know and was introduced to cousins, aunts, and uncles that traveled from California for the occasion. Most of the family was Alexander's, which was Pop's family, along with their extended family members. The children ran and played throughout the fenced-in backyard while the adults gathered at several tables, reminiscing. Do not forget about that uncle in the family that tooted his own horn when it came to telling tall tales. One could hear the women screaming with laughter as they challenged the men in a dance-off. Of course, the music of choice was anything from the '70s to include Marvin Gaye, Gladys Knight and the Pips, James Brown, the Commodores, and much more. Aunt Jennie loved to dance, and she would always grab her husband, Charles, to dance with her. It was like peeking back in time when one watched how the energy and love was shown that day. Nana only danced to slow songs that were played on the stereo.

Yes, there was an old-fashioned stereo with built-in turntable and eight-track tape players. Savannah was familiar with this type of stereo because her mom still had the same model placed in her living room. Of course, Jennie would switch dance partners when Charlie became winded. She and Bryson's dad stole the dance floor and always were the last to leave. It was literally a blast from past when those two got together to cut a rug. The younger generation did not have a say in what music was played and never had a choice in the matter. So what most young people would do was carry their party to the other side of the house. Some of the cousins had expensive car stereos, and they played their kind of music on the street. Along with the music, Bryson's cousins and family friends had their own minibar going on in the trunk of their cars.

It was summertime, and that was one of the things that people did in the neighborhood. One of the other choices was to take off to one of the local nearby parks in the northwest neighborhoods. Hanging out in the park was another habit that the younger generation was accustomed to. Savannah remembered when she was a teenager and every weekend she and her friends would go hang out in the park. Everyone knew one another, and the boys were always pursuing them. Savannah would always have older guys trying to get her attention, but she ignored them.

Although she was intrigued by the chase, she would never let anyone get close enough. She did not know Bryson, and it was a strong possibility that he was hanging out in the park as well. Savannah found herself remembering when she was younger, without a care in the world, although she was only nineteen years old in the present day. The time had passed so quickly, and people were starting to pack up and leave. Bryson's grandparents dropped her off at home since it was the way to their house. Mason was already asleep on the car ride home. She carried Mason upstairs to lie him on the bed. He was worn-out from the excitement and playing with his new cousins. Savannah undressed his sleepy little body. It was too late in the evening to put him into the bathtub. She just wiped him down with a nice wet warm washcloth and then pulled the sheets over him. At last, it was her turn to have some time to herself. The bathroom did not have a shower in the bathtub, but there was a showerhead attachment that was used in its place. It was still hot that night, so she left the bathroom window open as she climbed into the tub and turned the water on. She lay back into the tub as it filled with water, and she soaked.

The house was noticeably quiet as she closed her eyes and dreamed about seeing Bryson the next day.

Chapter 17

Bryson was up before dawn and called a taxi to take him to the Greyhound bus station in downtown Killeen. The moment had come where he was going to see his wife and son soon. Everything was going as planned; he would travel from Texas to Virginia on a full passenger bus for more than twenty-four hours. It seemed like eternity aboard and stopping at every little town on the way. The first stop was in Dallas, Texas, where there was a layover and then changed buses. He was prepared for the long trip based on the essentials he packed in his carry-on bag. To pass the time away, he listened to his genre of jazz and R & B on his Sony Walkman. It had been five hours since their last stop as they crossed the Texas state line into Texarkana, Arkansas, which was the gateway to Little Rock, Arkansas. The bus terminal was as busy as the one in Dallas with all walks of life. He was sure to keep his personal belongings close and to be watchful of his surroundings.

They were limited once they reached Tennessee; he was only two and half hours away from seeing his family. He called Savannah from the first stop in Memphis to let her know that he was a little over two hours away. It was about 8:00 p.m., and she called his parents to let them know what his expected arrival time would be into town. She had already put Mason down for bedtime and gave close attention to her appearance. It had only been a week since she last saw Bryson and wanted to look her absolute best. She felt a little anxious, with butterflies fluttering in her stomach. Why was she feeling this way? The answer to this question was simple. They have loved each other for what seemed like a lifetime, and the thought of being apart for any amount of time was a big deal. There was a car *honk* outside in front of the house; she looked out the bedroom window to see her mother-in-law. Savannah gathered her keys and jacket and told her mom that she was leaving to go pick up Bryson. She was greeted with a loving hug from her mother-in-law as they drove off. Nana told her that Grans wanted to come along as well, so they stopped by her house on the way to the bus terminal.

Within minutes, they had already arrived downtown and was searching for parking close to the bus terminal. Nana had already gotten out of the car, and she and Savannah were crossing the street. Grans decided to stay in the car and wait because the walk was a bit much for her at that time of night. It was only 7:30 p.m., but for her, it was a little late to be out although she had insisted on them picking her up. Bryson was everything to Grans and Pop, and he had always been their favorite grandson. It was obvious in the way that they talked about him. Although they did love their other grandchildren just as much, but there was something special about Bryson. The bus station was smoky with the smell of bus diesel fuel and the sound of engines running.

There was also the business of loading and unloading of passengers on and off the buses, preparing for the next arrival and departures. In the distance, there he was, smiling from ear to ear, as he was walking toward them. Bryson could not take his eyes off Savannah as she did the same. Nana welcomed her young with open arms and hugged him so tight as if she did not want to let go. Savannah waited patiently for her turn to show him how much she loved and missed him. Some would say that the wife should have been the first to greet her husband, but the circumstances were not always as easy as they seemed. Bryson has always been what some could say the *golden* boy in his family. He was not only the most popular and well loved in the neighborhood and school, but people also loved him and put him on this pedestal that made Savannah extremely uncomfortable at times.

Even when they dated in high school, she was always known as Bryson's girl. Savannah did not have her own identity when she dated him in school. It was a lot of pressure at times, and it annoyed her to the point that she wanted to end the relationship many times. The same attitude rolled over into their adulthood and married life. They had only been married one year, and there were things that they still needed to learn about each other. So she patiently waited for her turn as usual to greet her husband properly. He gently pulled her into him, never breaking his sight pattern on her. He kissed her like it was the first time again, and her body quivered and felt weak at the same time. After their welcome-home kiss, they walked to the parked car where Grans stepped out to give her grandson a welcome-home hug and kiss. The first stop was to his grandparents, and they all went into the house so that Bryson could visit with Pop for a moment. Savannah sat in the parlor as the two talked and caught up for a moment. It was then getting late and Nana had to get home, so she said that she would give them a lift to her mom's house.

Bryson decided that he was going to stay with his wife and son, and he told his mom that he would come to the house tomorrow. They both got out of the car and went into the house as his mom drove off. Bryson could not wait to see Mason, but he was still asleep, so he leaned down to kiss him on the forehead as he was bundled up with his favorite pillow. Savannah's mom was still up, so she talked with them for a while and decided it was time for her to go to bed, that was code for saying, "I know you two have some catching up" to do. Savannah lifted her eyebrow the way she always has done when she was sending him a message. Being back in her old childhood room again with Bryson was more than a blast from the past. This was where they hung out practically every day after school and week-ends. *Alone at last* was the thought that ran through Savannah's head as she pulled Bryson close to her. The house was dark and quiet as everyone else was sound asleep.

The two made up for lost time that night and held on to each other until the next morning. They were awakened by the sound of little feet running on the hardwood floors down the hallway to their room. The doorknob was moving back and forth with a little voice on the other side of the door asking where Mama was. Bryson got up half asleep and opened the door to find a wide-eyed Mason look-ing up with surprise. "Daddy, Daddy, Daddy!" was the squeals and screams that filled the hallway. He jumped up on his toes with arms stretched up for Bryson to pick him up. Mason wrapped his little arms around his dad's neck and squeezed as hard as his little body could muster up. Bryson carried him downstairs where Savannah had already started making breakfast. Savannah's mom had already left earlier that morning for work, so they had the house to themselves. They had a busy day ahead of them and wanted to get an early start. Bryson and Savannah were going car shopping today, and his mom had already agreed to keep Mason for them.

After they had breakfast, Savannah cleaned up the kitchen then got Mason dressed and then herself. Bryson's grandparents just lived a few blocks from Savannah's mom. It was a beautiful warm morning, so they decided to walk to their house. Pop had given Bryson a car for them to drive back to Texas, but it was not roadworthy. The only other option was to trade it for a safe and roadworthy car. The two dropped Mason off at his parents and went car shopping. It was a long day test-driving cars and talking with car dealership salesmen. Bryson did the talking, and Savannah just walked the lots, picking out cars that she liked. At this point, the two of them had become exhausted from all over town. They had to find a car before the day ended because they were due to go back home in a couple days. There was one last lot to visit, and it was about 5:00 p.m., and Savannah remembered that her grandfather bought his cars from this dealership.

As they pulled into the lot, there it was, a brown 1986 Brougham Oldsmobile Cutlass Supreme. This car was parked on the front row of the lot on the corner. Bryson parked, and the two got out of the car to take a closer look. Far in the distance, Savannah saw a salesman headed their way. She was not particularly thrilled about listening to another dealer. He approached like most car salespersons; he introduced himself as Bob, short for Robert, asking if he could help. Bryson asked him if he could test-drive the car. Bob asked for his driver's license and went to get dealer plates. When he came back, Savannah opened the door and sat up front in the passenger seat. Then Bob opened the back door, as it was a four-door car, and took a seat.

Bryson drove the car off the lot, and the ride was smooth. He then proceeded to take it onto the highway to see how it handled on the road. Meanwhile, Bob was giving them the specifications of the car along with city and highway miles. After the test-drive was over, Bryson asked Bob what the best offer he can make for him to take the car tonight. Before they knew it, they were signing the papers and driving their new car off the lot. Savannah and Bryson arrived at his parents' house to pick up Mason. They were proud of him making his first major purchase. Bryson had accomplished what he had planned for his family. He and Savannah decided they did not want to stay another two days and told their family that they would be headed back tomorrow. It was an awfully long drive, and Bryson would be doing the driving. The next morning, they packed up the car with their belongings and Mason. They said their goodbyes the night before and were prepared to get on the highway. Savannah was ready to go back home and could not wait to have this time with her family. She was the navigator and read the road map as Bryson drove them from Virginia to Texas. They made the necessary stops for gas and food.

Traveling with a toddler was an adventure, but Mason had been on long car trips, so it was not as difficult. It had been twenty-one hours, and they had made it safely back to Fort Hood, Texas. Savannah took Mason out of the car as Bryson was getting their luggage out of the trunk. She was already at the apartment door, letting Mason in as he was running around in the living room before climbing onto the sofa. It was so nice to be back home and doing their normal daily routine. It was Sunday afternoon, so Savannah needed to go to the grocery store to shop. She left Mason at home with his dad, and she was off to Winn Dixie. It felt different for her to be driving anywhere because she had been used to getting around town by taxi.

Finally, life was about to change for Savannah because she was no longer restricted from some of her dreams. Now that she had reliable transportation, she can now attend community college in the evenings when Bryson got off work. They had a system set up between the two of them where she only took two classes a week on Monday and Wednesday. She still would have the balance of being a wife, mother, and student without becoming overwhelmed. It was her own form of independence and some time to find herself.

Chapter 18

It has been nearly two years already, and Mason was growing like a weed. Savannah had completed six months of school at Central Texas Community College. There were other changes as well that they had to overcome with the leaving of Tony and Kristina. It was the end of Tony's tour in Texas, and he did not make any plans to reenlist. Savannah had become so remarkably close to them because they were the only family in Texas. She knew that it was going to come to the day that they had to move on with their lives, and that meant saying goodbye. It did not help matters that the two were having some marital problems, as do most couples. but overcoming them is what makes the relationship strong. Savannah could relate to not always agreeing on things in a relationship.

There were times she and Bryson had a disagreement, and because he was the more dominant personality, she would just shut down. It had been times they would argue over the most insignificant things that did not really have any warrant to them. With any couple, when finances are the topic or lack thereof, then the dynamics most certainly changed. In the beginning of their marriage, they did not have any issues with managing money. Bryson believed from his upbringing that the man worked and brought the money home. He expected his wife to pay the bills and take care of the home. Savannah accepted the responsibility without rebuttal because she was so used to taking care of family and home.

It was so especially important for her to be that wife who would make sacrifices for her family. Situations do change like the seasons with any relationship, and it can be challenging at times to work out differences. Bryson did have his friends on base that he hung out with some weekends. Savannah really did not care for it, but she never expressed how she felt about him coming home late some weekends. He did not hang out and drink with his friends most weekends, but when he did, she was never happy about it. She never knew where to reach him if she needed because he never left a phone number for emergencies while he was out. Savannah sometimes thought he missed being single, but he had never been single since they started dating in high school. She would have so many thoughts running through her head and wondered if he had any regrets with marriage.

The only way to know would be to bring it up in a conversation, but she knew that would not be wise. Of course, she felt so many insecurities with the relationship throughout the time they had been together. He did not intentionally make her feel insecure, but sometimes his actions opened that door. One Friday evening, when he came home from work, he mentioned that he would go play cards and hang out with some of the guys from the barracks. Savannah was not happy about it and did not share that information with him. As always, she kept quiet and went along with his wishes; she still could not escape the passive behavior. So it was about 8:00 p.m. when one of his friends picked him up. She knew that there would be some drinking involved, so he did not take the car. Savannah wanted so badly to ask him not to go because she wanted him to spend some time with her. He was on base all through the week, and sometimes he has overnight call duty and she and Mason were at home alone.

As the door closed behind him, she felt so empty and alone as tears fell from her eyes. She wiped them quickly because she did not want Mason to see his mama cry. It was Friday night, so she allowed Mason to sit up with her for one more hour before bedtime. She made some popcorn and snuggled up with Mason in her bed to watch a kid-friendly movie on television. The movie had not been on thirty minutes and Mason was out like a light. She did not want to risk waking him, and she did not know what time Bryson would be coming home. Savannah continued to watch television, but she was not truly focused on what she was viewing. Her mind was on her and

Bryson, and she was questioning why she never voiced her concerns and fears. She found herself thinking about what would be different if they were not together. How would her life be at this moment if she would have chosen a different path in life? One of her goals was to educate herself so that she would become self-dependent, and if one day she needed to leave, she would be okay financially. Savannah found herself thinking this way too often; it was not a good thing. She and Bryson did not communicate well, and at times they did not talk. Her escape would be thinking about Johnathan and if she should have just spoken up that night to let him know how she felt. Why she was still questioning her decision was what she asked herself, and why Johnathan? She continued to dream about him and wonder about what could be done differently.

He was not the only person that she thought about; she also played in her head numerous times the relationships that could have been with others. She also thought about both Cameron and Colby as well, and she knew it was not right to do that. The thought of them reminded her of the unknown, and it was risky. She was friends with Cameron since elementary school, and they remained friends throughout middle and high school. She remembered the talks they used to have on the phone and the silly laughter over nothing important. He was a true friend, and she had missed that once they went to high school and she figured one day that he wanted more. He did not say it in words, but his actions screamed it loud and clear. Savannah did not want to lose their longtime friendship and kept it that way.

Now Colby was a different *beast* of his own because the two of them had a very physical and strong chemistry. She also played the memory of them over again but still had the same result. Savannah did not trust him not to break her heart. Suddenly, she woke up abruptly to a loud knock at the door. Who could that be, she wondered, because Bryson had his keys to let him into the apartment. She looked over at the clock, and it was 2:00 a.m. As she stumbled out of the bed in the dark, the knock grew louder. She walked through the living room and cut on lights as she made her way to the door. Looking through the peephole, there was Bryson. She opened the door to let him in as he stumbled into the doorway. He reeked of the smell of alcohol as he tried to make his way to the bedroom. Savannah closed the front door and turned to see him lying on the floor. She told him to get up, and he just murmured something and then it happened. He vomited all over the carpet and himself.

She was livid as she told him that he would not be sleeping in their room that morning. She left him there in his vomit as she slammed the bedroom door closed and locked it. The next morning was not good for Bryson. She heard him stirring around and finally knocking on the bedroom door for her to let him into the bathroom. Savannah opened the door and told him to be quiet because Mason was still asleep. He made his way into the bathroom to take a hot shower. Savannah could not handle the smell that was in the living room or on him. When he was done in the shower, he came into the kitchen to apologize to her. She did not want to hear it; all she wanted was him to keep his distance. She told him that he was going to have the carpet cleaners come that day to clean the mess he left on the floor. She had already made a large pail of soapy water for Bryson to clean up his vomit off the carpet.

He continued to say that he was sorry and that he would never come home late and drunk again. Savannah was so hurt and disappointed with him because this was the first time since they been together she had seen that side of him. She heard Mason calling for her, and she did not want him to see this side of his dad. So she grabbed some of his breakfast favorites and brought them to the bedroom for him to eat. She closed the door behind her as she left Bryson in the living room where he fell asleep on the sofa. Later that afternoon, there was a knock at the door as the carpet-cleaning company had arrived to clean the carpets. Bryson allowed the workers to enter their bedroom as they were in the apartment.

Once they completed the job, Bryson paid and thanked them for their service. Savannah had already showered and bathed Mason so that they could go out for the day. She did not want to be in the same space as Bryson. It was Saturday, so she decided to take Mason to the mall to give her time to think. Her first stop was Walmart, one of her favorite places to shop, then onto the mall. The two had spent the entire day out and then stopped by the park that was close by the apartment. Mason was getting tired and irritable, and she could no longer keep him out. The time had moved so quickly, and it was 3:00 p.m. and time to head home. When she drove up to the apartment parking lot, Mason was already sound asleep. She turned the car off and took Mason out and to the apartment. When she reached for her keys, the door opened with Bryson standing there with a look of remorse and regret on his face. She walked past him and laid Mason on the sofa and turned to walk back out the door to collect her bags.

He grabbed her hand and pulled her close to him and repeatedly told her that he was sorry. It took everything in her body to hold back the tears as she fought them back. She did not want to show her vulnerability to him because, as always, he knew what it took for her to forgive him. Just like clockwork, he was back in her good grace again. They had problems in their relationship that had never been addressed and, at this point, will never be talked about. The one area of the relationship they could agree on was the physical and emotional chemistry. There was no doubt that she ever loved him, but at some point, she needed to have the courage to stand up to him on things that she did not agree on. For now, she just forbore the situation and hoped for change in the future. The two of them still had a lot of growing up to do, as she often reminded herself; they started out too young. She kept telling herself that it was all for Mason because she did not want him to grow up without his father in the household like she did. Even when there were times she was not happy, he kept her focused on what was most important to him. With time, there was change, and as expected, Bryson was up for new orders by spring.

It was already December, and Christmas was almost upon them. They were anxious to get home to be with family and loved ones. The plans had been made, and they were off to Virginia for the holidays. Bryson had a ten-day leave, and this would be the first vacation they had as a family. He learned that his next tour of duty would be in South Korea for eighteen months. It was important that they spent as much time together as possible. In a matter of weeks, they were all packed for their holiday vacation. Once again, they were on the road, traveling to Virginia. They kept watch for the changes in the weather traveling back east. Everything was good until they reached Tennessee, and then the road conditions changed. It was very cold that night with a combination of freezing rain. The car was traveling on Interstate 81 in Bristol, Tennessee, late around 10:00 p.m.

Savannah was extremely nervous and started to pray because it was bad; they had already seen accidents along the route. She read the map and navigated as Bryson drove. She used the dome light in the car to read the map. When she looked at the map, her left eye became blurry and she could not see. It was difficult to tell which exit to take as she knew the route very well from traveling it frequently. She told Bryson to take the next exit, and for some reason, her vision cleared. When he did, it was not the correct one and he became angry with her. He pulled off the road and took the map and read it himself. They got back onto the road and doubled back to pick up the exit that was missed.

As they approached, he slowed the car to a sudden stop, sliding a bit from the ice on the road. The two could not believe what they saw next; there were cars crashed onto the side of the mountain and a small pickup truck flipped onto its top. It was a horrific scene as they slowly drove through the wreckage. The two held their breath as the car traveled on the icy roads into Virginia. Savannah continued to pray as Bryson drove slowly until they were on dry road. They were only an hour away from home, and Savannah noticed that their side of the road was dry, and on the south-bound lanes of the interstate, it was sleeting. She could do nothing but give God the praise for their safe travels all the way into the city. God showed who he really was in the moment. This was the very first time Savannah had acknowledged the power of God. She knew who he was, but she did not have a personal relationship with Him. One thing to take from it was coincidences were not always what they seemed. One should understand that there was a purpose and reason for every step you take. For that reason, she felt in her spirit this was only the beginning of things to come.

Chapter 19

They finally made it to Roanoke, their hometown, and the weather was unusually warm for December, hitting the high at eighty degrees. Of course, stranger things had unfolded less than twenty-four hours since they had arrived. It was Christmas Eve, and that meant everyone was scurrying around to make those last-minute purchases. Bryson and Savannah stayed at her mom's with Mason in tow. The two went by his parents' house to spend a little time with them and for Mason to see his Nana. When they arrived, the front door was already open, and stepping across the threshold bought back so many memories. The house was filled with the aroma of holiday goodies trailing from the kitchen. Like clockwork, the Christmas music was playing softly in the background when they walked through the house to the kitchen.

It was the family tradition for each sister, and Grans included, to host Christmas brunch at their house once a year. This year was Nana's time to host, and she went all out with the preparations. Savannah had been coming to the family Christmases since she and Bryson were dating in high school. The day begins about 10:30 a.m., and all the family arrived with their gifts, which were placed under the tree. The table was set up buffet style, and the family would park wherever there was a comfortable spot to eat and enjoy one another. The food and good cheer would go on all day, then the moment would arrive when it was time to exchange gifts. The family was highly organized and creative with how the process began. Each family member and their immediate family would distribute their gifts, and everyone in the room would watch them open their gifts. This process took all day and part in the evening, but they kept it interesting with laughter and stories along the way.

In the end, everyone shared in the surprises and the amazing gift ideas presented. Mason was the only toddler in the family at the time, so he received the most attention and gifts. Savannah still had to make visits to her family as well, and it was still early. She knew that it would not be possible to visit with her grandparents on Christmas day because her entire day would be spent with Bryson's family this year. The first stop was at her granny's house, and Savannah was excited and looking forward to the visit. Mason had not seen her since he was about one year old, so it was a possibility that he may not remember her. The memories started to flood back to her when they drove through the project apartments, where she spent all her childhood summers.

The neighborhood remained the same with people sitting out on the porches and children playing in the yard. The back door was open with the screen door locked as she remembered. Savannah knocked on the screen door and listened for her grandmother as she heard her off in the distance humming a little melody. Granny smiled with great joy when she came to the door to see her granddaughter all grown up. The visit was not long enough as they talked about everything that had been happening in the neighborhood and the family. It was also good to see Aunt Joyce too. She had four children since Savannah saw her last, and it was a little different. Savannah remembered when she was the only child that got the attention. Granny was correct about many changes that had taken place since she got married and moved away. It was starting to get late, and she still had to go visit with Granddaddy and her step-grandmother. Everyone said their goodbyes and well wishes, and they hoped to see one another soon.

As they pulled up to the house, the living room lights were on, and the cars were in the driveway. When they reached the walkway, the door opened as they stepped onto the porch. Bobby was grinning from ear to ear, and he greeted them. He was Granddaddy's nephew by way of Savannah's step-grandmother. Everyone was there, including her mom and siblings, as they had just got up from the dinner table. Granddaddy was already sitting in his huge plastic-covered recliner. If you were a child in the '70s, this room was a blast from the past with the green carpets and cream flowers and green furniture covered in plastic. She remembered so well her legs sticking to the sofa in the summer months. Your clothes would be soaked if you were not careful not to sit too long. Her family loved Bryson, and Granddaddy herded him off to himself to talk and give unsolicited wisdom.

One of the things that made Bryson the person he was included his patience and respect for his elders. He genuinely showed interest in whatever the topic of the hour may be. Mason was growing tired from all the excitement and visiting. He was irritable and cranky, and it was time for a bath and bed. So another visit was cut short as he had already fallen asleep. Savannah stayed a few minutes more, waiting for Granddaddy to release Bryson from his tall tales. We all used to love to hear about his childhood going up on a farm and going to bed at first dark and rising to work the farm before sunrise. They finally made it through Christmas and were on their way back to Texas. Life, as they remembered, was headed for change.

Bryson went back to work on Monday and was given the details of his new orders. He would be deployed to South Korea for eighteen months. They were set to leave for Virginia in May, and he would leave in July for his deployment. The arrangements had been made for the movers to pack up and move their furniture and personal belongings back to Virginia. The decision had been made that she would stay with her mom for a while until she was able to find an apartment. The furniture would be delivered to Nana's and stored upstairs in the spare room until she was ready to move. The weeks were coming faster than one could count, and before you knew it, the month of May was upon them. Bryson did get some particularly good news a couple days before the movers were due to come. His absolute best friend from home, Roman, had just arrived for duty in Fort Hood.

When he got the call, he was overwhelmed with happiness and drove over to the barracks to visit with him. He also had gotten married and was waiting for his wife to come join him in Texas once he found an apartment. Roman did not want to live on base as Bryson did not desire. It was getting late, but Savannah was okay with it because it was Roman. They all went to high school together and lived in the same and nearby neighborhoods. When he finally returned home, he could not stop talking about his and Roman's days growing up together. He showed a little emotion because they were about to be apart again. Roman would be in Fort Hood for about the same length of time with Bryson. The next morning, Savannah waited for the final walkthrough with the apartment manager before turning over the keys. She did the last-minute check of everything to make sure the apartment was clean and ready for inspection.

Bryson already had temporary housing set up for them that day until he was fully separated from Fort Hood. Later that evening, they met up with Roman, and Savannah occupied Mason while his dad talked with Roman. It was a little emotional to see how the two best friends who called each other brother said goodbye. Real life was what they had to face; serving in the United States Army was not only an honor but a privilege. It was their duty to support and protect not only their families but also the families of this nation. The sun was coming up, and Savannah had not slept that night. She was not comfortable sleeping in military housing. People were noisy and walked about all night, and she was not used to living in such close quarters. Finally on the road and saying goodbye to Fort Hood. As they traveled a familiar roadway, there was laughter, talking, and singing to music that brought back memories.

Although the trip was a little over twenty hours this time around, they were happy to cross the state line into Virginia. Home again and thanking God for a safe journey. Bryson was on leave for thirty days before his deployment to South Korea, and he and Savannah were making the most of their time. She wanted to find a job so that she could contribute while he was away. She began searching for jobs, but due to her not having a college degree yet, she decided to try something at a sewing factory. It paid minimal wages, but it was better than nothing. The time was drawing near, and it was becoming more difficult for Savannah to let go. This would be the first time since they had been together that they been separated for over a year. His parents were planning their summer vacation to Hersheypark, Pennsylvania. Bryson and Savannah also talked about her looking for apartments once she got settled. She was called for an interview at Hampton Apparels, a sewing manufacturer in town. This was a big step for her and somewhat of independence of earning her own money. She had not had a job since after school on the weekends.

In the coming weeks, she had added more responsibility on her plate. She had to consider day care for Mason at this point because she did not want to overload her grandmother. She was already babysitting for Savannah's aunt that lived in the apartment with her. For the first week of work, Mason stayed at home with his dad until they could find a good day care. It was an experience working in a manufacturing facility, so things were quite different. The weekend had arrived already, and she had only a few days left before Bryson left for South Korea. He made sure that everything was in place as far as legal obligations.

With a blink of the eye, the day was here. Savannah and Mason were at the airport, along with Nana and Grans, saying goodbye to Bryson. It was one of the most emotional movements she had experienced and fought hard to keep from losing it in front of Mason. She kept a brave smile while falling apart inside as she kissed Bryson, and he hugged her and Mason so tight. The drive home was incredibly quiet as Mason was asleep in the back, and she thought about the next eighteen months without her husband. Of course, she will have the company of his family, but it was not the same. The next morning, she dropped Mason off at preschool before she went to work. The day was long, and she could not focus because her mind was on Bryson and wondering when she would hear from him. Savannah could not wait for the clock to strike 4:30 p.m. so she could pick Mason up from day care.

When she arrived home, her mother was already there, and they caught up on how her day went. She told her mom that she had been searching for an apartment and found one that was perfect for her and Mason. It was about thirty minutes away from her mom, and it was close to Mason's day care. The next Saturday morning, she paid a visit to the apartment complex and was given a tour of the model. It was in the perfect location, and the apartments were inside a building that you had to enter. One of the choices for her was a two-bedroom on the first floor which made it easy for bringing in groceries and transporting Mason. It had plenty of amenities to include a laundry room on each floor.

When she returned from the tour, there was no question that this was going to be home. Savanah did not waste any time filling out an application and placing a security deposit. She went home and began preparing for the move. Bryson's cousin and some of his friends volunteered to help her move the furniture and boxes from her mother-in-law's storage room. Within a couple days, she had a move-in date, signed the lease, and received the keys. One week had passed and she was all settled into the apartment, and Mason adjusted simply fine. They had a routine in place that would give him some normalcy. She talked to Bryson once a week although the phone bill was astronomically too high for her to pay at times. It did not matter because she missed him just as much as he did for her.

The days turned into weeks, and before she knew it, summer was here. It was July, and the weather was unreasonably hotter this year. Bryson's parents were preparing for their summer vacation to Hersheypark, Pennsylvania, and his mom was so excited. As always, she loved to go shopping and wanted Savannah to spend Saturday with her at the mall. It has not been long since the new mall was opened, and this was cause for frequent visits on the weekend. Savannah drove over that morning with Mason and unloaded his car seat and stroller into Nana's car. It was a particularly good day as they spent time with one another. This kept her mind off missing Bryson so much, and she loved window-shopping. She helped with selecting summer outfits for Nana's trip. They shopped at one of Nana's favorite stores in the mall. There was something about walking through the doors of Leggett Department Store. The first stop would always be the perfume counter. Nana loved to spray and test fragrances. Occasionally, she would purchase a brand that she could not resist.

After spending two hours in the store, they finally were done with the shopping. Of course, there were other stores to peruse, but they had their favorites. It was nearing lunchtime, and Mason had enough Cheerio treats to keep him occupied. Nana did not care for the food court, so they left the mall and went to have lunch at one of the local restaurants in the area. The day had come to an end, and Savannah was back home with Mason. She gave him a bath, and off to bed the two went. She could not go to sleep right away, so she stayed up and watched television. The phone ranged, and it was Aunt Pearl calling to check in on them. The two talked for what seemed to be an eternity. The one thing about Aunt Pearl was she loved to talk, and sometimes it was a little difficult to get her off the phone. Savannah still enjoyed talking with her because it gave her pleasure to learn more about Bryson's family.

The next day, she got up to make Bryson breakfast and to do laundry. The weekend would surely come and go as quickly as it came, and she had to prepare for the workweek ahead. Later that evening, she received a long-distance call from Bryson. She talked about how much Mason was growing and the time she had been spending with his mom and family. Mason wanted to talk with his daddy to tell him everything about preschool and his best friend. Once Savanah was able to end Mason's phone conversation with his dad, she continued her talk with Bryson. She told him about the upcoming trip his parents and brother were taking for the summer. He missed them so much and could not wait for his tour to be over. After being on the phone for about an hour, they had to say their goodbyes.

It was Monday, Mason was dropped off at preschool and Savannah was headed to work. She was already counting down to the hour that she would be reversing her route and coming to pick Mason up from preschool. She was grateful for the job at the plant, but she still wanted more. Maybe it was the fact she missed her husband terribly and wanted him to be there with them. They have reached the middle of the week already, and she had not heard from her mother-in-law. She was used to her checking in on them and to see if they needed anything. Savannah called her, but there was no answer, so she went by the house. This was some cause for concern, so she called Grans to see if she had heard from Nana. Savannah knew that they had not left for their vacation yet. The trip was coming up in two weeks, and Savannah would have loved to go with them, but she had not been on her job long enough to take off. It would always be another opportunity to go on vacation when Bryson returned home.

The doorbell rang, and she went to the door and it was Nana. She did not look very well as she came into the house. Savannah asked how she had been and that she was trying to get in touch with her. She told her that she had taken on a part-time cleaning job in the evenings. For some reason, Savannah did not understand why she would need to work so much. Nana continued to talk about what she believed was beginning to wear her health down. She complained about shortness of breath with chest discomfort when she would use the vacuum. This only caused more concern from Savannah because Nana had always been in such great health. Now she was a smoker, but Savannah did not want to say anything that would remotely be suspicious of her years of smoking. It was one week away from the vacation to Hersheypark, and Nana was not getting any better. She decided to pay a visit to her family doctor. The news was devastating to the family as she was diagnosed with stage four lung cancer. Bryson's dad came home on emergency leave for a couple weeks to take care of his wife. She was taking it well and went to her chemotherapy treatments as scheduled. Bryson's dad only was able to stay for a short period of time, so he contacted the Red Cross so that Bryson could come home for a month to help take care of his mom.

Chapter 20

The anticipation of the flight arrival from South Korea via California and then to Virginia was great. Savannah was sitting anxiously in the airport, waiting for Bryson's return home. It was the first week of August, and summer was coming to an end. The heat once again was hotter than usual, and the nights were suffocating at times. Sitting there looking out the window as the planes took off and landed onto the tarmac was an adventure for Mason. Finally, his flight was announced of its arrival, and her heart raced with anticipation of seeing her husband. When Mason saw his dad walking toward him, he took off running, yelling, "Daddy!" Bryson had a big smile on his face when he picked Mason up and kissed and hugged him. Savannah greeted her husband with the proper welcome-home kiss.

The first stop was to his parents' house to see his mom and then on to his grandparents. His mom was incredibly happy to see him and did not let on to how much pain she was in. Bryson was there to take care of her and to make sure that his little brother had everything that he needed. There were several family members and her best friend that took turns in shifts to stay with her before his arrival. Now that he was in town, Bryson would stay with her on alternate nights and switch off with his aunts. Tonight, he would spend it with his wife and son because they needed to be with him as well. Savannah understood the importance of him being there for his mother and did not have an issue with his duty as a son. At home finally, Mason was put down for bed, and Bryson was patiently waiting for his time with his wife. Savannah took special care of her appearance that night. She took a relaxing bubble bath and then pampered herself with a new body moisturizer and lingerie to welcome Bryson home properly.

Monday morning was a little busier than usual. Bryson was sitting with his mom today, so he dropped Mason off at preschool and Savannah at work. He made a stop by his grandparents first for a short visit and then on to his mom. Bryson spent the entire day in the upstairs den, watching movies and listening to his music. He made sure that his brother had something to eat while his mother went off to her chemotherapy treatments. She was picked up by the Radar bus twice a week. When she returned home, she would always want to continue her routine of cooking and cleaning. She was in no shape for this, and it was exceedingly difficult for her to adjust to not being helpful. Bryson shared these duties with his aunts and his mom's best friend.

Mostly, he kept his brother company, fed the dog, and took out the trash. From time to time, he would run little errands for his mom to the grocery store and pharmacy. It has been two weeks now, and the daily routines were to focus on making his mom feel as comfortable as he could. One night, his mom's best friend sat with her while Bryson took a break and went home. He spent a little time with Savannah and Mason before Kristina, one of his best friends, found out he was in town and came by the apartment. Savannah was not happy about this because she wanted to spend time with her husband. His friend talked him into coming out for drinks with her to catch up. At this point, Savannah was livid but did not speak up to let Bryson know that she did not agree with his decision.

He and his friend left, and as the door closed behind them, tears rolled down her face. Savannah waited up all night for him to come home. She was worried and still upset with him for not thinking about her feelings. Meanwhile, it was about 1:00 a.m., and the phone rang. Her first thoughts were not good. When she answered, it was Aunt Jeanie calling, asking for Bryson. Savannah told her that he was not there and did not know when he was returning. She told her that he was out with some of his friends, drinking. Well, that did not go over well with Jeanie. She called to tell him to come to the house because his mom was extremely sick and she was being taken to the hospital. There was no other there to watch his brother. Savannah could not leave with Mason to stay with him. Jeanie made a call to Auntie, and she came over to sit with him while Nana was taken to the hospital.

A couple hours later, she heard the keys to the door and jumped out of the bed to meet Bryson as he came in. She told him that his mom had become sick and that she was in the hospital. He was about to leave when the phone rang again, and it was Jeanie on the other end. She was not too happy, and she made sure Bryson got an earful. He did not need to come down to the house because someone was there sitting with his brother. Bryson was still not out of hot water because he still had to deal with Savannah and her cold shoulder.

It was already 2:00 a.m., and she did not want to get into it. The next morning, he received a call from his dad, and a reprimand as well, and was reminded the reason for him being on leave was to take care of his mother. The doctor told his mom that the chemo was not aggressive enough for treatment, and she did not have much time. It had been thirty days, and Bryson was due back in South Korea. He spent the rest of the week with his mom and brother. The day before he was scheduled to fly out, he and Savannah spent the entire day with her. He said his goodbyes, and she did not take it well. Once he left, she threw a tantrum because she knew that would be the last time that she would see her son. Within the hour, he and Savannah was at home, saying their goodbyes. His flight was leaving in two hours that night. She took him to the airport and waited until his plane left the gate and taxied down the runway. She stood outside the fence and waited until the plane sped by and up into the night sky. On the drive home, her mind was racing with the new information that had been loaded onto her. She was losing her mother-in-law, and her husband was thousands of miles away. Savannah could not sleep a wink, and she cried until her face hurt.

She knew that she needed to be strong and to carry on with her routine of life. Bryson called to let Savanah know that he made it safely back to South Korea. They talked for hours, as if he was just in another state. Their spirits were uplifted as they talked about his return home permanently. He asked her if she had received a package yet. She did not know what he was talking about, and she asked, "What package?" Bryson told her that she should have received something a couple weeks ago. She insisted that she never received anything in the mail. Savannah was expecting something special from Korea in the way of clothing. Bryson had a chuckle in his tone as he did not give her any more clues as to what he was speaking about. The hour came when they had to get off the phone; it was going to be an expensive phone call. He told her that he loved her and that he would see her again soon.

Savannah disconnected the call as she put the phone down onto the receiver. She had promised him before hanging up that she would check on his mom. So as promised, every day, she would drop by the house to visit with Nana and spend as much time as possible with her. When she pulled up to the house, there were several cars parked out front. The front door was open as she approached the front porch. After all those years, she still knocked on the door before entering. There was laughter coming from Nana's bedroom as she walked into the house. Everyone was gathered by her bed and laughed and talked to her about past times and current events. It was like old times again with Jeanie marching to her own beat. She was so amazing with her sister and did all she could do to keep her in high spirits. Of course, Grans wanted to mother her and bring food and some of her favorite treats. Savannah greeted her with a kiss and hug and asked how she was feeling.

One of the unique things that made Nana so sophisticated was the way she carried herself. A person meeting her for the first time would not have a clue that she was fighting for her life. Savannah had always admired and looked up to her mother-in-law. She was such an inspiration and a very classy woman. It showed in the way she dressed and how she kept her home and the values that she believed. No matter what, she always took the higher road and not entertain any negative vibes. The evening ended with more laughter, hugs, and kisses as her sisters, best friend, and additional family told her how much they loved her.

Saturday, October 8, 1988, as she walked down the corridor of the hospital's intensive care unit, she could hear the echo of respiratory distress. The closer she got, the louder the sounds as she stopped at the doorway of Nana's room. She entered the room to find Grans and Jeanie already there sitting by her bedside. Nana was fighting for her life as her eyes were rolled back into her head, and she was struggling with her breathing. Jeanie stated that she had a stroke. Mason held on to his mom's hand and stood behind her. He did not understand what was happening to his Nana. Jeanie spoke up and told Nana that her Bunkie was there. As soon as she mentioned Mason was in the room, Nana came out of the state that she was experiencing. Mason stood at the bottom of the bed as she smiled at him. There was one single tear that dropped from his big brown eyes. Soon after, she began to move her wrist alongside her waist as she was removing her IV.

At this point, Savannah became very emotional as did Grans because they could not accept the fact that she was saying goodbye. Jeanie, the stronger one out of the group, told Nana that she loved her and that it was okay for her to leave. Moments later, the heavy breathing ceased, and she was gone. It was like the life was ripped out of Savannah as she sobbed uncontrollably. She did know when she arrived at her mom's job to be consoled for the loss of her mother-in-law. The guard at the hotel knew who she was from the many times she visited. After she calmed down, she was able to tell her mom rationally about Nana's passing. Mason was with her, so one of the ladies that worked at the hotel kept him occupied with a special treat from the cafeteria. Savannah was able to pull herself together long enough to drive home.

Later that evening, family and friends gathered at the house to give their condolences. Bryson's dad was already on his way home, and he had contacted the Red Cross for his return. Savannah was holding up as well as expected. She had not been feeling well, and she thought maybe the stress of Nana's illness played a role. The house was filled to capacity, and she heard Jeanie calling for her and leading her into the bedroom. She closed the door behind her and asked Savannah how far along she was. Savannah knew something was off, and the fact that one of the great-aunts made a statement, that had her baffled. Auntie Verge said that she looked like she had *swallowed the grape*. Savannah needed translation because she did not understand the country lingo. Aunt Vergie told her that she was pregnant.

She did not want to share the news until she went to the doctor to know for sure. Jeanie was so excited and already was talking about Savannah giving them a little girl. Before the night ended, everyone in the family was talking about the possibility of a new addition. Savannah did not want them to focus on her when they had just lost Nana. She did get a surprise visit from Bryson's best friend, Roman, who was in town on leave. There was so much love and support given to Savannah, and she knew Bryson would appreciate his *brother* being there. The next morning, Savannah received a call from Bryson, telling her that he would be home later that night. His flight had left Saturday night coming back to the States. She was concerned with how he was feeling at the time. Savannah could hear it in his voice although he was trying to conceal how he was feeling. It was still difficult for her to accept, so she knew it must have been traumatic to Bryson remembering the last time he saw her.

The phone had been ringing all morning as Savannah was trying to prepare for her husband's return home. She wanted to be strong for both of them and be a supportive wife. She finally decided to answer the phone, and her mother was on the other end. Mom wanted to make sure that she was okay and if there was anything that she could do for her. Savannah did need a little time to pull herself together, so Mom offered to come pick Mason up for the day. Mason was super excited to be going to Grandma's house and wanted to pack everything he had in his room. Savannah checked his little dinosaur backpack to find every miniature car, McDonald's Happy Meal prize, he had collected. He could not leave behind his T-Rex Godzilla.

His room was decorated from the comforter on the bed to the curtains on the windows with dinosaurs. The colors in his room were bright and whimsical with four small chairs red, green, yellow, blue that were placed around a small white activity table. On the other side of the room was a bookshelf that was Mason's height for easy accessibility when it was storytime. Savannah was big about education and providing every learning tool available to her son. Once she had finished packing his clothes and substituting some of his toys, he was all set. The doorbell rang, and Mason was bouncing up and down, saying, "Grandma, Grandma, Grandma!" as Savannah went to answer the door. Her mom was not alone; she had Brandon, her other grandson, that she was raising with her. He and Mason were cousins that were of the same age and were best of friends. Mom stayed to visit for a short period before heading out with the kids.

Finally, the apartment was quiet, which left Savannah a moment to really focus on the things that she needed to take care of before Bryson's return home. She went to the grocery store to stock on his favorite foods. Savannah knew that it would mean everything for him to come home with some sort of normalcy. Even with the special circumstances, she wanted to be there for him emotionally and physically. The time had passed, and it was already 7:30 p.m., and she needed to be heading for the airport. This seemed to be a norm these days, traveling back and forth to the airport. She went alone this time, which gave her the time she needed to reflect on life while she waited. The airport was not as busy today, and she sat facing the runway as the planes were taking off and landing. She loved watching because it brought back memories of when she was a child with her dad.

The voice over the intercom announced the arrival of Flight 4650 from Fort Worth, Dallas, Texas. It was Bryson's connecting flight from Los Angeles, California, via Japan and South Korea. She patiently waited until the plane had disembarked all the passengers when she saw Bryson. He was smiling as he always did whenever he laid eyes on her. She approached him and held him tight and did not want to let him go. He returned the gesture, and they stood there for a moment, savoring every second. When they finally released, he asked why Mason was not there. She told him that he was sleeping over his grandma's house tonight. They left the airport and directly went home; this was their time to be together, just the two of them. He would call his family when he got home to let them know he had arrived and would see them tomorrow. The two needed this time to rekindle their relationship on an emotional level. They never had any problems in the physical capacity of their relationship. It had been a challenge emotionally due to the separation of his tour of duty and now the death of his mother. It was another test in their relationship, and they did not kid themselves that it would not be easy. Bryson was sitting at the kitchen table in the apartment as Savannah was preparing in plate. She had cooked for him earlier that day and knew that he needed a home-cooked meal.

When she brought the plate over to the table, he grabbed her around the waist and just held her. She placed her arms around his neck and just pulled him closer to her body. A moment later, he asked, "Did you receive the gift I gave you?" He looked up into her eyes, and a tear fell from his face. For that quick moment, the light bulb came on. He knew that she was pregnant before he left for South Korea the second time. Savannah burst into laughter as she told him that she was expecting some fabulous ensemble custom-made from Korea. Bryson was so tickled at her reaction and could not stop laughing at her. There it was, that boom of laughter and happiness she had missed in his voice. She had not been to the doctor yet to be certain. The next morning, she called her gynecologist's office to set an appointment for earlier in the week. Meanwhile, they went to pick Mason up from his grandmother's and then on to see his family.

The funeral arrangements had been set, and there would a graveside service on Tuesday, October 11, 1988. Only close friends and immediate family attended the graveside service. She was laid to rest at Sherwood Memorial Park on the very top and center of the hill. Nana had made that request before her passing, and the family honored her wishes that she would be looking over the city. The weather was perfect on that warm and sunny fall morning as the family gathered to say their goodbyes. Bryson was remarkably close to his mom, but he never let on how difficult it was for him to say goodbye. Savannah knew her husband very well, and he had not truly grieved his mother. The service was short and sweet as his mom requested.

The family left the cemetery and gathered at the house for the repass later that afternoon. People from all over stopped by to pay their respects and leave an abundance of food. A lot of Bryson's friends came over to spend a little time with him. He seemed to be okay, but Savannah knew better and was a little concerned. The day seemed longer than expected, and they both were exhausted from the heavy foot traffic at the house. As the last guest drove off, she could finally take a deep breath. The drive home was silent as they listened to Najee on the car stereo system. Bryson parked the car while Savannah took Mason into the apartment. She did not bother to wake him from such a peaceful sleep.

After taking the clothes off his tiny little body, she placed him in his bed. The door in the front room closed as she walked down the hall back to the kitchen. Bryson was bringing the rest of their bags into the apartment from their stop at the grocery store. He began to unpack the bags and helped to put things away. Savannah wanted to take a long hot shower to wash the long day away. She invited Bryson to join her because she knew he needed to decompress emotionally. It was not about sex that night; intimacy would be the medicine for the evening. Bryson was only in town for a few more days, and she did not know when they would see each other again. His tour of duty was for eighteen months, and he had only been there two months total. With all that had happened in the last three months, time will tell if they could survive these changes.

Chapter 21

It was no surprise that the pregnancy exam returned positive. The doctor told her that she was a little over eight weeks pregnant. Savannah was already feeling nauseous with morning sickness every day. She could not tolerate the smell of food, and she slept more than usual. Bryson was already back in South Korea, and she could not wait to confirm what he already knew. She did make the announcement to the rest of the family, and they were happy. His grandparents and aunts were already hoping for a little girl. She was not on board with planning for a baby girl just yet. Savannah wanted another boy and already was playing around with boy names. She never even considered any girl names or entertained the possibility that this child could be a girl. Bryson's dad talked with her on the phone every Saturday and Aunt Pearl called her every night. Although Bryson was not there with her during the pregnancy, his family was supportive.

It had been only a couple weeks since the passing of her mother-in-law. Savannah was resting in bed one night with her eyes closed. The television was on in the background, and the lamp on the table was turned on. She could not lie down due to the heartburn and nausea she was experiencing from the pregnancy. On that night, she had a visit from her mother-in-law. At first, she thought it was a dream, but she was not asleep. Savannah was not startled because this would not be the first time she had experienced a supernatural encounter. She recalled from memory Nana asking why she had dirt all over her new pink suit. It was so vivid and in detail, watching her pick things off her body. Savannah wanted to tell her about the baby, but for some reason, Nana already knew. The visit was brief but so fulfilling at the same time because she had one more memory to keep with her always.

Of course, she wanted to share this experience, and the only person that would not judge her about something like this was her mom. She had always told her mom about the encounters that she had in the past. The sun was rising on that Saturday morning, and she could hear Mason stirring in his room. She knew that it would not be long before he came running and jumping into her bed. Savannah got out of bed and peeked into his room, but he was still asleep. She decided to get breakfast and started making his favorite on Saturdays—pancakes with strawberries and a side of sausage links. The phone rang like clockwork, and it was her father-in-law calling exactly around 10:00 a.m.

They talked about everything, and she believed that it kept his mind off things and missing Nana. He also mentioned that the funeral director told him that he was looking for a secretary. This seemed very strange of conversation to her because she already had a job. It turned out that he was taking care of some final business at the funeral home and the subject came up.

So he mentioned that his daughter-in-law may be interested in speaking to them about the position. It had not been advertised, so it would be a great advantage in terms of seeking out the opportunity. She was skeptical about it, but he insisted that she would be perfect for what they needed. After selling her on the idea, she finally agreed to meet with the funeral director on Monday. The weekend had come to an end, and she dropped Mason off at preschool on her way to the interview. She arrived at 8:00 a.m. and met with one of the senior funeral directors, who was a partner in the business. Mrs. Russell gave her a tour of the facility and introduced her to the staff. She also showed her where she would be sitting and explained what the day-to-day would be like. After the tour, she was introduced to the chairman and senior partner, Mr. Hamilton. He was a very prestigious gentleman and well respected in the community.

Savannah thought it was appropriate to tell him that she was pregnant, and he was appreciative of her being forthcoming. She went back out to the front where Mrs. Russell was waiting at the reception area. Savannah was asked if she could see herself becoming an addition to their family. She accepted, and immediately Mrs. Russell told her that the position paid $10 an hour and payday was every Thursday. She would be working Monday through Friday with no weekends or holidays. Savannah was happy about the opportunity and could not wait to let her father-in-law know how things went that day.

One thing that she needed to do was give her current job at the apparel plant a notice. She did not give a two-week notice because her new job needed her ASAP. Savannah was starting a new chapter in her life—first, a new baby and now a new job in one of the last places she would have dreamed. The Christmas holiday was upon them, and at three months into her pregnancy, there was movement. She was already showing and looked to be further along than what the doctors told her. All she could think about was how big this baby will be at full-term. As the days turned into weeks and months, she was getting larger by the minute. She talked to Bryson on the phone once a week and wished that he was there during the pregnancy. It was difficult at night to get comfortable when she lay down. The baby was more active and did not like for her to lie on her right side.

There would be sharp kicks, and you could see an elbow or a foot and sometimes a little butt push out under her breast. This was cause for many sleepless nights, and she would need to sleep sitting up with four large pillows. Most nights, Aunt Pearl would call her and talk with her until she fell asleep. She was grateful to her and the consistency of the nightly conversations and stories about her life. Aunt Pearl was a *hoot*, along with sassy and classy all wrapped up in one. She had no problem telling you when she thought you were wrong about something and then she would move on to educate you. I guess she had that privilege since she had been on this earth for more than three-fourths of a century.

Every morning, Savannah would get Mason ready for preschool and drop him off on her way to work. Working in a funeral home was not the worst thing in the world. The staff was nice to her, and she was treated like family. Most of the time, the staff would pick her lunch up on some days. They all checked on her constantly to make sure she was comfortable in her present state of pregnancy. Savannah was much bigger with this child than with Mason.

Life was good, and she was happy with her job and the people that she worked with. Spring had arrived, and she had been working there for nearly five months now. Everything was going well as she thought, but she could not have been more wrong. She noticed that the former secretary was making more frequent visits to the funeral home. Mrs. Russell would come out to greet her, and the two would go back to her office and close the door. Savannah did not think anything of it and thought maybe they were just catching up or maybe she needed some help. The buzz around the funeral home was that the reason she was let go was because of some undesirable behavior. In the next couple days, Mrs. Russell asked to speak with Savannah privately. The office was quiet that day, and Mr. Hamilton was in his office working. They took a little walk down the hallway, and Mrs. Russell told her that she was not working out and that she would pay her severance pay.

This news was devastating to her, and she asked to speak with Mr. Hamilton. It felt like she had been punched in the gut without warning. She could not wrap her head around it and needed to understand. Savannah became emotional and started to cry as Mrs. Russell tried to calm her. She told Savannah that it was not a good idea to speak with Mr. Hamilton at the time and for her to pull herself together. Savannah was told to collect her things and take the rest of the day off to calm down. She made her way back to the front and gathered all her belongings. As she walked through the building, it was difficult to pull herself together. She reached her car and drove to Pop and Grans house because they lived just a few blocks away. When she got out of the car, she just broke down as she walked up the stairs to the front door. Pop opened the door and told her to come in and asked what had happened. She went to explain that she went to work today and was asked to leave without any explanation. Savannah sat at the kitchen table as Grans poured her something to drink. They told her that everything was going to be okay and not to worry.

It was getting close to the time for her to pick Mason up from preschool. She had plenty of time to pull herself together, and Pops and Grans made her feel much better. Savannah drove up to the building and walked in to pick up Mason. He was on the playground with his best buddy, Josh. Ms. Beamer alerted him that Mom was there to pick him up. In the car heading home, she decided to stop by his favorite place to eat—McDonald's for a Happy Meal. Savannah did not have much of an appetite, but the baby had other demands. She ordered something from the menu as well because it would not be long before hunger set in. Reaching for the keys to open the apartment door with her hands full, she was able to maneuver with a balancing act to manage Mason and her bags when opening the door.

Mason ran past her into the apartment and straight to his bedroom. She put everything down on the kitchen table and called for Mason to go wash his hands and come eat. It was already 6:00 p.m., and she knew her mom was home from work by now. Mason was in his room playing with his dinosaurs and the surprise toy in the Happy Meal. Savannah called her mom and gave the bad news. Mom was upset and took offense to the actions of Mrs. Russell.

She had always been very protective of Savannah although she was a grown-up and married with a family. The news had traveled fast because her call-waiting feature was activated. She switched over to find her father-in-law on the other end. Savannah switched back to her mom and said that she would call her later. Bryson's dad was not happy with the news and expressed that she was treated unfairly. He wanted to make a big deal about it and was planning to talk with Mrs. Russell and Mr. Hamilton. Savannah begged him not to go to that extreme on her behalf and that she would be okay. She was not telling the truth about her feelings and tried to hide them from her father-in-law.

It was getting late and she was ready for bed. She had given Mason a bath and put him to bed, and like clockwork, Aunt Pearl called. The entire family knew about her day, and she had to relive it all over again. She was exhausted from a very emotional day and wanted to retire for the evening. Although Aunt Pearl meant well, it was time to end the call, and she hoped that Pearl would understand.

The night was long and restless one for her as she tossed and turned. The baby did not allow her to sleep on her side and would stretch and kick. Savannah had to sleep sitting up with four big pillows under her back. At this point, she was already in the third trimester and had only a few weeks before her delivery date. The stress of not working and her husband not going to make it in time for the delivery wade on her constantly. Finally, she was able to drift off to sleep and the baby kept quiet throughout the night.

The next morning came as fast as the night ended for Savannah. Mason was already stirring in his room, and she knew it would not be long before he climbed into her bed. It was a task for her to sit up on the side of the bed, but with practice, she developed a unique way of getting out of bed each morning. Her pregnant form was too large for her to see her feet, and she needed assistance from little Mason with finding her shoes and slipping them onto her feet. Savannah had about thirty minutes to get him dressed and feed before taking him to preschool that morning. She was going to continue to take him to preschool because he needed stability and routine. The time had passed so fast, and she was at the end of her third trimester and ready to deliver. It was June 2, around 11:00 p.m. She was sitting up in the bed, talking with Aunt Pearl, when her water broke. Savannah called her mom to let her know that she was on her way to the house.

When she arrived at her mom's house, she took Mason out of the car and put him to bed. Savannah's brother was there to keep an eye on him while her mom drove her to the hospital. The contractions were really coming at this point, and Savannah took deep breaths to get her through them. They finally arrived in the emergency room department where she was taken immediately up to labor and delivery. The nurse had her undress and put on a hospital gown so that she could check to see how far she had dilated. It was 11:30 p.m. and she was at four centimeters, and the baby was surely going to be delivered. The monitors were hooked up so that she could see when the contractions were coming. Savannah's mom was in the labor room with her but did not do well with the process. She talked about when she delivered in the '60s and how women were given something to put them to sleep.

Well, Savannah was not going to take any drugs with this delivery as she did not with Mason. It was going to be a natural childbirth with no drugs for pain. She looked up at the clock, and it was twelve midnight, and she told her mom that the baby would be here around 6:00 a.m. Savannah was taking little naps in between contractions and just wanted to sleep. Mom was already asleep in her chair and missed most of the event. It was not like she wanted to be a participant. The contractions were very intense now as the nurse came into the room to prep her for delivery. Dr. Michael stepped into the room to check her and said she was ready to go.

The nurse asked Mom if she wanted to come into the delivery room, and she immediately declined. She stated that she would wait until after the delivery, but Savannah knew that she was tired and told her to go home and get some rest. She was rolled into the delivery room, and the doctor was already there, along with more staff. Two of the nurses assisted Savannah with transferring from the bed to the delivery table. She was asked to move her bottom closer to the edge of the table, but she was sleeping, so it became a difficult task. When the doctor told her to put her legs in the stirrup, she commented, "You do it. I am too tired." It was both hysterical and sarcastic at the same time under the circumstances. It was time to push, and as the nurse held her back and she began to bear down, she suddenly stopped pushing. The baby was too big, and she felt a tear, and she immediately stopped and told the doctor that he would have to cut her. Most would not ask to be surgically cut while in full delivery without anything for pain. She was determined that the baby was not going to cause a vaginal tear. She felt the sting and burn of the scalpel as it sliced through her like butter.

Now she was ready to push, and with one big deep breath and push, the head was out. Dr. Michael helped with the shoulders and then instructed her to give one more big push. The pain stopped abruptly, and she heard the boom of Dr. Michael's voice deliver the news, "It's a boy!" She had delivered a healthy son at 6:02 a.m. that Saturday morning. Savannah was exhausted from the delivery but excited to meet her new baby boy. He was laid onto her chest, looking up into his mother's eyes. She reached out to wrap her arms around him. Savannah did not realize how weak and tired she was as she held onto him. The nurse relieved her as she took him over to the table to give him a quick exam. Savannah had already chosen a name for him, but after seeing him face-to-face, she knew it was the perfect choice.

She could not wait to introduce Isaiah Micah to his father and big brother. Bryson was on his way home from Japan and was due to arrive later that day. She was rolled down to recovery where she would be prepared for a surgical procedure two hours later. Savannah had talked to Bryson about getting her tubes tied after she gave birth, but they did not agree on that subject. He wanted more children, and she did not want to have any more. She came from a large family, and two children were more than enough. Bryson did not have the final say as she signed papers months prior to have the procedure done. The complicated part in doing this would be she needed to have his signature and agreement. Right before he left for South Korea, he had given her power of attorney for emergencies. Savannah used this power to sign on his behalf to have the surgery. Of course, this would cause a rift in the marriage, but she did not want to compromise with the subject anymore.

She argued that it was her body and her choice. It was not fair to Bryson, but he left it alone, and they never bought the subject up again. Without realizing it then, this was the start of troubles to come in their relationship. Two hours later, she was back in her private room, waking up from the anesthesia. She woke up at the right time as the nurse was rolling Isaiah into the room. It was time for him to be fed, and she was anxious to see him again. There were family members lined up already to come into the room to visit with them. Isaiah was feeding as she was talking with her cousins and catching up. She looked up, and Bryson was standing in the doorway, smiling, with Mason's arms around his leg as they walked into the room. He leaned down to give her a welcome-home and congratulations kiss as Mason clung tightly to his dad's leg. She gave the baby to Bryson and held her arms out for Mason to come see Mama. It was the reception that she had expected from Mason. He took one look at Isaiah and burst into tears and clutched his dad's leg more.

Mason did not want to talk to Mom or anyone else in the room. Savannah's heart melted and filled with pain to see that her big boy was hurting. Although she was still weak from the delivery and surgery, she took his hand and pulled him onto her lap to hug, kiss, and console him. She let him know that he was her baby too and that she needed him to be a big brother to Isaiah. Savannah told him that she loved him very much. It was not long before he began to warm up to his little brother, but in small doses. The visitors were slowing down as the day was coming to an end. It was time for Bryson to take Mason out to feed him before going home. They would be coming back tomorrow to pick Mom and the baby brother up from the hospital. Savannah got much needed rest that night. The nurses made sure that Isaiah was fed for those two-hour feedings. She was truly appreciative of the nurses and the time spent helping her. Morning had arrived, and she was already up and dressed, ready to go home.

The doctor had to give Isaiah another checkup and perform a circumcision before discharging him. The nurse came in with the birth certificate to be signed and instructions on both their care once at home. Everything was good to go, and she called Bryson to let him know that she would be discharged by noon. She reminded him to put the baby car seat into the car before leaving for the hospital. Bryson arrived early because he had Mason with him, and it would take a little time with a toddler. Savannah was already packing up her things as Bryson walked into the room. "Mason is in a better mood today," she stated as he came running to her. He talked about being a big brother and sharing his room with him.

The nurse came in with the wheelchair as Savannah's form of transportation down to the lobby and to the car. She held onto Isaiah as they rode down the hall to the elevators. "Finally, we are on our way home," she stated as the big doors opened. The ride home was beautiful with the sun shining and the warm summer breeze flowing into the car windows. When they arrived at the apartment, Bryson took the baby and Mason out of the car first. Savannah took her time because she was still a little sore. She walked slowly with Bryson as she held on to his arm. As the key was put into the door and opened, Mason dashed into the apartment and straight to his room. Bryson sat the baby carrier down on the coffee table as Savannah sat down on the sofa. He turned the television on for her and returned to the car to bring in the rest of her things. Isaiah was still asleep as newborns do the first several days of life.

Mason came to sit on the sofa with Mama while she held Isaiah. She wanted them to bond early, so she had Mason to sit back on the sofa, and she laid Isaiah in his arms. He was so excited that he was able to hold his baby brother. Savannah reminded him to be very gentle as she held the back of his head for support. She asked if he would like to feed his brother, and Mason screamed with joy. Bryson had ordered takeout for dinner and went to pick it up. When he returned, the baby was sleeping peacefully in his new crib. She and Mason were still sitting on the sofa, watching a Disney movie. The food finally arrived, and she could not wait to dive in because one day of hospital food was enough for anyone. Life was good as she knew it, but she was cautious, knowing that it was not going to last long. She was elated that Bryson did not have to return to South Korea because that tour was done. All she wanted right now was to have her husband home.

Bryson wanted to wait to tell her about his next duty station. The most important thing to him at this point was enjoying this moment with his family. Later that night, after putting the children to bed, the two had some alone time. It was all about intimacy and cuddling, which was overdue. Savannah was having some fears and anxiety thinking about the possibility of them being separated again. He told her that he would be going to Colorado for about eight months. The idea of him being back in the States gave her hope. She asked if he would be taking her and the children with him. Bryson stated that since it was such a short-term that it would not make financial sense to uproot the family. She did not want to hear this news, not now. Savannah was still trying to cope with a lot of emotions that had not been resolved. She was known to hold in her feelings and did not talk about things that bothered her—the fact that she just had a new baby and she was still grieving the loss of her mother-in-law and the thought of being alone again.

Later that night, she lay in bed, going over in her mind the conservation she had with Bryson. It made her feel as if the things she wanted were not warranted, but she failed to remember that she never gave Bryson's feelings a thought at times. This marriage had been heading in the opposite direction for a while, but neither of them have taken the time to consider the possible damage. In the past, communicating with each other was not as strong as it should have been. Bryson always voiced his opinion, and she never fully expressed how she really felt about situations.

As she lay there, the memories from the past flooded her as tears rolled down her face. She was careful not to let the sound of sobbing escape from her. The sense of loss was overwhelming, and she did not know how to express them. Just as she was about to fall asleep, Isaiah was making his presence known. She got up to head for the kitchen to warm a bottle. When she returned to the children's bedroom, he was wide-eyed and letting everyone in the apartment know he was ready to eat. She reached into his crib and picked him up and carried him over to the changing table. After a quick diaper change, she cradled him in her arms and gave him his bottle. Mason was still asleep, so that gave her plenty of time to feed the baby and have a little downtime. It was a new adventure caring for two small ones at the same time.

She was confident that it was not going to be too difficult because she was used to caring for smaller children. She grew up in a large family with cousins of all ages and helped with diapering and feeding. Savannah used to babysit her younger cousins when she was just a young girl. She always had that nurturing gift and took the role of mentor and caretaker. Isaiah had finished his bottle, and she held him on her shoulder to burp him. The apartment was quiet, and Bryson and Mason were still sound asleep. Savannah used this time to reflect on her life and the changes she was about to go through. She was still grieving the loss of her mother-in-law, recent childbirth, and news that she will not be able to go to Colorado with her husband. She was filled with hurt, anger, loss, and disappointment. Soon anxiety set in, and this did not make things any better. She knew that it would not be long before Bryson was leaving once again. She did not have a job, and money was tight. It had been two weeks, and she could not take it anymore. She decided against Bryson's wishes to return to work. She called her old supervisor at the apparel company and got her old job back as a seamstress.

This was a big mistake because she had just delivered two weeks ago, and the normal return to work was after six weeks. She was desperate and too proud to ask for financial help. The money that Bryson got from the military was just enough to pay the bills and food. If she needed anything else outside of that, she would just go without. She could no longer pay for day care for Mason and now with a newborn. She called her grandmother and asked if she could babysit the children while she worked. Of course, she paid her grandmother and provided transportation for her back and forth from Mom's house. She did not trust for the kids to be at her grandmother's due to the circumstances in the household. Savannah did not trust many people with her children. The time grew near and Bryson was off to Colorado.

The night that she took him to the airport was one of the hardest things she had to do in such a long time. It felt like a lump was stuck in her throat as she struggled to say goodbye again. She wanted to scream at the top of her lungs and protest that he would arrange for her and the children to come with him. He hugged and kissed her and the children and turned to board his plane. She kept it together for the sake of the children as she watched him enter the door out to the tarmac. Savannah buckled the kids in the car and drove off, not knowing where she was headed at first. When the car stopped, she was parked in front of her mom's house. Mom opened the door when she heard car doors shutting and was happy to see them. Savannah was dying inside, but she kept a believable appearance as if everything were great. They all went into the house, and Mom grabbed the baby carrier because she could not wait to visit with her new grandson. Mason ran straight to the refrigerator because Grandma always kept his favorite goodies there. Savannah was thankful for Mom tending to the children.

She was emotionally not equipped at that time. After Mason got his snack, he went into the den and sat on the floor in front of the television to watch his favorite *Dinosaur* movie. Mom came back into the kitchen with the baby and sat at the table. She knew something was bothering her daughter, but she did not want to probe. It was already June and well into the summer months. Mom did not have air conditioning in the house. Savannah grew up in this house so it would make sense for her to be used to the heat. There would always be a box fan in the window blowing hot air into the house. Mom did upgrade to several ceiling fans over the years, but the intense heat could be unbearable at times.

The house was more than one hundred years old with the original hardwoods and trims. The walls were constructed with old plaster that had turned yellowish tint from the years use of coal burning furnace. Mom could sense that something was off with Savannah, so she tried to lighten the mood with how her workday went. It was difficult to put on a happy face when she was dying inside. Mason was in the family room with her little nephew, eating their snack and watching television. It was an event when those two boys were ever together watching the *Teenage Mutant Ninja Turtle* on VHS. Although she could hear the children playing and Mom talking, it was all a blur to her. Savannah knew she had to bring it together soon because she had to get the kids home. The drive home was the same as usual—Mason wanting to tell her everything about his day. She had already put the kids down to bed, so she had a little time to reflect on the events of the day. Savannah would not hear from Bryson until later that night due to time change in Colorado. She could not stay up any longer because she had to be up early to drop the kids off before heading to work. Before drifting off to sleep, she told herself that tomorrow was going to be a new day.

Chapter 22

The roar of industrial sewing machines was blaring in the background. She had put her headphones on to listen to her Walkman. She loved to listen to R & B, but today jazz music was her choice. One of her favorite artists was Najee, and his music would take her to another level of peace. It filled the void temporarily, and she knew that something else was missing but could not pinpoint it. As the day went by, she started to think about her dad and missing him. It had been years since she had seen him and wanted to reach out to him. If a girl ever needed her dad, it was now. She did not know how she was going to contact him, so she was going to take a chance and go by her grandmother's over the weekend. She did not have a relationship with her dad's mom and had always felt uncomfortable around her. Savannah had to find the courage and strength, and in doing so, she had to take the leap of faith.

There was one more hurdle to defeat, and it was hard. Telling Mom that she wanted to see her dad after all these years was a little intimidating. Her mother could always count on Savannah to take her side when opinions mattered concerning her dad. The separation and divorce were *messy*, and Savannah remembered so much about the effects it had on her mom. The nervous breakdown and the long days and nights filled with weeping could not be forgotten. Along the way, she had developed a strong dislike for her father based on what she saw or overheard her mother speak about. Now that Savannah was a grown married woman with children, it was time to hear her father's side of the story. She had always been told that there are two sides to a story. But this would not be the time to bring up such a complex situation. Throughout the week, she thought about how her reunion would be with her dad.

First things first, she had to make contact, and that meant reaching out to her grandmother. Later that week, she told her mom that she would be going to visit her grandmother. Mom was not all that excited about it, but she had to accept Savannah's wishes. On Saturday afternoon, she dropped the kids off to her mom's and made the journey to her grandmother's home. She drove into the street where the cars lined both sides. She was lucky to find parking across the street from the apartment that her grandmother lived. Her heart was racing, and she had about million thoughts rushing through her mind. She stepped out of the car and walked across the street. As she began to walk down the sidewalk, she noticed that some people were gathered outside on the porch where her grandmother lived. She recognized one of her uncles as she got closer. There was a man sitting in a chair on the sidewalk with his back to her. She approached, and her uncle looked at her with shock. It was almost as if he had seen a ghost. The man in the chair turned in his seat, and it was her father. He quickly got up from the chair and called her name as he hugged her so tight that she could barely breathe. Her other aunts and uncles came out of the house to see what was going on.

Everyone was surprised and overwhelmed with joy to see her. They had not seen Savannah since she was about eleven years old. Her uncle Donnie was the comedian in the family, and he could not stop laughing and joking about the look on everyone's faces when they first saw her. Savannah was always the spitting image of her mother. If you were to put them both in the same room, one would think they were sisters. She even sounded like her mom when she spoke. Her stepmother was especially nervous at first because she could not tell if Savannah was not her mother. Although the age difference of twenty years was a factor, her mom still looked so young. Her dad just could not get over how grown up she had become and the fact that she was a wife and mother and only twenty-one years old.

Savannah had so many emotions flowing though her and did not know where to begin. She told her dad that she had missed him so very much and wanted him to be in her life. They talked for what seemed to be hours before realizing she had to get back to pick up the children. There was not enough time to talk about everything. Her dad gave her his contact information and home address. He lived in Virginia Beach and had been there for many years. She remembered visiting him during the summer when she was young. Mom would let her, Miles, and Sapphire stay once for two weeks one summer. Dad invited her to come down and visit. She would need to make plans in the next two weeks and set up arrangements for the kids. This was the meeting that she had long awaited and could only imagine where the journey would take her. It had been a week already, and the arrangements have been made for the children. They would be staying with her mom for the weekend, and she would be driving down on Friday morning and returning on Sunday afternoon.

Her mom was worried about her traveling alone, so she insisted that her grandfather's step-nephew accompany her on the road trip. Savannah did not need a chaperone for this trip, but Mom insisted. She had packed the car with a weekend bag and the children and headed to her mom's house. When she arrived, Rob was already at the house waiting. He was thrilled to be taking a road trip to anywhere, which was to be a new adventure for him. Rob was a special character indeed. He loved to smile and was a big fan of WWF wrestling. Savannah's grandfather and his wife, who was Rob and his sister's great-aunt, were legal guardians when they were children. Their mother passed when they were young.

Rob and his sister Audrey had two other siblings, Margret and Gregory, that was raised by other family. They were on the road by 8:00 a.m. that Friday morning. Savannah had already called her dad to let him know that she was on the way down. He had previously given her directions to the house. The sun was up, and the skies were clear that day. Rob talked the entire time they were on the road. It had been only two hours into the trip, and she stopped for a bathroom break. The anticipation was building because she was only two and a half hours out from Virginia Beach. They were traveling on

460 east which was not heavily traveled that morning. There were many small towns they drove through which lowered the speed limits to 25–30 miles per hour.

Once she gassed up the car, they were on their way entering the Hampton Road area. She drove over the Elizabeth river bridge where they could see small boats and people out fishing. The lanes began to expand into several lanes as the traffic was increasing. Savannah was careful to read the traffic signs on the expressway to make sure that she did not miss her exit. Approaching her exit now, she made the right turn off the ramp and onto Indian River Road. She was used to heavy traffic midday because she learned how to drive in those conditions in Texas. Her dad's directions were exact as she turned into the neighborhood.

The home was beautiful as she pulled up to the house. Rob jumped out of the car with excitement. She turned the car off and walked around the rear to gather her belongings from the trunk. She and Rob walked up the driveway and to the front door. Savannah lifted her hand to push the doorbell, but the door was already open, and her stepmother, Gina, opened it with a big smile. She was greeted with open arms as Gina pulled her in too tight. Dad came soon after into the foyer and grabbed, hugged, and kissed her as if he was seeing her for the first time. Rob was greeted with a warm welcome as they all journeyed into the family room. It was still early in the day and so much to catch up on. Gina was about to make lunch and asked if she could make them something. Savannah was not that hungry and said she'd eat a little something later. She was so happy to spend time with her dad. Her stepmother showed them to their rooms and gave a tour of the house. It was an incredibly beautiful home, and the decor was every bit dad's taste.

He had always, from her memory, loved the finer things in life. Later that evening, Uncle Nathan and his wife Darlene came over to visit. The evening was filled with good food and plenty of laughter. It was getting a little late, and she was ready to retire. After all, she had been driving most of the day and needed a little downtime. Before going to bed, she did call her mom to check on the kids. She told her that she would call in the morning when they get up for breakfast. The next morning after breakfast, Dad and Gina planned to take them out for the day. They ventured down to the oceanfront and walked the boardwalk. Dad loved to fish, so they made their way onto the pier. He did not have his fishing gear because he and Granddaddy loved to fish at night. They had driven around, touring some of his favorite spots at the beach. The weekend was passing so fast, and she needed more time. Later that night, after dinner, she and Dad sat down in his study and talked about everything.

Of course, it was not nearly enough time, and she missed him so much. She told him about Bryson being in the Army and stationed in South Korea for over a year and was now back in the States. Savannah told him that Bryson was currently in Colorado for an eight-month tour and decided not to take her and the children. The visit was good; in fact, she decided to make another trip soon and bring the kids. Before she knew it, they were back home, and she made the decision to take one week off and take the kids to meet their grandfather.

Chapter 23

It had been two weeks since she had visited her dad, and she was missing him dearly. The decision had been made, and she packed the kids up in the car and headed to Virginia Beach to spend more time with him. She was so excited for him to meet his grandchildren and wanted him to build a relationship with her sons. When they arrived at her dad's house, she parked the car in the driveway and gathered the boys out of the car. Savannah had already talked to Mason about meeting his new granddaddy. He was so excited to have another granddaddy, and to a four-year-old, that was big news. It meant more gifts at Christmas and birthdays. Mason took to Gina immediately, but he was a little shy around his new granddad. It took only a moment for him to warm up to him. Isaiah was only four months old at the time, and he was happy to have someone feed him.

Whenever Dad would sit to have a snack or any food at this point, Isaiah made himself known to take part in the festivities. It was amusing to watch the interaction between the two. They stayed with her dad and stepmother for one week. Savannah drove around the city on her own to learn the surroundings. She even stopped by some apartments while she was out just to see how they were set up. At this point, she was becoming serious about moving to the beach. She was going through some changes and had not really dealt with the death of her mother-in-law. Bryson had not dealt with the loss either. They never comforted each other, and this was not good for their relationship. She was still resentful that he left for Colorado and did not take her and the children with him.

Yes, his explanation was that he was only going to be there for eight months. It was important to Savannah that they be together. So much time had passed while he was in South Korea, along with a great deal of loss. In her mind, he did not have any control of his overseas deployment, but he was back in the States now. They never discussed it any further, and he had made his decision final. She had just delivered Isaiah, and a couple weeks later, he was gone again. Now she was struggling with postpartum depression and was seeking companionship. All she wanted was a sense of normalcy and family life. She missed her husband and their relationship. Communication was not one of their strong points in the relationship, but she was counting on him to make her feel important enough to hear about her concerns and fears. Savannah was losing a part of her, and it was happening so fast that she did not know how to slow it down or stop it.

Later that evening, she had put the kids to bed and went back downstairs to talk with her dad and stepmother for a while. She talked about Bryson and how supportive he was about her moving to Virginia Beach. Savannah had even told her dad that she would be making plans as soon as she returned home. There was only a month left on her current lease, and she had to move fast. Little did her dad know of the reality of Bryson not knowing about her decision. The two never talked about her taking the children and leaving town. She still had power of attorney, and she used it to obtain another apartment. When Bryson found out about her move, it was too late to have any discussion. The week was coming to an end, and she needed to arrange for the move to the beach. She made one more visit to the apartment complex the day before leaving. She filled out an application and left a deposit for a two-bedroom townhouse apartment that was close to dad's house. After saying her goodbyes, she and the children were back on the road, headed home early the next morning. Savannah thought about her upcoming move and needed to figure out how she was going to tell Bryson.

For a moment, she tabled the thought and focused on the road and frequently asked Mason if he needed to potty. She did stop an hour later at his favorite place to eat, McDonald's, for a Happy Meal and, of course, the toy inside the box. One thing that anyone should know about raising a toddler is their sporadic eating habits. While they were in the restaurant dining room, she fed Isaiah his bottle. Once back in the car, she buckled the kids in their seats and was back on the road. They only had a little over three hours left on this trip, and she wanted to get back by 2:00 p.m. The kids were already napping as she was driving, so she did not need to make any other stops. She had gassed up the car immediately after lunch.

Finally, some quiet time. This was the perfect time to reflect on the events over the weekend. She thought about her decision to relocate and the expectations set for this new journey. Savannah still had not spoken with Bryson about her decision and was not in any hurry to tell him. She had been searching for jobs in the Wanted ads while she was at the beach. There were some promising leads, but she was faced with the cost of day care for the boys. She and the children arrived at the apartment a little before 2:00 p.m. Savannah unloaded the kids and their bags from the car. It felt good to be back home, and all she wanted to do was take a moment to kick her feet up from the long drive. The kids had slept in the car, so laying them down for a nap was out of the question. She fed Mason a light snack because dinner was going to take a moment. He was in his room playing with his toys, then he decided that Isaiah would enjoy some of his dinosaurs. Isaiah was only interested in his bottle at the time.

He was a baby, and that meant business when he was hungry. After settling down, she played a Disney movie for Mason to keep him occupied while she started dinner. Isaiah fell asleep as soon as he finished his bottle, so that gave her a little time to finish preparing dinner. It was a Sunday afternoon, and like clockwork, the phone rang. It was a long-distance call from Colorado. Mason was excited to hear that his dad was on the phone. He talked with Bryson for a while, filling him in on the road trip to see Granddaddy. Savannah gave him enough time to talk with his dad. Mason missed him so much and asked when he was coming home. He was satisfied with the answer that his dad gave him and handed the phone to Mom. Mason was so happy as he ran through the apartment, shouting, "Daddy is coming home!"

For a moment, when she took the phone, Savannah was rehears-
ing in her mind how she would tell him about the upcoming move.
The words did not leave her mouth when she said hello. One thing
that she thought would not change between them would be the love
they had for each other. But the relationship could not survive on love
only. It was a dangerous game when the trust in the relationship was
on the edge of coming apart. As expected, he told her how much he
loved and missed her. And she would respond with "I know, and miss
you too." The conversation never ventured on the topic of the loss of
his mother and how he really felt and was coping. There continued
to be many unspoken words. Savannah wanted to mention to him
about moving to the beach but could not find the confidence and
courage to say anything. She was still in her feelings about him not
taking her with him to Colorado. There were many opportunities for
her to say, "I am moving to Virginia Beach and taking the kids." But
she already knew that he would not agree with her decision.

For many years, she had never been able to voice her opinions
about things. She would be considered an introvert and passive and
did not speak up. The long-distance collect call came to an end soon
after thirty minutes. It was already October and the arrangements
had been completed for the move. Her dad and uncle came up to
help her pack and move her things. She said her goodbyes to Mom
and Bryson's family. She still had not told him, which made it difficult to mention anything to his grandparents and dad. They finally
arrived later that night and stayed at her dad's house until the next
morning. She was up bright and early and drove over to the townhouse to check things out before her dad and uncle came with the
furniture and boxes. The kids remained in the care of her stepmother
at the house. It did not take long for the truck and trailer to be
unloaded and the furniture placed in its proper place. Unpacking
the boxes could be done much later in the week. She was all moved
in by noon. Savannah stopped by the grocery store to shop for the
townhouse.

After completing her errands and unloading the groceries, she
went to pick the kids up from her dad's. The first night in their new
home was an adventure for Mason. All he could talk about was his

new bedroom that he shared with his baby brother. Savannah wanted to get some work done in the apartment, so she fed them lunch and then put them down for a nap. She unpacked the kitchen first and placed everything in the cabinets, cleaning as she went. Next, she headed upstairs to the bathroom to unpack and put away all toiletries. She hung the shower curtains and placed the rugs on the floor and bath linens in the closet.

Finally, she reached her bedroom to unpack and hang her clothes in the closet and fold and put the rest in the dressers. Savannah did not want to wake the children, so she decided that to unpack their room the next day. Two hours had passed, and it was time to wake the kids from their afternoon nap. She brought them downstairs into the living room, turning the television on for Mason to watch his favorite cartoon. Isaiah was put in his rocker while she started dinner.

Chapter 24

It had been a month now, and she had not found a job. Money was getting a little tight, and she had to sacrifice the luxury of spending on things that were not a necessity. Although she spent a lot of time at her dad's, she was lonely and missed Bryson. It was time to talk to him about her move. She knew that he probably already was told from his dad. He had been trying to get in touch with her for weeks now, but she had not given his family the new phone number. Her mom was the only person she had left contact information with, so he had reached out to her. Mom called her one weekend to relay a message from Bryson. She was not looking forward to that phone call. It was as if she was punishing him for leaving. Her emotions were somewhat extreme at times. And he did not deserve such behavior, but she was hurting and did not know how to fix it. She expected to receive his phone call later that evening.

Savannah was a nervous wreck all day, but she kept it together while she was with the children. The phone rang, and she picked it up to hear his voice on the other end. She was bracing herself for what she knew was coming. His tone was off a little as he asked when she decided to move and not consult him. She remained quiet as he spoke, and she struggled to respond with an answer. The first words that came from her mouth were she found a new job and it paid well. What he did not know that it was the furthest from the truth. She thought maybe this explanation would buy her some time until he was due back in four months. All she wanted to do was move on and change the subject. She asked how he was adjusting to Colorado and said that she missed him so much. He told her that he was thinking about reenlisting for another four years.

This was not the news she was expecting to hear, but it was their reality. After talking for an hour, it was that time. She had to put the kids to bed because she needed some time to reflect on what was next in her life. Falling asleep was quick as she drifted into a dreamworld. A stranger appeared, but you could only see blurred images of what seemed to be a man. Although being new to the neighborhood was evident, there was no time for meeting and becoming friends with any of the other tenants. *Maybe my mind is playing tricks on me*, she thought. Life was complicated enough without entertaining any suggestive notions.

So in her own typical way, she ignored it. Days turned into weeks and then it had been two months already. The job search was becoming discouraging because she was faced with not enough experience or the hours did not coincide with her needs. Spending most of the time with Dad, kids, and family seemed to ease the anxiety at times. On nice days, she would take the children across the street to the park. Most of the time, they would be the only people there in the early afternoon. The other parents and kids were at work and school that time of day. Mason played on the jungle gym as she held Isaiah close to her on the swing.

The next day was just as nice, and she took the children back to the park just before lunch and laying them down for a nap. The park was not empty as she noticed the stranger with a small child; he was gingerly pushing in the toddler swing. She approached to place Isaiah in the swing as well while Mason raced to the jungle gym he loved. The stranger spoke, and she returned the gesture. There was no further conversation as she tended to the boys. After all, she had enough on her plate and did not give it another thought. Each day apart from her husband was becoming more difficult. She was lonely and needed that physical and emotional companionship.

The memories of her mother-in-law continued to haunt her. It was difficult some days when she thought of her often and missed her so much. Savannah had never witnessed someone's death, and it was very traumatic to her. The pressure of trying to hold on to hope was a challenge, and there were times that she just wanted it all to go away. The one thing that kept her going was the love for her children. She did not call home to talk about how she was feeling with Mom. Savannah did not trust to express her feelings with her mother. She did not want to hear negative things about her dad and their relationship. Her in-laws were out of the question although her husband's grandparents were always understanding and talked about life's lessons.

They were a strong family support system, if not anything else. She cut herself off from everyone back home. She would spend time with her step-cousin mostly on the weekends. She had a daughter that was close in age to Mason. They were inseparable and did a lot of things together. Time was pushing along rapidly, and it was Christmas. Savannah packed the kids in the car and headed home to spend it with Mom and her in-laws. Dad had left a day before and spent the holidays with her grandmother, aunts, and uncles. She was happy to be home; it had been three months since she last saw her mom. The kids were also happy to see their grandmother and cousin. After settling in and unpacking their bags, she called her father-in-law to let him know that she was in town for the holidays.

The family Christmas brunch was being hosted at Bryson's aunt's at her new house this year. She really was not jumping at the thought of having to answer a lot of questions. But for the sake of the children, she brought them to the house and the family went bonkers over how much they have grown. The family commented on how well she and the kids looked. Savannah had lost a lot of weight, and her hair was down the middle of her back. As usual, there was the huge buffet with every kind of food you could imagine. Then it was time to exchange gifts. She did not have the money to purchase gifts this year, but she stretched her funds to not be empty-handed. Her family would not have been good with that decision if they knew she had made that choice. One thing about her in-laws was that they were givers and not takers. And they would give you the shirt off their backs. Savannah, at this point, continued to make bad decisions. The move was the first, not telling her husband or dad the truth, and the list started to build. Her emotional state was all over the place, and she did not know how to deal with it. She was good at covering up how she felt and what was really going on in her life. She was afraid of judgment and disappointment.

After visiting everyone, she made it back to Mom's and took the kids in the house. She would normally park the car in the driveway and remove the portable car stereo. With all the excitement and running around all day, she left the car on the street and forgot to remove the stereo. The next morning, she got up and packed everything after feeding the kids breakfast. She was planning to leave a little early. As she was walking down the stairs, she looked out from one of the windows on the lower landing and noticed something odd about the car. She opened the front door and stepped onto the porch to see that the rear passenger window was broken. Panic sat in as she called to her mom, stating, "I believe someone broke into my car." As she ran to the car, the baby's walker had been tossed to the front of the car and the stereo was gone. She went into the house to call the police.

When the dispatcher answered the phone, she was frantic as she told them someone had broken into her car. What made her angry was the fact that it did not seem as urgent to the officer. She was told that due to the nature of the crime and with the possibility of her prints on the car that it would be difficult to separate hers from the offender. This really took her to the next level of anger and feeling she had no control of what was happening to her at that moment. She could not believe they were not going to send a unit out to take the report or investigate. She was told to just file with her insurance. Talking about injustice! She was beside herself with grief. She could not take one more thing happening at this point. She loaded the car and headed back home. There was a tremendous amount of fear, anxiety, depression, and guilt summed up in one big emotional storm.

As she drove over the Hampton Road tunnel, all she could think about was, *What I am going to tell my husband?* He had spent a lot of money on that stereo system which was a pullout to prevent theft. When she pulled into the parking lot at the townhouse, it was still early in the afternoon. She unloaded the kids out of the car and carried them into the house, turning the television on and opening curtains to let the sunlight pour into the living room. She went back out to the car which was parked directly in front of her door to unload the rest of their things. When she closed the trunk of the car, she heard a male voice say hello. She looked up to see the stranger whom she found out to be her neighbor.

He lived in the townhouse on the end of her building. She never noticed due to the fact she was not interested in getting to know her neighbors. She spoke back because it was the polite thing to do. He responded with a flirtatious smile. Savannah was not amused because she was used to guys *hitting* on her since she was a young girl. She walked into her townhouse without any regard to his flirting. Once settled, she called her mother to say that they made it safe and sound and that she would call her by the end of the week. Finally, she had a moment to relax and did not want to go upstairs to her bedroom. Curling up on the sofa in the living room was her other option. The room was lit by the glimmering lights on the Christmas tree. She had the stereo turned down low and listened to the Quiet Storm hour on the radio. Savannah was not a drinker, but of late, her palate danced around with the blackberry-flavored Bartle's and Jayme's wine coolers. Most would probably say that was not a choice for serious drinkers. She had never been one to indulge in any form of alcohol. On her wedding night, the hotel sent a complimentary bottle of champagne to the room. She did not care for the taste, but the experience was not bad. In the moment of stepping out of her comfort zone, life appeared to be more complicated than expected.

There was still something missing, and she did not quite know what it could be. *Is there a moment of regrets or wish I could have done this differently?* Then she found herself questioning the decision that was made years ago in her life. No, there were no regrets for having her children or even marrying the man who was the father of her children. Of course, life was not always perfect and will certainly be unpredictable. Playing it smart and safe was always the objective for her. Savannah was always put on this pedestal by friends and family. She never got into trouble or hung around the wrong crowd and was always setting examples of what was expected in life. But this time around, she did not want to be what some would say goody-two-shoes. In this moment, all she wanted to do was scream for freedom from the overwhelming expectations of others. She wanted to experience something different, and she was feeling so alone. She was missing her mother-in-law terribly, and on top of that, she missed her husband. But right now, the marriage was headed for trouble. The lack of communication was truly a factor, along with intimacy. Now please do not misunderstand the difference between intimacy and sex. They never had a problem with a physical connection, but it was a void lately due to the eighteen months he was abroad and the eight additional months here in the States.

There was just not enough time between leave time and going off to the next tour of duty. She understood it came along with the job in the military. The family was left with the sacrifice as well because they could not always travel with their loved ones. She was still bitter because there was never an in-depth discussion about leaving her and the kids behind for an additional eight months. There continued to be so much resentment and unforgiveness she was feeling within. By this time, she could feel the wine coolers setting in, leaving her a little drowsy and eventually closing her eyes to dreamland.

Chapter 25

The chatter of little ones echoed in the distance as Mason was calling for Mama to come get him. The boys were awake as Mason saw that his baby brother had plenty of toys in his crib. Isaiah reached up with arms open to greet Mama as she reached down into his crib to change his diaper. He was a happy baby and apparently wanted to tell Mom about his morning so far. Of course, baby talk babble was taken to another degree. The more she asked how her baby boy was this morning, the more excited he became. Mason decided he wanted to join in and interpret what Isaiah was saying to Mama. To hear the dialogue between the two was hilarious. Moments like this were what kept her happy despite what may be happening in her life. She took the boys downstairs to the kitchen and placed Isaiah in his high chair while she prepared breakfast.

Today was going to be a great day. It was something in the air that made her feel that things were going to be okay. The sun was shining bright, and it had warmed enough to take the kids across the street to the playground. It was apparent that many of the other mothers were thinking the same. The park was filled with little children and school-age kids. Most of the moms were sitting on the benches, chatting away, while the kids played. Savannah went along with her normal routine with the boys. She put Isaiah into the toddler swing while Mason made friends with the other kids in the sandbox. She had been there awhile before she noticed that the stranger was there with his little girl. He approached the toddler swings with his little one and asked if it was taken. Savannah was polite and told him that it was free. He introduced himself as Malik with his hand extended as a friendly gesture.

Without thinking about it, she shook his hand and introduced herself as well. He also introduced his little girl as she introduced Isaiah and pointed out Mason in the sandbox. All was well as the two made short conversation based around their kids and spouses. She told him that her husband was in the military, and he shared that his wife was in the military as well. The day was going very well, and she let her guard down just a little. He would be the first neighbor that she had spoken to while she lived in the townhome community. Before she knew it, the polite hellos turned into light conversations at the park. It was becoming frequent that he would show up at the same time as she did.

Of course, she knew it was not a coincidence at this point and was aware of the overwhelming attraction between the two. This was the making of a dangerous situation that would lead to a profoundly serious repercussion. The more dangerous it became, the more she was intrigued by the attention. She had been longing for some type of emotional and physical attention for quite some time. There was no doubt that she loved her husband, but those feelings were slipping away with no recourse. She kept telling herself that maybe it was some phase and it will pass. She had never experienced what it would be like to let go and not worry about how others expected her to be. Savannah did not kid herself about any fairy tales because she was not searching for one. She wanted to feel free for just a little while and not think about her current situation. It was more like this man was an out even if it was temporary.

There were no expectations as she was very vulnerable, depressed, and lonely and needed to feel alive again. The casual conversations became frequent, and she enjoyed his company. She was becoming too comfortable with his presence and, in the back of her mind, thought it was harmless, not until late one night when there was a knock at her door. Her first reaction was to question who could be coming to see her that time of night. Hours ago, she had come home from her dad's and just wanted to put the kids down for bed. Earlier, her cousin that was stationed at the naval base stopped in to check on her and the children from the request of Mom. She knew it could not have been her dad or cousin. Her sister-in-law just lived across the street behind her building. She worked at night, so she knew it was not her either. Looking through the peephole of the front door, she discovered it was Malik. A thousand thoughts ran through her head within a few seconds. She was asking herself why he was at her door that night. She did not recall inviting him. The attraction to each other was obvious and intense. It was like her brain shut off as she opened the door to find him smiling with those hazel color eyes.

Letting him into the townhouse was a big mistake, but she did so anyway. She walked back to the kitchen to grab a glass of water and asked if she could get him anything. He followed her into the kitchen, and when she turned to address his visit, he was there in her personal space. She could feel his breath on her face and the warmth of his body pressed against hers. *This is not happening* were the words that she was trying to force out of her mouth. In that moment, her life changed forever, and time slowed to a complete stop. All she felt was Bryson's eyes set upon her with disappointment, hatred, and betrayal. She could not imagine facing him with such a traumatic and selfish act. Could this all just be a dream that she seemed to not be able to pinch herself to bring her back to reality. In that moment, she rejected his advancement and asked him to leave. She felt such a tremendous amount of guilt for allowing him to get too close. *What was wrong with me?* questioning her judgement.

The next few days were rough as she was out of touch with possible repercussion to her actions. She wanted to talk to someone about what had happened, but she could not trust this information with anyone. Savannah did know that whatever was starting up had to stop immediately. This was what she had agreed with herself to do. The one thing she did not expect was a part of her still wanted the danger and thrill of the chase. Yes, it was crazy and selfish to not be considerate of others. Her actions were not alone, and the blame was to be shared. Weeks have passed and her communication with Malik had come to a halt. She wanted to avoid any contact or even passing in the parking lot. She also changed the schedule of when she took the kids to the park across the street. Bryson was coming home, and she was excited but paranoid about his arrival.

It was February, and he arrived as promised. She picked him up at the airport on a rainy evening. The anticipation was getting the best of her as she waited for him to disembark from the plane. How was she going to put on a happy face when she saw him again? This was harder than she could imagine, but as soon as he appeared in the doorway of the ramp, she pushed all those anxieties aside. She was holding Isaiah on her hip and holding Mason's hand with him, bouncing up and down when he saw his dad. He pulled away and was off running to greet his dad. The reunion was worth the wait as Bryson kneeled to his son's height and closed his eyes as he held him tight. Savannah approached with Isaiah in hand and greeted her husband as a wife should after returning home from deployment.

Although the embrace was much needed, it felt as if two strangers were meeting for the first time. There was a moment of awkwardness as she recognized the look of pain and disappointment in his face. The car ride home was off as well as she tried to keep a genuine conversation flowing so that Mason would see that his parents missed each other terribly. She was not looking forward to going home right away, so she suggested that they stop by her dad's first. When they arrived, Dad had already heard a lot of good things about him. It was a matter of sizing him up to see if he, indeed, was deserving of his daughter. The introduction was great as the two sat in the family room becoming acquainted. They did not stay long because she knew that he was a little jet-lagged and needed some rest. The drive home was a little lighter as she pulled into the parking lot of the townhome; she noticed that Malik was also returning home with his family. Savannah's heart was pounding as she put the car in park and opened the driver-side door. They took the kids out of the car and were walking toward the sidewalk. She noticed from the corner of her eye that Malik looked over as he was picking his daughter to carry her into the house.

It was all she could do to keep it together and hoped that Bryson would not catch the glimpse. A sigh of relief overcame her as she was able to stick the key into the door and open it. They entered the living room where he put his bags down at the door. She gave him the grand tour of the townhouse as Mason was pulling at his shirt to follow him into their bedroom. She let the kids stay up a little while longer so that they could enjoy being with their dad. They had already eaten dinner, so it was bath time for the kids and then off to bed for the kids. The night was going to be a long one, and she was not looking forward to it. The one thing that she did know was the fact that it was time to face the music. She turned the bed down while Bryson was taking a shower. Her heart was pounding again from the fear of having to talk about their problems. There was no way other way of dealing with what she knew was broken. When he was done in the bathroom, she told him to get comfortable and to try to get a little rest. She tried to stay in the shower longer in hopes that he would already be asleep when she was done.

To her surprise, he was still up, as she knew he would be. For a moment, she allowed herself to forget that they were in tune to each other. He would know that something was off just as she would know. The mood in the room felt like they had just met for the first time and were waiting for whoever was going to make the first move. She lay down in the bed and turned away from him. You could feel the heat radiating from his body as he pulled her close to him. One thing she could not deny was the way he made her feel whenever he was that close. Longing for his touch again was overwhelming. She was having a difficult time opening to him, but he always had a way of persuading her. Because the two were so in tune with each other, he already knew there was something wrong.

He asked that question she did not want to be faced with: "Who is he?" She knew that it was impossible to make up a lie because it would be pointless. Sitting up in the bed, she began to talk about the events that led up to the casual conversation. For the entire time that she spoke, it was difficult to look him in the eyes. The pain alone was heartbreaking for her to watch, but she knew that he deserved the truth. When she had hoped the conversation was done for the night, there was an interesting turn of events. He asked how long and if it was still going on. As she began sobbing, trying to give him an answer, he pulled her close and comforted her. This really sent her into hysterics because it was not the reaction she was preparing for. He also had something to share with her. The first thing that crossed her mind was he was asking for a divorce. Yes, he was upset and angry because his trust was betrayed.

Then he told her that while he was overseas, there was another woman that wanted to be more than friends. He said that it could have developed into something, but he told her that he had a wife and family. Of course, this was not what she wanted to hear not right now. Is this a pass because they both were in a vulnerable state? It scared her to death to hear this because it was not only confirming there were some major issues in their marriage but also that these were some pretty serious changes. Hours had passed and then it was dawn. The children would be getting up in another four hours and they both needed the rest. The two drifted off to sleep in each other's arms.

Chapter 26

The next morning was the start of a new day, and the expectations were set. The kids had not awakened yet, so this was the perfect time for some additional alone time. They had a lot more to talk about and needed to decide what was going to be their next move. The night before was highly emotional, and the intimate time they very much needed was not addressed. The house was quiet, and the sunlight peeked through the window blinds on the cold February morning. Savannah certainly did not expect what happened next. Bryson deliberately kissed her on the shoulder and neck as she was turned away from him.

After all that had happened, he still was very much in love with her and wanted to show her how much. Savannah had no choice but to give in although she felt as if it was not deserved. She was very submissive to his will and silently cried as he made love to her. She was convicting herself for him. An hour later, you could hear the boys stirring around in the next room. It was time to get up and tend to the kids and start breakfast. Bryson went into their room to spend a little daddy time. Savannah was already downstairs in the kitchen, preparing breakfast and cleaning as she goes. The commotion of kids playing and the television on was the much-needed distraction at this point. The phone rang, and Bryson answered to find his father on the other end. The two had talked for a length of time, discussing what our plans would be. Bryson was just out of the military, and there was no immediate income coming in. Savannah's job situation was still in limbo, and there were no prospects yet.

After breakfast, she sent Mason into the living room to watch his favorite Saturday-morning cartoon. She and Bryson remained in the kitchen with Isaiah sitting in his high chair as they discussed what their next move would be. Her father-in-law stated that he would bring a truck down and help them pack up everything and move back. Savannah did not want to leave; she wanted to at least try to make it. The first thing they had to do was find Bryson a job and a cheaper place to live. When he finally found a job and things began to look up for a while, then the baby got sick and had to have surgery. He was admitted to the children's hospital to have an inguinal hernia repair. Savannah had never been so scared in her life. She did finally find a sewing job making less than minimum wage, but it was a start.

In a few weeks, the baby had fully recovered, and they moved into a new place. She worked during the day and Bryson worked night shift. This worked out best for them because they did not need to pay full-time day care fees. Their relationship was still on the rocks, and the stress of medical bills was steadily piling up. It was already spring, and the warm weather was truly welcomed. Her cousin also lived in this apartment community with her young daughter. So some evening, she would take the kids over for a while to visit while Bryson was at work. The neighborhood was not the best, but they had to do with what was within their budget. In the evenings, one could see people walking around outside, kids running through the playground, and some sitting out in the parking lot in cars, listening to music.

One evening, she was taking the trash out to place in the dumpster when she looked up to see a small group of people gathered around some cars in the parking lot. To her surprise, she recognized someone and was in disbelief, saying to herself it could not be true. A gray Audi was pulling into the parking lot and stopped by the group of people. She already knew what was true that it was Malik. How could this be? She had not seen him for a moment and thought that she would never laid eyes on him again. Hurrying back up the stairs, hoping that he would not notice her, she closed the door behind her. Savannah wanted so much for the past to stay in the past. It had been a couple months, and she needed to reconnect with her husband.

What she didn't need right now was any more complication. She had already spoken about him to her husband and had casually pointed him out from the previous home. *What was I thinking?* she asked herself as she paced back and forth in the living room of the apartment. Who was she kidding? When she laid eyes on him again, it was evident that there was still a strong attraction. She continued to try to fight it, but it was like a magnetic pull that she could not break.

The next day, her cousin came over to visit. Bryson was already at work, so that gave her time to talk with her cousin. She had to tell someone what was going on, so she confided in her. Later that evening, she walked her cousin back to her apartment building, which was just a few buildings over. And of course, they had to walk past that same group of people. Savannah avoided contact as they passed when she heard someone say hello. She turned to find Malik with that flirtatious smile as he spoke to her. There was no response from her as she continued her walk with her cousin. They arrived at the building and said their goodbyes, and she hurried home before it got too late. The kids were bathed and put to bed, and she poured herself a glass of wine and lay on the sofa, listening to a little jazz on the stereo. This habit had become her go-to when she needed to relax. Just when she thought things were headed in the right direction, here popped up things from the past.

Although it was not long ago and still very fresh, it was still a problem. At some point, she drifted off to sleep and was awakened by her husband who had just come in from the third shift. He was tired from working such long hours and wanted to hit the showers and then to bed. She went to the kitchen to fix him a little breakfast while he was showering. The kids were still asleep, so she could be quick about it. While he was eating breakfast, she went to take a shower as well because it was soon time for her to be up and getting ready for work. Once done, she got the kids up and fed and dressed them to be ready so that she could drop them off at day care. They were only there three days a week when her husband was working.

He worked three twelve-hour-shift days per week and had the weekends off. So two days of the week when he was off, the children stayed at home with him. The commute to work was like any other typical day with the bumper-to-bumper traffic, horns honking, and people in a rush. The ladies at the shop were already wired for the workflow today, which made her optimistic. She enjoyed working with these ladies because they became more than just coworkers; she looked at them as friends. Savannah had not met anyone else since she moved to the beach. She only spent time with her immediate family, which left no room for socializing outside of that circle.

The day was running smoothly as promised, and she felt enthusiastic about working on some of the current issues in her life. It was time for her and Bryson to have some quality time with each other. So she thought about calling her mom and asking if the children could come up for a few days. When she arrived home, Bryson was getting ready for work, so she mentioned that she wanted to talk over the weekend about taking the kids to her mom for a while. He said that would be a good idea because they needed to work through some things. Savannah was feeling happy and optimistic right now because they both wanted to work on the marriage. Well, that was what she had hoped would be the case. Old habits and desires are sometimes hard to shake when there are constant reminders. She packed his lunch as she was preparing dinner so that later she could take the kids to the park. The evening was nice with a mild warm breeze, which was perfect for a good night's sleep for the kids. Sitting on the park bench, watching Mason play with the other children, was soothing. Isiah was still young, so he sat in his stroller and played with his favorite toy. One of the other mothers sat down beside her, and they started a very casual conversation. The two ladies introduced themselves and shared a little about each other. They both were married and had not lived in Virginia Beach long.

The other mother was there due to her husband being in the Navy. Savannah shared that her husband was in the Army recently but decided not to reenlist. Savannah enjoyed socializing with someone other than family and coworkers. It was starting to get late, and the mothers gathered their children to take inside. They said their goodbyes and promised to see each other again. Savannah brought the boys in and started their bath. It was always fun time for them splashing in the tub with a bubble bath. Sometimes she would have a time getting them out, but it was worth their little bit of happiness. Children are so innocent and precious. Later that evening, it was her turn to shower and relax for the night. She loved to watch one of her late-night shows *Arsenio Hall* just before drifting off to sleep.

There was a knock on the door that woke her; at first it sounded like across the hall, but it was more prominent to her door. Who could be at her door this time of night? She knew that Bryson was still at work, and he did have a key. She tipped to the door and looked out of the peephole. How was it possible? She never spoke to Malik or told him where she lived. Who could have told him which apartment she lived? All these questions came rushing to her head as she could feel her heart racing. Without using her better judgment, she opened the door to find him giving a stare of puzzlement. She asked him why he was there and for what reason he thought there was still something there. His response did surprise her as he moved closer to her in the doorway. He asked if he could come in because he needed to talk to her. She did not want to fall for his charms, but the magnetic attraction was still there. So she asked herself, What was there to lose?

She was going to make her point clear and tell him that whatever this was had to stop. Here was his opportunity to talk, and she made it clear that he had to make it quick. He started with telling her that he missed her, and he did not like the fact that she completely ignored him. He was not used to being rejected and did not know how to deal with it. She told him that it was a mistake between the two of them and that she was working on her marriage. He failed to mention that he should be giving more attention to his own marriage and family. Just before she suggested that he leave and to never come back, he grabbed her gently and pulled her close to him. She could smell the light hint of beer on his breath where he had obviously been outside with his friends socializing. She backed up and asked him to leave with a firm tone that anyone could not mistake for just a kind gesture. Although he offered an apology, she did not receive it as intended. Her face was cold as stone, showing no remorse for the words uttered. The look on his face proved there was an unbelievable chill in the room. She opened the door for him to exit, and he said his very last goodbye to her.

This could not be happening again; she was still very attracted to him but knew that this could not continue. Why was he so irresistible? She had been up all night thinking about what seemed to be a never-ending cycle. She did not want to develop feelings for this man because there was nowhere to go with it, and she wanted very much to save her marriage. The next morning, she wanted so badly to talk to her husband about what had been going on, but it would be best once the kids were out of town. So she held that information until the time was right, but when was it going to be the right time? The weekend had arrived sooner than she expected, and Bryson packed the car and took the kids to her mom's. He asked her to come with them, but she did not want to go because she did not want to face her mother with the guilt that she was filled with. He was to call her once they arrived and again that night so the kids could say good night. She was feeling depressed and needed someone to just listen. Her cousin came over and invited her to come out to a club. Savannah had never been to a club in her entire life and was more than skeptical. She wanted to try something new so that, for a little while, she can forget about her current situation.

The last twelve months had been difficult with the passing of her mother-in-law, postpartum depression, feelings of abandonment, loss of communication in the marriage, and now adding more complications to her life. As they pulled into the parking lot of the club, she felt butterflies in her stomach. There was a great abundance of anxiety and fear wrapped up into one big emotion. She followed her cousin to the front door where they both showed their IDs. They entered and walked through another set of doors where they could hear the music behind them. The gentleman standing by the door opened as he was inviting them into the club. Because she had never been to a nightclub before, she did not know what to expect. The lighting was dimmed, and there were small tables around a dance floor.

There was a bar setting off to the side with additional seats. She and her cousin grabbed a table where they sat, and not long, a waitress came over to take a drink order. Savannah did not know about any types of cocktails, so she ordered a glass of white wine, something she was familiar with. After sitting for a while, a gentleman came over and asked Savannah to dance. At first, she was hesitant but accepted, and he escorted her to the dance floor. It was a fast-paced song, so there was no physical contact. She had not danced like that in such a long time. Savannah had never danced with Bryson like this for the entire time they had been together. Maybe there was a slow dance or two, but she had never had so much fun in that moment. The song ended, and she was escorted back to her table.

The gentleman thanked her for the dance and returned to the table with some of his friends. For the entire night, she could feel eyes on her, and as she thought, it was him. Savanah had enough on her plate and did not want to add any more than she needed. She and her cousin talked for a while and danced a little more. Her cousin went to the bar for another drink, leaving her at the table alone. This was where the gentleman made his attempt to come sit with her. He asked if he could spend a little more time with her and if she would accompany him. She refused and asked him to leave her table. When her cousin returned, she told her that it was time to go. On the way home, all she could think about was the people and the atmosphere at the club. She soon realized that going to nightclubs was not all it seemed to be and that she had not missed anything. It involved guys *hitting* on ladies and trying to get them to go home with them. And most of the women traveled in groups and had their personal agendas as well. The club scene was not for her, and it was the first and last time visiting one.

Once she arrived home, she entered the apartment and lay on the sofa and went straight to slept. The next morning, she got into her bed and slept for the rest of the day. It was nearly 7:00 p.m. when she woke up, and it felt like she had slept for about a week. Maybe that was what she needed—to rest both her body and mind. Bryson was due home tomorrow, and she was a little nervous about facing him. Mom agreed to keep the children for two weeks while they work on their marriage. That was the idea until he came home; it was difficult for them to even have a conversation without an argument.

And she would just shut down and not talk at all. Apparently, he had a lengthy conversation with her mother about the current situation with their marriage.

On his return, he had a written letter from her mother that he was told to give Savannah. She did not read the letter right away because she was not ready hear the disappointment and judgment from her mother. One thing she was good at was putting on a face that appeared as if everything was okay. Some days they would just take long drives out to the beach to just walk and take in the ocean breeze. But something was still missing, and the two of them did not know how to fix it. Sometimes she felt as if she did not want to fix the marriage.

Things were becoming worse and not better between them. Savannah distanced herself more and was not intimate with her husband. She did not feel anymore. It was as if everything was dead. She often asked herself if the entire relationship was just a smoke screen, hiding her true feelings. The one thing she was sure of was that she was not looking for any new relationships or to be emotionally involved with anyone. All she wanted was her freedom and independence, but she did not have any prospects for a good-paying job. After spending several years together, it was evident there was some codependency in the relationship. She never finished college because she had to put things on hold while trying to raise their family.

Savannah knew that was just an excuse because she feared trying to make it on her own. And she did not want to be a cliché, like most of the women in her family. It felt as if she was suffocating, but how do you tell your husband, a person you have been with all your teenage and adult life, at this point that you want out? The children would be gone for two weeks and something had to give. Her habits continued to change to the point that she was getting behind on bills and paying the rent. They were extremely in debt with medical bills from Isaiah's surgery because there was no health insurance after Bryson was discharged from the military. He chose not to reenlist, and it took him about two months to find a job. He was ready to move back home when he got out, but she talked him into staying. It was against his better judgment, but he would have done anything to make her happy, not knowing that it was too late; and this was for her own selfish reasons. Although he did make decent wages, the bills were more than what he was bringing into the household. She was only making minimum wage, and it covered groceries for the week.

The goal was for them to spend more time with each other on his days off. She would find herself outside late in the evenings, sitting with some of the ladies of the apartment complex, laughing and talking and having some girl time. Occasionally, there would be some of the husbands and their friends gathered in little groups as well. It was like she wanted to spend her spare time with them and not with her own husband. In such a short time, she developed friendships with most of the people in the group. Savannah had always been comfortable being around guys due to, all her life, most of her friends were males. This was her comfort zone, but there was always someone attempting to change the dynamics. And she would also find herself flirting a little. It was always never intentional; it was like she had this magnetic pull that just drew attention. Growing up, she never wanted to be in the spotlight, and even now it was not her choice.

Remembering being a young girl, guys would stop in their cars to talk to her. Boys in the neighborhood would hang out at her house. She never put any thought to it until she started showing interest. Savannah was always discreet with her flirting, and one would never know outside of the person she was flirting with. She never initiated the mild flirting, but if she was interested in that person, he would not miss the hint. It almost never failed, and it was true this time around. One of the gentlemen in the group was becoming friendly, and she took it as that—just someone to cut up with and, as a group, talk about many things of interest. Everyone pretty much knew one another's name at this point, and being in a military town, most came from other parts of the country. For most, they either worked at the naval shipyard, railroad, Ford truck manufacturing, or in the military. He had introduced himself on a previous day, but it just did not stick because she was not trying to befriend everyone. Savannah did not want to come off as a snob, but she did not want to send the wrong message.

Chapter 27

Today was going to change their lives forever. She was getting ready for work and had finished cooking breakfast and packing a lunch. He was sitting at the dining room table, eating his breakfast, while she was in the bedroom dressing for work. It was nearly 8:30 a.m., and she did not need to be at work until 9:30 a.m. In the back of her mind, she was still processing how she would bring up a conversation about how she was feeling. She knew it was already going to be difficult due to her passive behavior. Sometimes that shy little girl that she knew many years ago would resurface, and that was a challenge at times. Savannah said goodbye to her husband as she was going out the door.

There was a piece of paper taped to the door, and she grabbed it and stuck it in her purse. It was recognizable because she had seen this before at the townhouse apartments they used to live. She knew it would be a matter of time before receiving a notice that they had to vacate the apartment. As she got in the car and started it, she opened the notice to see that in five business days the full rent was due. She had already received a thirty-day notice last month, and this was the follow-up of the impending eviction. She was hoping that the money would be saved in time, but as she could see, time waits for no one. Now was the time to figure out how to tell her husband. The entire day she was a nervous wreck and could not focus. Savannah did not have an appetite and felt sick.

The workday had come to an end as quickly as it began. On the drive home with the traffic hurrying along and horns honking, she replayed in her mind how she would break the news to her husband. As she entered the apartment complex parking lot, her heart started to pound faster. Getting out of the car and walking toward the stairway seemed like a mile. Opening the main door to the building, you would see more than two dozen stairs that appeared to her as climbing a steep mountain. Reaching the top and putting the key in the door was one of the many hard things she ever had to do in quite some time. What she was about to do would change her life forever. Savannah entered the apartment and placed her handbag and keys on the dining room table. She slipped her shoes off as she walked down the hallway to find her Bryson already up, watching television in the bedroom.

He was in a particularly good mood and asked how her day at work was. Savannah was reluctant but said that everything was good. She sat on the bed beside him while bracing herself for delivering the bad news. He asked what was wrong and that if she had anything to tell him that it was okay. Bryson was very caring, and his tone proved to be sincere. *Here goes*, she thought as she swallowed a deep breath. She began with, "We received a notice on the door this morning stating that we have five days to vacate." The temperature in the room dropped instantly. It was not due to a climate change but the mood of the atmosphere, which set the tone for what was about to happen next. It felt that the roof was being ripped off the apartment building from the raging roar that was released from his voice. He wanted an explanation as to why this was happening when he went to work every day, performing a backbreaking job.

There were words coming from his mouth that she had never heard him expel, and it terrified her. She believed that everything he was feeling from the time he returned home was released. He grabbed the car keys and left, slamming the door. She did not know what was going to happen; she knew that he would be too upset to go into work, but he would never miss work. It had been an hour, and she began to worry more now than ever. Her first thought was to call her dad, but that would mean that she would have to 'fess up to what had been happening all along. Savannah called anyway, and Gina answered the phone. She asked if everything was okay because

Bryson had just left their house. Savannah asked if she could come over because she needed her. In about thirty minutes, Gina was there, trying to make sense out of what was happening. Moments later, the door opened, and Bryson came in with rage in his eyes. There were so many scenarios running through her mind regarding what could happen at that moment. Gina tried to talk to him, but he was not interested in anything she had to say.

Savannah begged Gina to stay because she did not want to be left alone with him. She had to face the consequences alone and trembled with fear as Gina closed the door behind her. Savannah went to the bedroom with her head down so that she would not have direct eye contact with him. Bryson followed her into the room and asked her why. She turned her back on him because she did not want to face him with the shame and guilt she carried. She did not see it coming as she felt the blow knocking her down; as she felt herself falling to the bedroom floor, everything was spinning as she was trying to get up off the floor.

As she was sobbing uncontrollably, he told her that he went to his house and dragged him out into the yard and beat him until he told the truth. This was it. Life as she knew it was over in a swift instant. She lay in the floor until she heard the apartment door close again. Savannah was too afraid to move in fear of him coming back and touching her again. The memories of their teenage years came rushing back from the times he was physical with her. She was terrified then and more afraid now than ever. She finally found the strength to get up and go to the living room to find that he had not returned. Sitting on the sofa in the dark gave her plenty of time to think about what was next. After sitting there for a while, she decided to start packing up her things in suitcases. She did not have any boxes, so she had planned to go early the next morning to the U-Haul store to buy some.

The kitchen was the next room to start packing up appliances and dishes, then she moved to the living room. By the time Bryson had returned later that night, she had all the pictures off the wall and curtains off the windows. He was a different person when he entered the apartment. He approached her in a gentle and caring way and pulled her close to him. She resisted as he held her tight and told her that he was sorry and that he loved her. Savannah was still shaken from the blow he delivered to the back of her head. All she could do was sob quietly as he tried to apologize for hurting her. He pleaded with her not to leave him and that everything was going to be okay. She had heard this before, except the difference was she betrayed his trust and their marriage. When they were kids in high school, she wanted out of the relationship due to his possessive behavior. Yes, he was sweet and caring then but also jealous and refused to let her leave him then. The next morning, around 7:00 a.m., they went to the U-Haul and storage place to rent both a truck and unit.

They returned to start moving the furniture into the truck. It took them every bit of four hours to completely empty the apartment. By 1:00 p.m., the sheriff had shown up with the warrant to vacate, but they had already officially removed their personal items. Savannah drove the car and followed him to the storage unit to place their things. Once the truck was unloaded, they drove to her parents to say goodbye before getting on the road headed back home. The car was packed to the brim with clothes and some of the children's toys. It was only a four-and-a-half-hour drive back, but it seemed as if they were on the road for twelve. Savannah never spoke a word as the music played on the radio as they passed through each small town on Route 460. They did stop once for food and bathroom break and continued their journey. When they reached her mother's home, it was late, and the kids were already in bed. Mom did not know that they were coming tonight; it was her understanding that it would be by the end of the week. Bryson told her what had happened and that they had to move back. Savannah was too embarrassed to say anything to her mom. She already knew Mom had been privy to some of what had happened.

When Bryson dropped the kids off a week ago, he talked with her mom and told her what was going on with this other man. Bryson had returned with a handwritten letter from her mom speaking on the subject. It was settled that they were staying with her mom until they could get back on their feet. She and Bryson both found jobs and worked to pay debts and save money for them to move. Things were worse before they seemed to get better. The two fought all the time, and at one point, she secretly contacted a divorce lawyer. She had a consultation with the attorney and was given a brief review of what would take place and the difficult challenges that she would face in a custody battle. Within a few days, she received preliminary papers in the mail from the lawyer, which laid out the details of filing for a divorce. She did not want to fight anymore and wanted out of the marriage. The one thing that kept pulling at her heart was the kids. She did not want them to grow up like she did—in a broken home. So she called the attorney and told him that she wanted a little more time to think about it. Now they were living life day by day and putting their differences aside to keep the family together. It had been eighteen months since they moved in with her mom, and now it was time to move on.

Savannah had started searching for two-bedroom apartments that were affordable. After a week of calling and visiting apartment complexes, she found a neighborhood that was kid friendly and had good schools. The application was processed, approved, and the security deposit paid. It was early May and perfect for moving. The two made the trip back to the beach to pick up their furniture. Savannah was happy to be in her own place again. She was grateful to her mom for letting them stay until they could get back on their feet and work on the marriage. The boys were happy to be living in the same house as their grandmother, and it was some form of normality for them. Although their parents were not at their best, they worked hard to not show any difference in the relationship around the kids. The next day was move-in day at the apartment, and the boys were excited about having their own room again and playing with their toys. Finally, they were settled into the apartment with everything unpacked and put away. Now the next chapter for them was beginning.

Chapter 28

Finally, things were beginning to turn around. Although the relationship was not great, it was better than what it was eighteen months ago. The kids were settled into a routine with school and meeting new friends at the playground across the street. Savannah got a new job and befriended several coworkers that had become close girlfriends. Her husband, too, had gotten a new job with better pay. They were on the grind throughout the weekday, and on the weekends was family time. On Friday nights, dinner at their favorite restaurant, Western Sizzlers, and then over to Blockbuster to pick up a half dozen VHS movies. She always would let the boys pick at least two PG movies that they would enjoy watching all day on Saturday. Summer and fall had come and gone, and now the Christmas season was upon them.

The Christmas catalog from JCPenney arrived on schedule along with Toy "R" Us *Big Book*. And as expected, the boys held both catalogs hostage as they repeatedly made a list and left them on their parents' dresser every week until Christmas. It was adorable that Mason and Isaiah would include the page number and detailed descriptions of the items they wanted for Christmas. Life was good at this point but not long-lived. The two still had some issues they had to deal with but were put on the table. They were not communicating in a conducive manner, especially when finances were involved. Savannah decided that she was going to open a separate savings account she identified as an *escape* account. She did not make good money at this time, but every little bit she had to put aside was acceptable for her goal until she was able to do better. Then the light bulb came on one day, and she decided to return to school.

They had been living in the apartment for about three years now, and she needed to take a chance on working toward her dreams. Bryson was working in the textile industry where he worked four twelve-hour shifts a week and had alternating weekends off. His schedule enabled her to work during the day and take classes three nights a week when he was off. Some weekends, the boys would spend the night with their grandmother and cousin. This was a big deal for the boys because they would consider this a treat. Savannah hardly ever let them stay overnight away from home although it was at her mom's or their grandfather's. She had always been very protective and did not trust many with her children. On those weekends, when the boys were at their grandparents, it gave her and Bryson some alone time, but they never used that time to work on the marriage.

Of course, the intimacy level in the relationship was never an issue. The one thing that would have made a major difference and breakthrough for them was communicating—talking to each other about their current relationship. It was always the same thing going out to dinner or ordering out on Friday night and watching movies. They did not go out on dates or entertain any friends, so their social life was nonexistent. It would be occasions where Bryson would go over to one of his friends' place and stay all night. She did not care for that because he left her at home although she would not have cared to be around his guy friends. He would come home with the smell of beer on his breath, and she would not approach him with how she felt about that. She would always go to bed without saying one word or asking where he had been all night. Sometimes she would not sleep in the same bed and would take her pillow and blanket and spend the night in the living room, watching late-night television until she fell asleep.

Savannah would find herself thinking about how her life would be if she had chosen someone else. She thought about her what-ifs more often now than ever. Savannah continued to dream about Colby, Jonathan, Donovan, and Cameron, asking herself if she made the right choice. This seemed to be a never-ending desire, and she wanted an answer. She had not seen any of these guys in years and often wondered what she would say to them if the universe afforded her the opportunity to make things right. Although it had been nearly ten years, her remorse and guilt over hurting these people stuck with her. Donovan was a couple years older when he started to pursue her, but she did not have any feelings for him. She never admitted that if he were not also entertaining the company of another girl, she would have given him a chance. She was young but not stupid, and she was already being pursued by Johnathan at the time and he was becoming a permanent fixture at her house.

And although he drove her crazy at times and asked her numerous times to be his girlfriend, she repeatedly would tell him no. She did care for him but was afraid to act on those feelings because she was not ready to date. On the other hand, she did not want her heart to be broken. She would always go back to that memory of him and the last night she witnessed the hurt on his face that she was responsible for. Then she often thought about Cameron as he was an awfully close friend, and they talked on the phone a lot when they were in junior high and the beginning of senior high. She felt that he wanted to be more, but she was not going to cross that line because he was a friend. Then there was Colby; she knew that her life would not have been a rainbow if she would have chosen him. She was caught up in the magnetism that put them together. The physical attraction was intoxicating, and she could not trust herself alone with him. She also never admitted to herself that she was beginning to have feelings for him too. He had the reputation of being a bad boy, and she did not want to be a cliché. Dreamtime was over when she heard Bryson calling her name as he rubbed her shoulder, waking her from a private trip down memory lane.

Like clockwork, she woke up with haze in her eyes and followed him back to bed. She was so used to the same routine when sex was the buffer to the elephant in the room. This was how they have always dealt with the adversities in their relationship and marriage. Sunday morning was welcomed with the warm sun breaking through the window treatments in the bedroom. She woke finding his arms wrapped around her as he still slept. Savannah eased out of bed to make her way to the bathroom. Sitting there, she was replaying in her mind the night before and tried to convince herself that things will somehow get better. She was raised in the church, and for the first time in several years, she thought about being in the house of the Lord.

When she finished up in the bathroom, she called Mom and asked if she was on her way to church that morning. Of course, the boys were going to attend as they did every weekend when they stayed the night with their grandmother. Savannah wanted so much to tell her mom that she wanted to attend as well, but the words would not leave her lips. Instead, she told her mom that she would come by and pick the boys up after church. Most of the time, she would tell her it was okay and that she would drop the kids off before she went back to church that night. After hanging up the phone, she sat at the dining room table, pondering about what to cook for breakfast this morning. Bryson was up now and made his way to the kitchen, asking her, "What was for breakfast?"

In return, she responded with both shoulders shrugged and replied that her guess was as good as his. With a unanimous decision, they both opted for the breakfast buffet at the Sizzler. The two got dressed and gathered the rental movies to return to Blockbuster after they had breakfast. It was nice to spend some time with each other, and she was pleasantly pleased with how the morning was headed. Once finishing their breakfast, they dropped off the movies and made their way to the grocery store to pick up some items for her to prepare for dinner. When they returned home, Bryson sat at the dining room table and read the Sunday paper while she began preparing dinner. It was getting close to time for the football game to come on, and she already knew his focus will be on the game. This would not be a good time to talk about her wanting to go back to church.

Once again, another missed opportunity where neither of them was willing to take a risk and communicate. She did not want to watch football, so she went to the bedroom and watched television and put away the laundry from the day before. Savannah found herself daydreaming once again about a better life and how important it was for her to think about her future. The objective remained the same, but she was still very much codependent on him. She had learned over the years to put on a happy face even though she was dying inside. Now that children were a big part of the equation, what was she going to sacrifice for them? Her happiness and needs were put aside to make sure the children did not grow up in a one-parent house like she did. Sometimes you read about or hear stories of couples staying together for the sake of the children. She was living that reality. Savannah loved him, but she was no longer in love with him. She does not remember when she had stopped loving him, but it felt like an eternity. Why was she feeling this way? It had been over two years or more since the indiscretion, yet she was still empty. She, at times, would just pray for a way out. Savannah was so unhappy and depressed.

By the next Sunday, she made it a point to go to church, and she did. It was the best homecoming that she could have ever imagined. She was embraced with open arms and love from people she had grown up with in the church. She did not have much to wear, so her aunt took her dress shopping the following weekend. They met at one of the local women's clothing store in town where she spent hours trying on dresses. She was so appreciative of her aunt that she would spend the time and money on her. Feeling so loved and excited about attending her childhood church on a regular basis left her with many thoughts and uncertainties at first. Those insecurities left once she made the choice to reaffirm her relationship with God. She returned as a functioning member and even joined one of the choirs.

Savannah had purpose now, but she did not fully understand it yet. It was important that she took baby steps at this point. She still had problems at home and in her marriage, but for the meantime, she put them on the back burner. Savannah had been going to church on a regular basis now, and even the boys had joined the children's choir. Life was changing again as she and the children had busier schedules now. The weekends were no longer redundant, and she was not left with the normal routine. Time had passed so swiftly, and she and the kids were functioning like a well-oiled machine. She wanted to invite Bryson to church, but he would not hear of it and chose to hang out at the basketball court on Sundays. Savannah was in hopes that things would get a little better, and sometimes it seemed as if things would turn around for them. The elephant was always in the room with them because they still have not dealt with it. There was also the financial hardship they had to overcome.

Yes, their finances were better, but the aftermath of their financial woes was still haunting them as well. One evening, the hair that broke the camel's back came tumbling like a wall of bricks. Bryson and Savannah got into a verbal fight which led them to the bedroom, closing the door so that the kids would not hear. They both were selfish in not considering the kids on the other side of the door that could be listening to them shouting at each other. Savannah had reached her point and shouted that she wanted a divorce. The room felt like time had stood still as Bryson had a look of shock as he had never heard her raise her voice, let alone asked for a divorce verbally. He responded by asking her if this was what she really wanted. She said yes as tears rolled down her face while he gave her this look of disappointment. She was removing his clothes from the dresser and the closet as she told him that she was tired and wanted out. His entire demeanor changed as he saw that she was serious.

This was the first for him because she had been so passive in their relationship and never expressed her feelings. There was a tremendous weight that had been lifted from her shoulders after she told him that she did not love him anymore and wanted out. He reached for her, and she pulled away. He responded with the question, "So this is what we're doing now?" This was all too familiar and then she would turn herself to being submissive, and things would go back to the way it always been. Maybe if she had the courage and strength all those many years ago when they were dating in high school or maybe if she had chosen another, it would be different. The fact was that she spoke the words that had been trapped inside her for a long time. What were they going to do next?

Chapter 29

There was an extreme weight lifted from her shoulders, but she was conflicted with making the right decision. Savannah was still battling with separating from her husband and raising her children in a single-parent home. Her memories of being raised in a single-parent home haunted her, and it was one of the sole reasons it was so difficult to make a choice. It was a matter of her happiness or the children's. One thing that most parents would agree on is the protection, happiness, and well-being of their children. She was not happy and was miserable in her marriage, but putting her children's needs before hers was complicated. Savannah promised herself that she would not let her decisions affect the children. Bryson would not agree to her decision to leave because he, too, was not going to sacrifice the happiness or stability of the children.

It had been a few days since she and Bryson had spoken to each other. They only kept up false pretenses around the children, and she put on the happy face when they were all together. The two did not change the routine of their family outings on the weekend because they wanted to maintain a sense of stability for the boys. Savannah usually kept her feelings within and did not talk to anyone about things. She decided to call her mom one afternoon because the pressures and anxiety were overwhelming. It was obvious that she needed her mom. But she was still guarded and would not be opened to expressing her feelings completely.

Olivia picked up the phone and was happy to hear from her daughter. She sensed in her daughter's voice that something was wrong. It has been a few days since they last spoke to each other. When her mother asked what was wrong, she immediately felt the anxiety and buildup until she could no longer control it. Savannah began sobbing uncontrollably and could hardly catch her breath as she tried to find the words. This was a big move for Savannah, so she began talking to her mom and expressing how much she wanted out and was tired of the fighting. She told her mom that she wanted a divorce and that he would not agree to it. Olivia listened and suggested that she pray about it. Although she knew her mom was correct, this was not the resolve that she was ready to try. Her mom suggested that the two at least try talking to each other. This was hard for Savannah to take advice from her mother on marriage and relationships.

At this point, Mom already knew most of the situation and was supportive regarding their marriage and family. One of their issues was the lack of communication, and she knew this was not going to be the path she would take. It was mostly he did the talking and she would just shut up. Some would be familiar with the silent treatment, but this was not the point of punishment; it was more like not having the voice to express herself verbally. Something had to give, and she did not know what else to do. Mom suggested that she and the children come to church on Sunday. Savannah knew that being raised in the church was a safe zone and sanctuary.

After agreeing to attend church on the next day, she said her goodbyes and hung up the phone. She went into the bathroom to freshen up and pull herself together and put on that happy face when she went into the living room where the boys were watching television. Her husband had not returned home, so that gave her plenty of time to get Sunday's dinner started and have some downtime with the boys.

Tonight was going to be a treat for the boys as she ordered pizza, one of their favorites. They meant everything to her as she sat observing how much they have grown. The daylight was passing quickly, and a part of her was a little worried that her husband still had not come home for dinner, and it was getting late. She fed the boys, gave them a bath, and let them sit up a little longer to watch one more

DVD before putting them to bed. Savannah finished cleaning the kitchen and putting all the food away. She turned the light on over the stove and the lamp on in the living room as she checked the door before heading to her bedroom to get ready for bed. After showering and getting dressed for bed, she climbed in on her side and cut the television and watched until she fell asleep. She did not know how long she had been sleeping when she heard the front door shut.

It was Bryson returning from wherever he had been all night. She did not want to deal with him, so she turned away from his side of the bed and pulled the covers close around her, lying very still, as if she was still sleeping. He entered the kitchen and opened the refrigerator door, searching for something to eat because she could hear the cabinet drawers opening and closing. He made his way down the hallway to the bathroom and then into the bedroom. She did not move and just led him to believe that she was still asleep. He had changed out of his clothes, showered, and put on his pajamas before heading back to the kitchen to heat the dinner that he had missed earlier that day.

After finishing his meal, he came back to the bedroom, climbing in the bed beside her after turning the television off. He moved up close behind her and wrapped his arms around her and whispered that he was sorry and that he loved her. She continued to lie very still and pretended to be asleep. This, too, was also familiar whenever they had a fight and she was not speaking to him. One thing that you could count on was he was not giving up his need for sex. It did not matter how bad the disagreement or argument had become; he would never cut himself off from that privilege. And like many other times, she was submissive to his need, and all was well for his benefit. She finally drifted off to sleep for real this time, and Sunday morning arrived just as it was meant to be.

The alarm went off as scheduled, and she climbed out of bed to get showered and prepare breakfast before getting ready for church. The boys were running around the apartment, playing in between eating, as she was telling them to finish up so they could get dressed for church. Mason did well with putting his clothes on although she still checked behind him and brushed his hair. Isaiah, who was independent and always said he could do it himself, needed extra checking behind him. It was getting near time for them to be leaving, and she did not want to be late. The drive to church was about thirty minutes, and she had to account for a little Sunday-morning traffic. The morning service began at 11:30 a.m., and sometimes she still did not arrive until 12:00 p.m. on some Sundays. The boys knew to be well-behaved while service went on as she made them use the bathroom before service to limit distractions during service.

On this Sunday, she had a purpose—more like a mission—she was intent on accomplishing. When the prayer line was called, she stood up, and as she began to make her way down the aisle, the nerves and anxiety set in. She could not turn back now as she was next. Savannah kept her eyes closed as she prayed before reaching the elders and ministers of the church. There were ushers on either side, and they motioned for her to set up. She walked up to the group as they all surrounded her, and she leaned forward and whispered into the elder's ear that she wanted God to save her marriage. He anointed her head with oil and laid his hand upon, as all the others, and he prayed for her. Tears streamed down her face as she felt the presence of the God.

All she could do was give him praise for what she knew he could do to save her marriage. As she walked back to her seat, the tears flowed more when she lifted her head to see the boys watching their mother with concern. They had never really seen her cry or become emotional before because she always put on her happy face for them. The rest of the service was uplifting as she did get a lot out of the message because it was meant for her to hear that day. Savannah wanted to feel better, and the only way she was going to have peace was to seek God. So she made a commitment to work on her relationship with him, and everything else would fall into place. What she did not know that it was going to take some time. Each week, her journey had its moment, but she kept going, which increased her faith. After a while, she joined one of the choirs, which was one of her favorites out of all of them. The weeks turned into months and then a year had passed already.

The boys had joined the children's choir, and it was a very productive routine and introduced them to new friends. Finally, there seemed to be a light at the end of the tunnel. Even she had noticed a little change in her relationship with Bryson. Instead of disliking the situation she was in, it became apparent that God can fix anything or anyone, including her. Her life was changing before her eyes as she was in a different place than a year ago. The church was packed with people every Sunday, some she remembered from her childhood, and there were many that she did not know. Mom tried to introduce her to some of the members in the congregation as well as one of her aunt's longtime friends. She surprised her one day by mentioning that someone from Savannah's past childhood was attending on a regular basis. She did not know at the time that Mom was speaking about Donovan.

Savannah had never noticed him, but Mom said that he sat behind them every Sunday. She had not seen him since high school and did not recognize him right away when she saw him the following Sunday. Savannah did not make any attempt in speaking to him, and she did not expect him either. As Mom mentioned previously that he always sat behind her during service, she was not one to turn around in her seat once she was seated. Even when it was offering time and, as routine, everyone stood up, lifted an offering, and then moved along in a single-file line to walk up to the front of the church to leave their offerings and tithes in the collection plate. Savannah had more important things to think about than an old childhood friend or would-be boyfriend sitting on the row behind her. Church service was awesome again today, and her soul was fed.

There would always be a night service, and she also would attend as well. At night, dress attire was less church formal and very casual for some. She could not wait for night service because this would be the time that people tarried for the Holy Ghost. Most Pentecostal Apostolic churches believed in both water baptism and fire baptism with the Holy Ghost. On this night, she went to the altar to pray and ask God to save her marriage but, foremost, prayed for forgiveness. Savannah knew that she could not fix what was broken in her or the relationship with her husband. It took a moment for her to realize that God was the only one that was going to bring her out of this nightmare.

Instead of focusing on running and giving up, she was given another view to what the possibilities could be if she only believed. So that night, she was determined that God was going to fix it. She was desperate and wanted the emotional pain to stop. There was a void, and every time she tried to fill it, nothing or no one was efficient enough to satisfy the emptiness. As she was kneeling at the altar and focusing on being in God's presence, one could feel the atmosphere changing. It was not only spiritual but also supernatural as she heard the other members around her giving God the praise and glory. The one thing she did learn from Sunday to Sunday and Bible study was that God is always amid the storm. Savannah continued to pray and ask God to heal her mind, body, and soul as she repented for her sins and asked to be saved. With all her efforts, it did not seem that God was listening. It was disappointing that she did not hear from God that night. But she was determined and was not going to give up so easily. The plan was to go to church every weekend until she was able to tap into what everyone else around her had accomplished. There were times that she was jealous of others because they had that one-on-one connection with God. She wanted that relationship badly but did not realize at the time that she would have to let go of everything and focus. To some, it was not rocket science, but she continued to need the encouragement and guidance from the church mothers.

For some that do not understand, it simply was an honor to be taken under the wings of the elderly in the church. Most were what one would label as Bible scholars and had been serving the Lord since they were small children. And then there were those that had not been in the church exceedingly long but were just as helpful as the next person. The entire week, she was optimistic and could not wait until Sunday. It seemed as if she was looking out of a newly installed glass window. Everything looked brighter and full of color. When she was at work during the day, she would read selected scriptures from the Bible on her breaks and lunchtime. This was her designated time to commune with God as well as continue to pray for herself and family. She always had known who God was and honored his presence in her life. Somewhere down the road, she became sidetracked and followed another path.

Since she had been on this path, there had been a significant change in her thoughts about marriage and relationships. Savannah knew that it takes hard work and sacrifice to make anything work, but at this stage of the journey, she was up for the challenge. To prove to herself that this was the path that she wanted to follow, she not only prayed for her husband and children, but she also anointed them each day. Now Bryson never had a clue that she was anointing him as he slept. He would not understand because he grew up in a Methodist church and had never been introduced to any other faith or worship. The entire time she had been a part of his family, she used to hear his grandmother and the rest of the family speak about Sunday services. Later, she did find out that his father's parents were a pastor and ministers at a local Pentecostal church. Bryson had never been really exposed to that level of religion and faith. She continued to pray and anoint him and her children because the power of prayer superseded all obstacles. In time, she began to see a change in him as well, and it was evident that her constant prayer and anointment over her family proved that God was listening.

One weekend, Isaiah had a conversation with his dad about coming to church with him. This astonished her because he was only five years old at the time and talked to his dad about being baptized so that he may be saved. All she could do was give God the praise in her own special way. See how God works? Out of the mouth of babies. It had been a couple weeks before little Isaiah mentioned to his dad again about being saved. Savannah could only hope that God would continue to work with his heart. The following Sunday, she woke the boys up so that they could eat breakfast before getting ready for church. Bryson told her that he was coming to church with them that morning.

The boys were ecstatic with joy as their eyes lit up like lights on a Christmas tree. She did not want to overwhelm him with too much information about what to expect. Savannah was happy and pleased that he wanted to join them that morning. Everyone dressed and

IMPERFECTIONS BUT GIFTED AND CHOSEN

was in the car on their way to church. It was a beautiful day with the warmth of the early spring sun shining and the sound of birds chirping. They pulled into the church parking lot where some members unloaded from their cars and were entering the church. Savannah was a little nervous as she walked with her family up the stairs to the double doors. You could already hear the music playing and the choir singing. She was always running a few minutes late and arrived just in time before morning prayer.

As she and her family entered the building, two ushers were standing on their post, greeting them and other members and guests. She greeted them with a "Praise the Lord." This was how the congregation greeted one another. The church was filled to capacity as always, and she made it down the aisle to the pew that she and her family always occupied. Mom was already seated and was thrilled to see her with her family. She had been praying, too, for this day to come. Service was about to start, so the small talk and greetings ceased as the minister called the congregation to order. As they sat there, she could see the wandering eyes focusing on her and, most importantly, Bryson. Besides her immediate family and a few close friends, no one knew that she had a husband. The minister asked everyone to stand as the pastor and other elders took their place around the altar for the prayer line. As the choir sang softly, a line formed in the aisle with people that were requesting prayer. One could feel the energy in the atmosphere as the prayer went forth and people were getting delivered. The altar was lined up with people kneeling and praying about the concerns in their life.

Once prayer ended, the choir continued to sing softly until the very last person returned to their seats. The choir prepared to sing another selection, and then it was offering time. She looked over at Bryson and asked how he was doing. He responded with a head nod that he was okay. Of course, she could tell by the expression on his face that it was far from the truth. He had never experienced being in the presence of God and his Holy Spirit manifesting through true worship. The house of the Lord was filled with the anointing and those that were gifted with the Holy Ghost's evidence of speaking in tongues. It was now offering time and then on to the Word of God delivered by the pastor. The congregation stood to their feet once more to lift an offering and then made their way down the aisle to the front of the church to leave their offerings and tithes. Savannah stepped out of the pew first, and Bryson followed behind her. As she walked down the aisle, all eyes were on her and what some figured was her husband. One of the members she worked with reached out to say hello as she passed. He was startled when her husband gave him a look that was not welcoming.

When she left offering on the table, she walked past some of the members and greeted them on her way back to her seat. She smiled at her aunt and cousins and stopped briefly for a hug and kiss. Finally making it back to her seat with her husband and children, Donovan was sitting on the pew just behind them. She did not make any contact with him as she took her seat. She had come too far to regress back, and God was doing so much on her behalf. She was given a blank slate and was on the straight arrow. The service has been amazing, and the church was filled with a special presence from God. When it was time for altar call, Mason told his mom that he wanted to be baptized, and she stood up to take him to the front of the church. Savannah never questioned him because he had been going to church for a while, and his little brother had made that decision weeks prior. Once she reached the front of the church, she turned and motioned for Bryson to join them for support of their son. Little did she know that, on the same day, he would be giving his life to Christ. She never spoke to him about being saved or getting baptized.

Once the benediction was made and the church dismissed, she and her family made their way downstairs to prepare for the baptism of both Bryson and Mason. Savannah believed more than ever now that God can do all things. The next week, she was determined this time she was going to receive the Holy Ghost. God had been blessing her family and there was a positive change in her relationship with Bryson.

Chapter 30

This was going to be the night that she gave herself fully to the Lord. The choir was singing and the music playing and the voices of the elders praying for those in need of a blessing from God. Here she was, on both knees with hands lifted toward the heavens, giving God the praise, the ultimate words of worship rolling off her tongue, "Hallelujah!" repeatedly as she closed her eyes and focused on God repenting of her sins and casting all her cares upon him. All she could remember was saying, "I surrender my all to you, Lord." She continued to hear the music and the altar workers praising God and encouraging those on the altar to lift him up. Savannah repeated saying *hallelujah* over and over until she felt the quickening of the spirit as her body began to tremble and the presence of God upon her. She no longer had control of her tongue as *hallelujah* changed to something else. She was speaking in an unknown tongue as the spirit of the Holy Ghost fell upon her. The anointing was so powerful that she fell on the floor as she was filled with the spirit.

Although she did not have control of her body, she could hear the congregation erupt into a thunderous roar of praise, shouting and dancing in the house of the Lord that night. As things were winding down, she could not pull herself together to rise to her feet. With the assistance of the altar workers and a couple ministers, she was placed on the front pew as the service was ending. This was an experience that she would never forget and could not wait to learn more about being saved and filled with the Holy Ghost. The entire week was brand-new to her; it seemed as if she was seeing everything for the first time with a new set of eyes. Bryson had noticed the change as he, too, was seeing things differently. He was going to church on a frequent basis and even started working with the deacons and driving the church bus every Sunday. God continued to manifest his power in their lives.

Savannah participated in going to Bible study every week so that she may learn more about God's teachings. And the more she sought the Word of God, he continued to manifest and bless her. He was also working in their marriage, and that, too, was viewed with a new set of eyes. The two were communicating more and spending more time with each other. They knew that their problems were not going to be fixed overnight or by taking a magic pill, and *poof*, all better. But the two did agree that hard work and dedication and trusting in God and allowing him to guide and counsel them was the key ingredient to their marital success. As the weeks passed, she was becoming more in tune with God and allowing him to use her.

The first encounter took place during benediction one Sunday night. The pastor was dismissing the church after the altar call. She was standing in her pew with eyes closed and hands lifted to the heavens, and the anointing fell upon her. She heard wings roaring in her ears, and then she felt the presence of someone or something surrounding her as the wings wrapped around her body. She did not have control of her body as she was moved out of the pew into the aisle and down to the altar. There she continued to hear an unknown tongue as she spoke, and the presence answered in return. Now she was given instructions, but in her mind, she was hesitant because she did not want to be out of order. There, waiting at the altar, was a church member kneeling and seeking God for answers. She had no way of knowing what this individual was going through or if she could be of any help. The more she allowed herself to receive the anointing of God, the more she heard the roar of the wings and tongues becoming more profound.

As the church was becoming empty, there was still a couple dozen people still present. She was still under the anointing and could not drive herself home. Bryson was out driving the church bus, taking people home, and it would be a while for his return.

So her cousin volunteered to drop her and the kids off that night. Savannah was still feeling something with great intensity after she arrived home. She gave the boys their baths and put them to bed. Bryson arrived home feeling a little exhausted as he showered and prepared for bed. Savannah was not ready for bed, so she sat at the dining room table to study some scriptures in her Bible.

She turned the television off so that she could focus on her studies. Sitting alone at the table, she began to feel the anointing upon her again, but this time, she heard the wings roaring in her ears at the same time as she felt a presence enter through the front door. Although her back was to the door, there was no doubt that she was not alone. Her Bible lay open to no preferred book, but what happened next was unexplainable. The pages began to turn as the movement of the sound of wings grew louder. She was not afraid because, throughout her childhood until present day, she had always experienced the abnormal. When the roaring in her ears stopped, the pages in the Bible stopped in the book of Ezekiel chapter 1. She did not understand, but as she began to read from chapter to verse, little by little, her curiosity got the best of her. Savannah knew that it would take some time to be edified for her understanding, which made her hunger for more for the Word of God. From what she knew thus far was that Ezekiel was called to prophecy by God which he communicated through visions.

Months had passed and things were changing at a fast pace. She did not complain about the change; in fact, she was overwhelmed and somewhat confused and asked herself why had God chosen her. Her marriage was taking a positive turn in the right direction, and they were communicating more and fewer to no fights. Savannah was beginning to have dreams or visions that were coming to pass. God was speaking to her frequently the more she allowed herself to be submissive to his Word and his will. The next spiritual encounter took place months later at a church choir road trip in one of the next counties. Her choir was invited to perform at a church to help celebrate one of their choir's anniversaries. It was an exciting time, and there were approximately six to seven guest choirs, including some from her church. The hosting church was filled, but they did not mind as God was being lifted in praise and worship.

As the service was ending, most of the members from her church all agreed to stop at one of the favorite places to eat which offered Dairy Queen and Bojangles restaurants about twenty miles from the guest church. That night, there were two choirs from her church, along with many church members, that also attended. Everyone made it safely to the restaurants and was having a good time fellowshipping. Savannah had her nephew, another young man with his aunt, who, too, was a member of her choir, and her mom with her that night. The boys sat with some of the other kids from church at a table, and Savannah sat with her mom and two others at a table. The building was filled with a lot of church folks that night, and the laughter was contagious. Savannah was enjoying herself until she began to fill the presence of God in the restaurant. She leaned over to her mom and told her that God was here. Savannah looked over the crowded establishment, and her eyes became fixed on one of her friends.

This was one of her closest friends who was on the choir as well. She was laughing and having a good time. Savannah kept telling herself, "Not now" and asking God, "What is it?" over and over. Her friend got up from her table and headed to the ladies' room. When she passed, the anointing fell upon Savannah. She followed her friend into the bathroom where there were other choir members. As soon as she entered, the tongues fell, and she could hear God speaking to her and telling her things. Savannah tried to fight it because she did not want to deliver the message, but she was overcome with the power of God. She heard her mother ask another member to go out and to collect one of the ministers who were traveling with them. He came into the ladies' room to begin praying over her. She was moving throughout the bathroom, and when she stopped, it was in front of her friend. Savannah's friend began crying because she knew that, whatever it was, God was amid it. Savannah told them that there was danger and they had to leave immediately. Everyone left the bathroom and began going around the restaurant, telling everyone to gather their things because they had to leave. Savannah was still under the anointing when everyone gathered outside in the parking lot. The minister asked everyone to join hands, and they all began to pray. He prayed for traveling mercies and to protect them from both seen and unseen evils.

The church members all began to load up into their cars where there was a line of cars back-to-back to follow one another home. Savannah's friend was in the first car with her children and a couple of friends. She was in the second car and so forth as church and choir members were ready to make the trip home. It was about a thirty- to forty-five-minute drive on an extremely dangerous highway at night where it was so foggy that you could not see the markings or signs on the road. It looked as if they were in a funeral procession as they traveled into the fog. Savannah kept looking into her rearview mirror to make sure everyone was still with her. Meanwhile, her friend's boyfriend was driving her car, which was the first car ahead of them. He was speeding that night well over the limit. Savannah tried to keep up with him, but for some reason, the more they tried to accelerate, the more her car slowed down. She held the steering wheel with both hands as the anointing was still upon her. Everyone in the car was quiet, not one sound, as she knew that they were praying. She tried again to mash on the gas pedal and nothing; the speedometer would not pass thirty-five miles per hour. She also noticed there was a thick cloud of fog all around the car, but she could see the car in front of her clearly. Then her friend's car pulled away from them, and she only could see a faint glimmer of the taillights. Savannah tried to speed up once more, and the car responded in the same manner.

The anointing was getting stronger, so she let off the gas and continued at the speed that she was going thirty-five miles per hour. At this point, she looked up and saw that her friend's car slowed as well, and then something unbelievable happened. Right when he dropped his speed, a car, coming out of nowhere, appeared in the thick fog in front of them. She saw the brake lights of her friend's car brighten. If it were not for God slowing her speed which prompted the other car to do so, their car would have been hit on the passenger side at an extremely high speed. After that near miss, Savanah was beginning to feel like herself again as she drove into town. But that was short-lived; as she drove closer to the church and parked the car, she was under the anointing once more.

This time, she was out of the car and over to her friend's passenger side of the car. Her hand was all over the entire passenger side as she moved under God's power. This was when Savannah understood the severity of what was happening and foreseen through vision and prophecy. It was surreal that God had given her the gift of prophecy and the things that he had shown her, indeed, came to pass. It did not mean that all things came to pass, but for the most part, she knew things that no one else could possibly have known. Once again, her close friend was crying and did not know what was happening. Savannah hugged her very tight to give her comfort and that everything was going to be okay. A few days later, her friend was in a car wreck and her car was hit on the same side and place where Savannah had foreseen. She was okay and walked away from the crash without injury. Life, as Savannah had known, was not the same. All eyes were on her every time she entered the church.

Most were envious of the gift that God had bestowed upon her, and then there were some that were afraid of what she may see in them. Repeatedly, she had to tell people that it did not work like that, and she only was moved by the power of God. Yes, she had visions and messages from God, which made it difficult for her at times. Some accepted her, and then there were those that did not. She felt judged and scrutinized all the time because of people's thoughts about her. She never asked for attention and was not seeking approval. She just wanted people to not treat her like something was oddly wrong with her. Bryson did not understand it either, but he was supportive because he loved her, and their relationship was becoming stronger than ever. God had answered their prayers as well. The two had found their happiness again and had fallen in love again. She discovered that the more she was obedient to God's Word through fasting and praying, the more he blessed her spiritually. They learned that to know how to love again, the requirement would be to love God and he will do the rest.

The visions continued, and God always put her on assignment for his purpose. There were dozens of spiritual encounters to name as God placed her into people's lives for his purpose. He would give her a vision and she would prophesize to an individual, and yes, that, too, would come to pass. Sometimes, the delivery of the message was good and sometimes it would not be. She also had seen both life and death, which was a little overwhelming, but God kept her. Savannah did not always want to be the messenger, but she had accepted God's will.

Part 2

Chapter 31

They had a second chance of happiness, and the two were sure not to take it for granted. Everything was falling into its proper place as God had promised. She wanted to experience everything with her family, which meant living outside the box. The boys were in elementary school now and were learning at a fast pace. Savannah always rewarded them for doing such a great job in school, taking special trips to the toy store to select a special gift. So this year, she wanted to up the reward and take them on their very first vacation. The family had never been on vacation, so this was new to them all. One Saturday evening, they sat down with the kids and asked how they would like to spend a few days at the beach and go to their first amusement park.

The boys were overexcited and could not wait to see a roller coaster and other theme park rides. Of course, Isaiah was too small to ride a roller coaster, but there would be plenty for him to enjoy. The following week, Savannah made the arrangements, and she and Bryson requested time off from work. Because this would be their first journey, it was decided to take a trip close by. So of course, they headed to Busch Gardens Williamsburg and then onto Virginia Beach. The four of them were set to go as they piled into the family car with packed bags and snacks for the road trip. It was only a three- to five-hour drive, but it seemed like a lifetime. Traveling with small children meant frequent bathroom breaks and stretching of your legs. The boys talked and played in the back seat while their parents listened to music and navigated them to the theme park.

Once they were getting close, Savannah informed the boys that they were almost there and asked what some of the things they would like to do first. Each of them named things, with Mason commanding his mom's attention to the things he wanted. Isaiah just repeated everything that his big brother stressed as he wanted to feel included. As they drove into the parking lot, the excitement was high and the expectations were overwhelming to them all. Savannah unloaded the boys and covered them with sunscreen as it was a hot July summer morning already. Bryson told her to remember where they had parked so at the end of the day, they would have a general idea where to locate the car. The family walked toward the shuttle, which was a train system that would take them to the entrance of the park. The train made numerous stops at different sections of the parking lot to pick up passengers. They finally arrived at the park entrance where there were lines at the ticket office. Bryson approached the ticket counter to purchase two adult and two children tickets and followed the signs to the turnstiles. Wow, it was beautiful, with hundreds of families, along with perfectly designed landscaping and rows of all tree canopies above.

The first order of business was to locate the biggest roller coaster in the park. Because Isaiah was too young, Savannah decided that she would stay with him in the kiddie ride area. Before dashing off for the big-boy rides, she talked Mason into spending just a little time with his brother on the kiddie rides for a moment. As the boys got onto the little plane ride, she took dozens of pictures of them. Their smiles of happiness were priceless, and she wanted to record every moment. Although the rides were for the smaller children, Mason had just as much fun as the next person. He laughed and played with Isaiah on every ride that was available. When it was his turn to ride the big-boy rides, they all walked over to that section of the park. It took a while to reach the first roller coaster, but they did not mind. They took in everything as they passed carnival-style vendors to include cotton candy, large ice-cold drinks, corn dogs, and much more.

One of the stops before the roller coasters was the Anheuser Busch Clydesdale Horses exhibit. These were the most majestic animals she had ever laid her eyes upon. A few of them were grazing in the enclosed grassy area of their home. People were also viewing some in the stables where each horse's name was beautifully labeled on each stall. They were gentle giants, and she could imagine how people must look to them as the horses seemed to be towering over the visitors. One of the caretakers walked one of the giant animals to the fence so that spectators could feed him carrots. Savannah was not too sure about that, so she was viewing him from afar. Mason and Isaiah were so excited and even asked if they could ride on one of them.

Of course, Mom said absolutely no way she was going to let her babies get on those horses even if it was allowed. But these horses were not part of the package to give patrons horse rides. After leaving the Clydesdale stables, they continued their search for the Big Bad Wolf roller coaster. The park was becoming more crowded as many families and large groups of people entered the park. Bryson noticed on the road signs on the walkway that they were getting close, and Mason could not control himself with enthusiasm. Savannah stopped at the concession stand to make sure everyone was well hydrated and to take a bathroom break and then off to the roller coasters. Although it had been years since she had rode a roller coaster, she was extremely nervous for her baby riding for the first time. Savannah waited at the exit side of the Big Bad Wolf as Bryson and Mason got in line to ride.

Meanwhile, she and Isaiah played while they waited for Dad and Mason to finish their ride. The screams from above were intense as they passed with great speed, falling into triple loops. She knew that Mason was having the time of his life. At the end of the ride, she could see them approaching, and the smile on Mason's face was priceless as he ran to her with excitement. All he wanted to do was ride again, but Savannah was not eager to let that happen.

So they continued with their day in the park, enjoying all the rides they could handle in one day. It was starting to get late, and the boys were beat and Savannah and Bryson as well. Making their way back to the shuttle area and waiting for the train was a relief. Arriving at the car, the boys climbed into the back seat where they each fastened their seat belts. They still had another forty miles to drive until they reached the beach where their hotel was located. Bryson decided to stop at a drive-through restaurant to pick up a quick meal for the trip across the bay. It was already 6:00 p.m., and the sun was still up, which provided plenty of natural light for them to look out over the Chesapeake Bay Bridge Tunnel. It was beautiful as always and brought back some happy memories. But of course, four years ago, there were some unhappy times, but the good outweighed them. Finally, they reached the hotel and unloaded the car and kids before checking into the hotel. This was the first hotel stay for the boys, so it was an added adventure for them. The room had two queen-size beds with a microwave, refrigerator, and television. Savannah was eager to get out of those sweaty clothes and take a long hot shower before bed.

But first things first, wrestling up the boys to take a bath and into fresh pajamas and down for bed. After the kids were put to bed in one of the queen beds, it was her turn to shower and prepare for bed. She could not wait for her head to hit the pillow. Bryson was watching television and catching up on the local news and sports. Once she was done in the bathroom, she tidied up a bit and Bryson went last. As she pulled the covers back on the plush bed and began to yawn, the sleep monster was already upon her. The night came and went as fast as the morning sun was peeking through the window. She had not realized how exhausted they were because as she rolled over, the kids were still asleep and it was 9:00 a.m. Savannah stretched her arms and legs while cozying up to Bryson, hoping to lie in bed for a little while longer. That dream was short-lived when the boys began to stir, and she heard a little voice calling for Mama and saying, "I'm hungry." The hotel did serve a nice continental breakfast with freshly made waffles, but she was outvoted. There was a Denny's across the parking lot, and the food had more of a home-cooked meal feel. Everyone was up now and dressed and ready for the short walk over to eat breakfast.

They were all seated in a booth with the boys on one side and Savannah and Bryson on the other. The room was filled with the aromas of freshly cooked bacon, along with brewing coffee and the sound of clanging dishes and the buzz of conversations flowing throughout the restaurant. The waitress arrived with paper placemats with crayons for the boys to color while she asked their parents what they liked to order. Once they had placed their order, the two discussed how they were going to plan the day. First, she was going to call her dad and stepmom to let them know that they were in town. The next and most important to the boys was to make the trip down to the beach to hang out and play in the water most of the day. The meal arrived, and everything was delicious and had the boys asking for seconds. Savannah was full after the first plate of pancakes and sausage and did not have room to finish off her eggs. Looking at her watch, it was already 11:00 a.m. and the day was passing by so fast.

They finished breakfast and walked back to the hotel to change into their beach attire. Bryson packed the car with a cooler, beach towels, and the boys' sand pals and shovels. Savannah double-checked to make sure she had the sunscreen and other must-haves before going to the beach. When drove down to Atlantic Avenue and the boardwalk, it was buzzing with street vendors and tourists. They parked in one of the parking garages to keep out of the hot sun. Savannah took Isaiah's little hands, and he took hold of Mason's as they walked the crosswalk. Bryson was leading the way as he found the perfect spot on the crowded beach. He set up under an umbrella and laid the large beach towels out under them. The boys were anxious to get in the water, but Savannah was cautious about that because they were not swimmers. So she and Bryson made their way down to the waterfront with both boys. She knew the water would be cold at first, so she just put her toes and feet in at the ankle. The boys went full steam ahead, splashing in the water and screaming because it was cold. Isaiah found him the perfect place on the wet sand to collect into his buck, along with seashells. Mason was not concerned about sand; he was focused on what he called swimming for Mama. I guess it was his style by way of lying on his belly in the wet sand and letting the current wash over him. Bryson laughed as he watched his son move around like a fish out of water, flailing as such.

It turned out to be a perfect day as they walked the beach down to the pier and back, watching people parasailing along with other water sports. The day was nearing dinner, and she wanted to get back to the hotel to clean up and then go to their favorite seafood restaurant, Captain George's. Before heading back to the parking garage, she wanted to stop by the souvenir shop to purchase gifts and saltwater taffy. The return to the hotel was quick, and she put the boys in the shower to wash the salt water and sand off their skin and hair. She and Bryson were next, and once cleaned up, they all were ready for dinner. The line at the restaurant was already out the door and around the building. This was normal for this time of year as vacationers packed all the seafood houses around town. Finally, they were in after a forty-minute wait and was seated at their table. The buffet served over 270 items made fresh daily, and you could go back as many times as you wanted or until you were about to bust. The star item on the buffet was the snow crab legs, and people waited in line for them. The desserts were out of this world and intoxicating, as well as everything else. Savannah was pleased with the atmosphere and took a moment watching the joy in her children's eyes. She noticed that Bryson seemed happier than he had been in a long time. His family was complete, and they were all happy. She was having the same thought as she glanced over to him and gave him that flirtatious smile. Their relationship was getting stronger, and they were more in tuned with one another. It was to the point that they could finish each other's sentences or more profoundly feel what the other was feeling. Savannah remembered an incident a while back where she was at work, chatting with coworkers about what she would make for dinner that night. She told her friends that she would stop by the grocery store on the way home to pick up items to make spaghetti. When she arrived home and went into the kitchen with the groceries, Bryson already had a pot of water boiling on the stove for the spaghetti noodles. She never called to ask him to get things started or that she was stopping by the store. She asked how he knew, and he responded with he had a taste for spaghetti and decided to start the water while searching the cabinets for the noodles. There had been other occasions when she could feel him thinking about her, but he was in another room. She would respond verbally to whatever she felt he was saying to her, although he never uttered a word. Yes, it was creepy at first, but she was used to the strange and unbelievable events in her life. Until this day, the two can be hundreds of miles apart and still feel one another and hear one another's thoughts. Savannah gave God all the credit for the things that were taking place at that moment and beyond. The two learned how to listen to one another, and most of all, fall in love with each other all over again.

Memories of those moments when they were kids came flooding back all at once. It was true that they were getting their happiness back. The next morning was an early rise because she was eager to see her dad and stepmom. The day was already going to be filled with numerous activities for the kids. She called her dad before breakfast to let him know that they would stop by to visit later that day. Savannah was able to get a little school clothes shopping done in Virginia Beach at the Pembrooke and Lynnhaven Malls. They were not going to the beach today because she wanted to take them to the local zoo in Norfolk and then the next day to the aquarium. She promised that they would go to the beach once more before vacation was ending. After such a long busy day, they still made time to go by Dad's house.

When she arrived, her dad was so happy to see them. The boys were thrilled to see their granddaddy as they hurried out of the car, shouting his name. Savannah was still gathering their things from the car as the boys were already knocking on the front door. Her stepmom opened the door with a big smile and hugs for them. Bryson and Savannah were walking up to the front door when her dad appeared in the entryway. It was a new house, and they had just moved in the day before, so everything was still in boxes and the larger pieces of furniture were placed in its designated location. Bryson found his way to the family room with her dad to catch up and watch *SportsCenter*. Savannah stayed in the kitchen, her stepmom catching up on what had been happening in the past few years. They had not seen or talked to each other since moving back home. It was nice seeing her family and hoped to be keeping in touch more often. Dad kept her up on current events as to how the rest of the family was doing. She did not get to see them on this trip but was counting on seeing them the next time around.

The evening was filled with laughter and good food as Dad broke out the grill to showcase his cooking skills. He had always been a great cook, and Savannah loved watching him work his magic in the kitchen. It was already 10:00 p.m., and it was well past the boys' bedtime. Although they were on vacation, it did not mean that staying up late was an option for them. One could see the evidence in both their little eyes and the attention span was already done. Savannah told her parents it was about that time and they had an early morning. They did have one more day of vacation and planned to spend it on the beach. Pulling up to the hotel, they could see that the parking lot was full, which meant a longer walk to the front of the hotel. Bryson lifted Isaiah and carried him from the car and into the hotel lobby as Savannah and Mason followed.

The boys were exhausted, and she was too, so putting them into the shower was left for the morning. She pulled their clothes off and just wiped them down with a wet soapy washcloth, and into bed they went. The next morning, as promised, they had breakfast and off to the beach early morning to gain a head start before the tourist arrival. As a family, they spent the entire day playing, relaxing, and doing a little more souvenir shopping. Before you know it, vacation was over, and they were checking out of the hotel and on the road headed back home. Savannah went by Dad's house on her way out to say her goodbyes, and then they were off. This was the beginning of a family tradition and every year to come to vacation in Williamsburg and Virginia Beach.

Chapter 32

Life was looking great and their family was growing in so many ways. The apartment had been home for about six years, and it had reached the capacity for them. The boys were growing up so fast with Mason in junior high school and Isaiah already in the fourth grade. Savannah had been in her new job at Allstate for over two years now and was doing well financially. Bryson, too, worked for Virginia Transformer for about two years and was also doing well, but he wanted more. He always talked about going to truck-driving school for a better opportunity but never acted on it. Savannah had already followed her dreams and completed college and landed her job at Allstate. Now it was his turn to pursue the things he wanted out of life. So the two sat down and hashed out a plan and put money aside for at least three months. By February, he had enrolled into a truck driving school in Salt Lake City, Utah.

He was there for three months and returned with his Commercial Driver License, known as CDL. Part of the program required him to drive for the company that sponsored the school for at least one year. The agreement was in place for the student drivers to pay back the loan they acquired through the school's private lender. Bryson only kept off to that bargain for just one month, then he decided that he would leave and return home. When he returned home, there was no prospect of a job right away, so he contacted Savannah's dad. He was a truck driver of over thirty years and took Bryson under his wing at his company. The two teamed together for a while, but it was over-the-road, which was okay for a moment. Bryson missed his family and wanted to find something local. So he visited the Virginia Employment Commission, seeking dedicated truck-driving opportunities. At first it was tough, but finally, he broke through and was called by a very prominent company. He went to the interview and, within a couple of days, accepted an offer. That year was great for them both spiritually and financially. One day, Savannah decided that she wanted a home to continue raising their family. So they decided to start aggressively saving for a new home. Of course, God was in the center of it all and Savannah bore witness to that fact.

As a family, they still showed a strong presence in the church. Savannah and the children were on two of the choirs, and he was serving as the church bus driver and recently becoming the sound system operator. She continued to save as well as fast and pray, asking God for guidance. His presence was always evident of everything that had taken place thus far with the new jobs and increase in their finances. One weekend, she had decided to lie down and take a nap when God sent yet another vision to her. It came as a dream, but it was so real, which startled her when it was over. She did not realize how tired she must have been. As she drifted off, memories of her late pastor, who was the senior elder in the church, flashed upon her. But then within moments, what she thought was memories was indeed a prophecy. Savannah could see that she was surrounded by white clouds, and out of them appeared her late pastor that had passed earlier that year. She wanted to tell him everything about what was happening with her and the church. He comforted her and said that everything was going to be okay and not to worry.

Elder Englewood told her to get the house that she wanted; all she had to do was pay her bills on time. Savannah did not understand why he would be instructing her to do this. She was shown a vision of the house from the color of the exterior to the carpet color on the floors. What she saw next was unbelievable, even to her, as several hands appeared out of the clouds, each covered with white gloves, holding a scroll. When the scroll was opened, there was a deed to a house, her house, and when she tried to ask elder Englewood to explain, he disappeared. But what happened next was truly surreal as a white-gloved hand reached out and held her face, squeezing tightly.

A face appeared that was not of God and spoke to her, saying, "Don't you not know that I know already?" It was something evil, and as he kept a tight grip on her face, she began to call on the name of the Lord.

The words could not leave her mouth because she was bound by hands and feet and mouth. Savannah tried with all her might to break free and call out until the words became a mumble in Jesus's name. Then as soon as *Jesus, Jesus, Jesus* poured out of her mouth, the entity let loose. She leaped up, finding herself sitting in the middle of her bed as she still felt the physical pressure of fingerprints on her face. This was the very first time that she had encounter both sides of spiritual supernatural events. Her heart was racing and could not wait to tell someone about this experience.

The next day, she called the mother of the church, Mother Englewood, and asked if she could stop by to talk. She had been at work all day, thinking about what had happened, trying to make sense out of it all. Savannah fasted and prayed throughout the day, hoping to get some resolve to her questions. When the workday was over, she went home to pick up the kids to drop them by her mom's while she went to Mother Englewood's to talk. The two talked for what seemed to be hours as she retold her experience. She was told that there was a visiting elder out of Virginia Beach who had many experiences with the subject matter. He was due to come to town for a convention in a few weeks, and Mother Englewood said that she would call him later during the week to fill him in on what had happened.

Although she was overwhelmed with what was happening, she never gave up on the dream of purchasing a home. Savannah was even more determined now than ever. She contacted one of her choir members, Rosa Garnett, who turned out to be a real estate agent. They set up a meeting the following weekend to start viewing homes. Meanwhile, she stayed on the course, saving money and buttoning up things on the credit report as well. Everything was coming together, and she was getting closer to finding that perfect home. Life was always unpredictable in her case, and every so often, she was happy to welcome a little surprise here and there.

She was busy in the kitchen preparing dinner when the phone rang. Savannah answered and was genuinely pleased to hear Dad on the other side. It has only been a week since she last saw him while on vacation. She was so happy to hear his voice, but she did not expect that he would contact her so soon. The two talked for a while and then he told her that he was thinking about moving back to Roanoke. Savannah was happy, but she thought it to be strange because he had just moved into a house when she visited a week ago. She did not want to pry and ask what the purpose of the sudden move.

He went on to explain that he took another look at where he was in life and decided that it was time for him to return home. Within the month, he had moved back and was searching for a new home as well. He did not find one right away, so he and her stepmom moved into a townhouse on a temporary basis. Savannah stayed the course as she continued her search for a new home. She was bringing home boxes every day and packing up things that were not for every-day use. At some point, she was beginning to run out of space due to all the boxes that had begun to accumulate. Once Dad had totally moved into his townhouse, she visited him very often. Savannah and her dad grew closer as their relationship was becoming stronger. They talked about a lot of things, especially concerning why he was not in her life as a child. She had always heard one side of the story from Mom, which alienated her from dad. He shared some secrets with her that shed light on some things she had always questioned in the back of her mind.

For some reason, she believed him as she looked him in the eye and he started telling his story. This must have been the most honest he had been in his entire life. Dad also talked about having lower back pain and stated that he visited the doctor. He told her that they were running some tests, and he should hear back soon. The doctor did talk to him about his smoking, but he was not going to give that habit up.

There were some concerns about his diabetes and heart health because many years prior, he had a heart attack. She wanted to stay optimistic and pray for a good report. Before she realized the time had passed, it was already Christmas. *Where did fall go?* she asked herself as she was making preparation for a move. The boys did not let her forget about the extensive Christmas list they left on the dining room table every week. There was always an addition to the list as they held the JCPenney and Toys "R" Us catalogs hostage. Once they arrived in the mail, she never laid eyes on them again until Christmas. This year was extra special because Dad was here, and she was so looking forward to spending it with him. She missed so many as a child, and this year was important. All was good and sometimes seemed to be too good to be true. She was holding on to it for as long as possible. Savannah had looked at dozens of homes and had not come across the one.

So she decided to take a little break over the holiday and would resume in the spring. In six months, the search for a new home picked up again, and they had saved more money as well. As she thought things were too good to be true, Savannah received the most devastating news one evening while sitting on the sofa. The boys were at their grandmother's for the weekend, and it was Bryson's weekend to work. Gina had called her to report that Dad had another doctor's appointment, and more test was completed, and he was diagnosed with pancreatic cancer. She was told that he had maybe a few months to live. All at one time, it felt like the planet had fallen from the universe. Savannah repeatedly shouted, "No!" believing that the news was not true and if she continued to plea that the delivery of the news would be different. She did not remember hanging up the phone as she cried uncontrollably and begged God to not take her dad.

Savannah asked for his life to be spared because she had just gotten him back into her life. She was in the apartment alone and needed someone to be with her. It was natural for her to call Mom for comfort and assurance that everything would be all right. As soon as Olivia picked up the phone, she knew that something was wrong. Memories flowed back to when Savannah lost her mother-in-law all those many years ago. Although Olivia had her unresolved issues with Miles Sr., their daughter's needs were more important. She was very empathetic and gave her daughter the support that she needed. The next morning, Savannah broke the news to Bryson that her father was terminally ill, and she did not know, besides what the doctors said, how much time she had left with him.

For the next several weeks, she spent time with him after work and on the weekends. She would fast and pray that God would deliver him although she knew that whatever God's divine will, she would have to accept. When things could not get any worse, Dad was admitted to the hospital. He was suffering with diabetic complications due the pancreatic cancer. The doctors wanted to treat him with a surgery, which would be complicated. Savannah arrived at the hospital to sit with him, but when she entered his room, he was asleep. She always was in the habit of bringing her Bible with her, so she read a chapter and verse to him. She also would sing some of her favorite hymns to bring comfort to herself and Dad. Although he was asleep, she knew that he was listening. The next day, he was scheduled for surgery, but she was not able to get the time off work to be there.

When she arrived later that day, she learned that he had a massive heart attack. The doctors had done everything they could to save him, but it was too late. Learning that her father had passed was a devastation she could not recover or prepare for. Here she was again in the same place as when she lost her mother-in-law, feeling helpless and broken. All she needed was to be around family. So she asked Mom if she could take the boys for a while so that she could meet with the other family that night. Everyone was gathered at her dad's place where all her aunts, uncles, and some cousins were already there. She was happy to see some of her family that she had not seen in many years. It was a night of sorrow, but there was laughter oddly enough because her dad's side of the family always had big personalities that could sometimes be contagious.

To most of them, it was a time of celebration of a homegoing. He did not have to suffer and no more pain. She continued to see that fact, but it was still difficult. This was her dad, and at that point, she could not see anything else but her loss. Savannah went to the funeral home with her uncle and stepmom to make the arrangements. She helped pick out his casket, which made her feel a part of the process. On the day of the funeral, she did not ride in the family car; his sisters and brothers took their place. When she arrived at the church with Bryson, she lined up with the family so that they would be led into the church. She was from a large family, which filled the entire church. She was sitting on the front pew with her other siblings as friends and family came by to give their condolences. The service was about to start as people packed into the church. Her father was well-known as people from his past poured into the church as well. When she glanced back, she saw that some of her church family was there, too, including her pastor and first lady. Her cousin was a pastor, and he was due to deliver the eulogy.

As the prayers were brought forth and the choir sang the praises of Zion, she could feel the presence of the Lord. Her cousin took his place at the podium to deliver his message. He brought forth a message that was powerful in God's Word. She could praise throughout the church as she closed her eyes to meditate on the goodness of the Lord. Savannah praised God until his spirit fell upon her. While under the anointed, she approached her father's casket to say her goodbyes. There was something different in the way she moved and spoke in an unknown tongue. She had never experienced this before while under the anointing of God. She was being edified by God right there in the moment.

Of course, she was consumed with emotion, and that would account for the most part. Savannah was in mourning and was taking the loss of her father with such a heavy heart. She felt someone come to assist her back to her seat, and there she continued to communicate with God. He was delivering a message of comfort to help ease the pain. Her cousin concluded a spirituality-filled eulogy that lifted and delivered comfort to the congregation, family, friends, and loved ones. The funeral director concluded their part of the service, asking would-be pallbearers and flower ladies to take their positions. The funeral procession was well on its way with the family following the casket, escorted by the pallbearers, then followed by the flower ladies.

With everyone now in their cars, the local police department provided an escort service to the gravesite. There were more than a few dozen cars in the procession as people parked along the narrow roadway at the cemetery. It was February, and the ground was frozen over as people made their way to the tent area where her dad was going to be laid to rest. The sun was shining, which offered some heat for those that stood around the casket. There were chairs placed upon a green outdoor carpet rolled over the unearthed dirt for family to be seated. The minister gave his last remarks and, once again, offered condolences and comfort to the family as the graveside ceremony came to a closed. People were still standing around socializing and reacquainting themselves. Some had not seen one another for many years and were so happy to see one another.

Finally, the family was escorted back to the funeral limousine and off to the church for the repass, where family and friends would meet them there. Once Savannah had arrived with the rest of her family, everyone greeted one another with hugs and love. Folks were laughing and talking and having a good time fellowshipping. There were tons of food and drink it almost looked like a Thanksgiving or Christmas dinner that was being served. So many items to choose from, and the desserts reminded you of Grandma's house. Her uncles were huddled up, telling their usual jokes that made you bust a gut with laughter. And her cousins from each age demographic, too, enjoyed one another.

Of course, the women of the family did what they did best—organize and instruct the flow of things. Savannah's aunts were comical as well and had her laughing at their antics too. This was what she needed to be surrounded by family who shared their love with a little laughter. She was feeling better for the moment. A week had passed, and she was still mourning her dad, but she was determined to move forward with life. Savannah called her realtor to set up new appointments so that the search for a new home can continue. It was not soon after she found the house of her dreams, literally as it had been shown to her through vision. It was the month of fall, one of her favorite seasons, as the leaves were beginning to change to different shades of red, burgundy, yellow, and brown.

They all arrived at the property for their first viewing. The realtor put the key in the lock and opened the door to their future home. Savannah made her way up the stairs into the kitchen, opening drawers and cabinets and visually placing her dishes and glassware. Then she went down the hallway to see the first bathroom, which was decorated with a country blue and pink wallpaper. The three bedrooms were as expected, and the master bedroom and bath were sufficient for their needs. The house also had a two-car garage downstairs to the right, which also had a space for the washer and dryer. The other side of the basement was not finished but had the plumbing roughed in for a third bath and family room. She and Bryson went outside on the large deck where there was a spectacular view of the mountains around the entire house. There was also large backyard which most of it was on a hill.

Bryson was not too happy about the hill because his first thought was who was going to cut all that grass. Savannah's mind was made up, and this was the house. They returned to the apartment where an offer contract was written. The realtor was presenting that night and would get back to them as soon as possible. Amazingly, the next day, the first offer was accepted. The financing for the mortgage had already been approved with a VA loan. Their realtor delivered the news when the closing date would take place. She informed them that it would be anywhere between thirty to forty-five days to close on the house. They were told how much money that was needed to bring to the closing. Savannah gave notice to the apartment manager that they would not be renewing their lease.

Everything was all set as the arrangements had been made for moving and changing school systems for the kids. Mason was in junior high now, and he did not want to leave his friends. He was in a magnet school baccalaureate program, so Savannah made the sacrifice and changed her work schedule to accommodate the new schedule. The boys were excited about the new house as later that week they took them back to the house for a second look Mason had already picked his room, which was the larger of the two and leaving Isaiah's choice obvious.

The next few weeks were busy, leaving no room for her to ponder. She still thought about her dad from time to time and missing him, but this stage in her life had kept her preoccupied. The closing date had finally arrived on October 28, 1998, a day that would never be forgotten. She and Bryson met the realtor at the closing that morning after the boys were off to school. The two were excited and nervous at the same time because this was one of the most important milestones in their lives. Everyone was seated at a long table in this very professional conference room. The nerves were building as she sat on the edge of her seat with feet crossed at the ankles. Her realtor asked her to relax, and this was the easy part and she explained they would be signing a lot of papers. The mortgage closing officer, along with the listing and selling agent for the property, was also in attendance. Once the legal documents were signed and then copied, Savannah and Bryson handed over the closing check and the deal was done. They received the keys their new home and a congratulations from all parties seated at the table. It was done they were now first-time homeowners, and it felt so rejuvenating.

The first order of business afterward was to pick the children up and celebrate, but Bryson had to work that night. So instead, she picked up her mom and called her aunt to come by the house to help her clean before moving in the next day. Bryson had taken two days off so that they could start moving early the next morning after sending the boys to school. The day began early as planned; she and Bryson were up at 6:00 a.m., preparing for the long day ahead of them. Savannah prepared breakfast for the family before she went to wake the boys up for school. By 7:30 a.m., she had the boys dressed, fed, and on their way out the door to catch the school bus. Once the boys were gone, she and Bryson got into the car and drove to the U-Haul center to pick up the truck. She waited in the car while he went into the store to do the paperwork and collect the keys. Bryson had rented the biggest truck they had because he figured they could get everything in one trip.

When they arrived back at the apartment, the sectional sofa was the first piece of furniture loaded onto the truck. The plan was to load the furniture, then the boxes last. Once they began to load boxes, it was evident that everything was not going on the first trip. So leaving the car behind at the apartment the two rode together to the house. When they arrived, Savannah opened the garage doors and then the front door to the house. The two started unloading the boxes and placed them in the garage.

Next was the bedroom furniture, which was placed in their respective rooms. Savannah decided to leave the sectional in the garage because she had planned to purchase new living room furniture. It was nearly 11:00 a.m., and they decided to take a little break to grab a bite. The boys got out of school around 3:00 p.m., so they wanted to be fully moved before picking them up. They returned to the apartment to gather the last of the boxes and to clean up any trash that may have been accumulated. Savannah ran the vacuum over the carpets once more and checked all the cabinets and closets to make sure everything was out of them. The time was drawing near for the boys to get home for school, so they decided not to leave yet. About twenty minutes later, there was a sound of someone relentlessly knocking on the door. Opening the door, there standing with a huge smile on his face was Mason. He had beads of sweat rolling from the temple of the head down his face. It was obvious that he ran home from the bus stop. He could not wait to be in the new house. He went into his old bedroom, looking around at all the emptiness.

Maybe he was reminiscing about the times he and his brother spent in that room. There were going to be a lot of changes with moving to a new place. He would not be losing any of his friends because he will continue to attend his old school. Finally, Isaiah was home from school, and they closed the apartment door, saying goodbye to many memories. The boys wanted to ride in the truck with their dad, but they had to make one last stop to the apartment management office. She entered the office to turn in the apartment keys and to say goodbye. They were now on the way to their new home and new beginnings.

Chapter 33

It has been six months since they moved into their new home. The boys have adjusted and made new friends. Bryson and Savannah's relationship continued to thrive, as well as their spiritual growth. Although life was well for them, there was still a part of her that was not complete. Savannah still missed her father and thought about him often. God continued to use her as a vessel for his overall purpose. Sometimes it was a challenge for her to separate from the things that were necessary. She knew that, at some point, getting over the death of her dad would not last forever. The more she thought about him, the more she mourned over the loss. Savannah found herself slipping into a slight depression where she cried herself to sleep.

The visions were more vivid than usual, and this time around, she was seeing her paternal grandfather. In these dreams, he was terminally ill, and he wanted to see her. What made these events so interesting was the fact that she had not talked to or seen her grandfather since losing her dad. It had come to the point that the spirit of the Lord was so intense that she had to act on it. At this time, she could feel the sorrow, loss, and grief from her grandfather, but there was something else more prominent. There was a sense of urgency, and it could not wait another minute. So she planned a trip to Virginia Beach to get a better understanding of what God wanted her to know. For the next few days, as she prepared, she continued to have visions and the same strong feeling that something was not right. The day of the trip, she cried from the moment she rose from her bed and on the entire four hours it took to arrive. Bryson wanted to check into the hotel before heading over to her grandfather's home.

When they checked in to their room, she could not leave the car and she began to cry uncontrollably. She did not want to enter the room and refused to get out of the car. At some point, they finally arrived at the apartment complex where he lived. Savannah got out of the car with red puffy eyes and a terrible headache from the continuous crying. When they reached the front door, she knocked and waited for it to be opened. There standing in the doorway with an unwelcoming expression on her face was Beverly, who was married to her uncle Milton. Savannah was never fond of her and had always felt a dark karma about her. She entered the apartment to see one of her cousins sitting on the sofa. Brenda, who was married to her grandfather John, was also on the sofa beside him. She was greeted by Brenda with a hug that was welcomed. Savannah asked where her grandfather was and was directed down the hall.

As she turned the corner to walk down the hallway, there was a heavy presence. When she stopped at his bedroom door, he had his arms stretched out toward her. He had been waiting for her arrival, and Savannah embraced him and held him tight while she sobbed. There was no way possible that her grandfather would know that she was coming because she had not told anyone. But like everything else with Savannah, she was led by the spirit. Her grandfather talked about receiving visits from her dad that had been dead for more than six months. This did not frighten her because events like this had happened to her personally in the past. As he went on about leaving this world, he asked her to pray with him, and she did without hesitation. He also spoke about missing her dad and wanting to be with him.

The two talked for what felt like hours, but she knew that he was growing tired and weaker. She said her goodbyes and hugged him one last time before leaving. Savannah entered the living room where she left Bryson with the rest of the family. It was such a relief because she made it in time to say goodbye. It was not long after she had returned home to get the call that he had passed. The following weekend, she returned for a small funeral that was given to honor him. Savannah was filled with so much grief with the loss of her dad and grandfather. When she thought that things were beginning to look better, it all went downhill. She had fallen into the depression stage again, calling out from work past bereavement.

One morning, while still asleep, she was shown a vision of her grandfather when she was a toddler. The visions were vivid of her grandfather with her dad and uncles laughing and talking. She was seeing things that took place that she could not have known about. Then she felt a light touch on her face and heard him say thank you for the memories. Savannah continued to lie in bed with covers over her head. She wanted to grieve, but that was not going to be an option or choice for her to make. Savannah was alone in the house that morning because Isaiah had already caught his school bus. Bryson was en route to dropping Mason off at this middle school across town. As she continued to lie there in self-pity and fully awake, there was a presence in the room with her. But she was determined not to get out of bed.

Then something happened that she was not expecting. The sheet that was covering her was abruptly removed, as if someone held each corner with force. She knew that no one else was in the house as the sheet laid back over her. From that moment, Savannah felt that her dad was telling her to get out of bed and live her life. She sat up in the bed, trying to focus on what had just happened. Bryson was just returning from dropping off Mason as she heard the front door close and his keys placed on the table. Savannah climbed out of bed to go greet him, and he was pleased to see her up and about. She sat at the kitchen table with him to eat the breakfast he had picked up on the way home. He asked how she feels and if there was anything he could do to make it better. She reluctantly answered because she was unsure how he would feel if she told him about her experience that morning. So she responded that everything was fine and that she felt good enough to return to work the next day. He asked if she was sure and that there was no rush. Savannah expressed that she had to get back to a normal life and become active again. Later that evening, as she read her Bible, Savannah realized that the answers to her questions were there. She had to rekindle the relationship she had with

God. He never stopped communicating with her even while she was grieving. There were many questions on the table, and she desired a fast-track lesson.

One chapter that piqued her interest in the Bible was Revelations, which some fear because it speaks of dark things to come. She wanted to understand the mark of the beast and how to recognize a false prophet. These things were extremely important to her because of the past supernatural experiences in her life. Savannah was prepared to seek God in a way that she had never in her life. The lessons began around 11:00 p.m. every night for a week. She would be in bed with her Bible open with a notepad and pen to record passages. Savannah anointed herself with consecrated oil each night while preparing to receive God's Word. It was only the middle of the week, and she studied until six the next morning.

At some point, she would drift off to sleep, and like clockwork, she would feel a warm tingle up her leg and the light in her room brightened. When she looked down at her Bible, it was like she never lost her place. By Friday, she was driving to work when she heard a voice tell her that he would always be there and never leave her. When she pulled into the parking lot, she gave God the praise because she heard him and trusted the path he laid out for her. She knew that he had something big planned for her. In the next several months, God had been using her in a way that led her to people in need. It had been recognized that she was a vessel of God.

There were events where she dreamed visions and they came to pass. Now people in the church had their opinions, and some judged harshly. She had to deal with ridicule from members in the church, along with some not believing that God was manifesting in her. Some called her a prophet and others were afraid that God had revealed something about them to her. The only thing that Savannah recognized was that although she was imperfect, God had chosen her to be blessed with an abundance of gifts. She knew that he was not done with her yet.

Part 3

Chapter 34

Fifteen years had passed and they had been married over thirty years. The boys were young men now and have completed their journeys in college. Isaiah was in the Air Force now, and Mason was working in his field of information technology. They could not be prouder of their sons and the path they were on. All was well in the family as Savannah had started her own business, and it was doing well too. Bryson was also doing well financially at his company, and the family was in a good place. She and Bryson went on more dates every weekend now that they were empty nesters. They also traveled every year to some tropical island, which increased the romance in the relationship.

There were many times they reminisced about how they met in high school. It was always a form of *foreplay*, remembering who was chasing who. He was the popular guy and star athlete, and she was quiet, smart, and known by all her friends as one of the nice girls. She never felt that she was popular, but she had many friends. Savannah had always had boys pursuing her, but she was not ready to date. Sometimes she did think about what her life would be like if she chose the other guy. She accepted that what was meant to be was just that. She never told Bryson about the other guys that were serious about her. There were three to be exact; one of whom was Cameron, longtime friend, then Ronald, just a friendly guy from another neighborhood.

And then there was Colby that was, indeed, aggressive with his intentions, but she did not trust with her heart. The attraction and connection were there, but they were not enough for her to give in to him. Often, she did think about Johnathan and wanted to know if he was doing all right. One night, while lying in bed, they both were talking about old times when they were in high school. He continued to say that she was always a trophy girl, and Savannah would deny it. The two had shared the story with their sons numerous times and the versions differ but with the result being the same. They were high school sweethearts and were reminded of how long it had been. At first it was cute as they teased each other about their pursuers.

Savannah had a moment of truth and tell that night. Bryson had always suspected she had many suitors but really could not confirm. He told her that he did not believe that she was not seeing anyone before him. Savannah vowed never to kiss and tell, not even her best friends. So as the conversation continued, she finally confessed that Colby was the person of interest. He asked if she had ever kissed him, and she reluctantly admitted that he was her first. Bryson did not believe her and kept pushing for more information. She did not want to hurt him because he already knew what her answers would be. He just had to hear them for himself. She asked him about past high school girlfriends, but he would never admit or deny who he was involved with before her. He kept pressuring now about anyone else, and she told him there really was not anyone serious.

In his mind, he always thought Johnathan was closer to her than she would admit. These were the games they played with each other and laughed about it. For some reason, he was feeling a little jealous although it had been over thirty years since high school. He went as far as to ask if she had feelings for these guys. She admitted that there were some sort of feelings for Johnathan but expressed they were young, and she never told him. After a while, she wanted to stop with the interrogation because it was headed down the wrong road. But he wanted to ask one more question and would not let it go. He asked if she kissed Colby the same as him on their first date. Savannah did not want to answer that question because she knew that he would not be happy with the answer. It really did not matter because it was over thirty years ago, and she ultimately chose him instead. She said yes and that they were in the beginning stages of exploring a possible relationship.

And as she expected, he had an attitude and did not want to talk anymore that night. Savannah had finally put that part of her life to bed, and now he had opened Pandora's box. A couple weeks later, all was forgotten, and they were in the car driving through the shopping center down the street from the house. Savannah was driving, and he was on the passenger side. As she was coming to a stop before proceeding, Bryson yelled out to her and pointed backward as she drove off. She asked him why he was pointing and making a fuss. He said, "There is your old boyfriend" as she drove past several stores in the outlet. She did not show any interest and did not ask who the person would be. Bryson could not keep that to himself as he stated it was Colby. She replied with a nonchalant attitude, reiterating the point that he was not an old boyfriend and continued her journey. Why would he continue to push that issue? He should not have any insecurities at this point in their relationship.

The past was what it was and should remain there. She had left those memories where they belonged—a *memory*. Savannah dismissed all of it and continued with her day. It had been a few weeks later and that nagging feeling reappeared as she trolled through her Facebook account. She thought that those feelings of the past had been suppressed in her memories. Savannah never wanted them to surface again, but that trip down memory lane a few days ago triggered her curiosity. While surfing the internet one evening, she googled his name Johnathan. The return generated numerous people with the same first and last name.

What was she doing? This was insane and reaching too far into the past, and it was dangerous. But the temptation was overwhelming as she tried to fight the urges of finding him. It had been more than thirty years since she saw him last, standing in her living room with disappointment and hurt all over his face. Now she had reached the point of no return. She was able to locate where he was currently living. The powers of the internet, what an invention. You can find anyone or anything if you put the time and effort into it. Great, she found him but could not confirm unless she laid eyes on him.

This was extremely bold and risky with the thoughts that flooded her brain of doing the unthinkable. She was contemplating conducting her own investigation and track him on her own. But the insanity switch shut off at the right moment, saving her from making another big mistake. She had not seen this person in decades and did not know if he was a crazy person, murderer, or worse.

So she killed that idea of momentary insanity and went a safer route, Facebook. Savannah began her friend search on Facebook and could not come up with anything. She used his nickname Clay. Still nothing, and for days she checked and no return on the search. Savannah thought to herself that it must not have been meant to be as it was all those years ago. But with her can-do personality, it was not going to be an easy quit on the mission. So she waited another week and tried again using his full legal name, and bingo, there was a match. She was so excited as she opened his profile to sneak a peek at his life. This was her moment. What did she have to lose? She did it, pushed the friend request button, holding her breath and then releasing as it sat in a request sent status. When she thought the universe could not be any stranger, it proved to be accurate with timing. Savannah decided to stop by the bargain discount store one evening after work. She had only visited the store maybe three times since they opened a couple years ago. She took her time to scan every aisle, finding great bargains at a great price. Savannah especially loved the book department mainly because she was a total book guru.

Reading was one of her favorite things to do from the time she was a small child. The shopping cart was filling up fast as she stocked up on scented air sprays and household cleaners. Before she realized the time, it had been an hour since she first entered the store. She proceeded to the front of the store to check out. While she stood in line, checking her phone for messages, she looked up to see him walking through the door. She had not laid eyes on him in decades, and her heart raced. A tingling feeling rushed from her head down to the pit of her stomach. She could not take her eyes off him as he passed through the door with an employee uniform on. Savannah was shaking as she moved forward to the register to pay for her items.

Why was she experiencing these things over someone she had not seen in so many years?

Yes, they had a past, but she did not feel that it was significant enough to make her react the way she did. As she drove home, the images of his face continued to haunt her. Later that night, as she lay in bed, trying to make some sense out of it was a challenge. The one thing she did feel that would bring some closure was to face her mountain. She decided to make another trip to the store over the weekend, hoping to run into him. The first time she saw him, he did not know that she was in the store and probably would not have remembered her. At some point, would Savannah realize a pattern with her behavior? She was very much married to her first boyfriend, but why did she feel like something was missing? It clearly was not appropriate to feel something for another no matter if there was history. Maybe there was some weird unresolved emotional attachment. She could feel the pull and could not control it. It was Saturday morning, and as usual, she started her day with her weekly 9:30 a.m. hair appointment. She had a stand-in appointment every year at the same time.

The salon was busy as always with the waiting room filled with clients and some children. She assumed that most of them did not have babysitters, so that would be one of the reasons for them being there. Savannah would carry on with her weekly routine, sitting in Trevaughn's chair as he created a masterpiece. He had been her hairstylist for many years, and she trusted him. There was always the usual chairside gossip that she never wanted to take part in but often was amused with how the other stylist interacted. Savannah would always have that "hear no, speak no, and see no evil" attitude. She did love Trevaughn very much as a friend and respected him the same.

The appointment would last about one and half hours, and then she was off to her next errand for the day. The next stop would be the dry cleaners and then to the bargain discount store, but this visit had a specific purpose. She had a fresh haircut and style and was feeling extra appealing that day. Entering the store, which was always filled to the brim, grabbing a shopping cart to make her rounds, she perused through the bedding and linens department, searching for new decor for her bedroom. Savannah took her time because she wanted to select the perfect ensemble. But the true reason for such a lengthy lingering was in hopes of seeing Colby. At last, she saw him as she was traveling down one of the aisles. She passed him but did not speak in hopes that he would recognize her first. As she passed, their eyes met but no verbal exchange of words. She continued thinking, *Why he would not speak?* Or maybe he just did not remember her. She found this to be strange and could not understand why. Most people from her neighborhood or past friendships would acknowledge one another and have a happy brief reunion. She did not want to read too much into it, but it was too late. Maybe he did remember and chose not to acknowledge her for his own personal reasons.

Once she completed her shopping and made it to the front checkout, she saw him again at one of the registers. Savannah tried not to make eye contact as she chose another register to check out from. She could hear him talking to the customers as he checked them out. After completing her errands, she returned home to do her weekend house chores. She could not get him out of her mind and played it over again of a better way of handling it. The weekend was over, and it was Monday morning already. The workday began the heavy traffic in the interstate as she drove into work. She always tried to leave a bit early to beat the high school traffic right by her job. Some days she was lucky, and then there were those days that could not be avoided. The workday went well at the office as she caught up with her coworkers about one another's weekend. She had an executive assistant position, which demanded a lot of her time and attention to detail. Savannah supported the chief of staff and director of the hospital, which granted her with great responsibilities.

With many projects going on throughout the week, she nearly had time to focus on anything else. Finally, Friday had arrived, and she could not wait for some downtime. She lay in bed a little late on Saturday morning, trying to steal that last couple hours before her day began. The alarm on her phone went off exactly 6:00 a.m. as she continued to hit the snooze button up until 7:00 a.m. Savannah just wanted to lie in bed all day, but she knew better with the laundry list of things to be done. She rolled over to the nightstand, reaching for her phone as it pinged, announcing she had a message. With eyes half closed and fuzzy from the needed sleep, she managed to grab the phone. She sat up in the bed with a quickness and disbelief.

It could not be as she tried to widen her eyes to adjust to the light in the room, opening her Facebook page to find an acceptance of a friend request to Johnathan (Clay), his nickname that she always called him, filling her with excitement. It had been decades since she seen him last, and over the years, she often thought about him and if he was doing okay. There were overwhelming emotions that overcame her because she cared about him. Rather, it was just a simple childhood friendship, he was important. Savannah immediately began surfing through his post to find that he was happy, and that pleased her. She messaged him, stating that it was so good to know that he was blessed and doing well. He replied, "Yes, I'm doing my best to be a blessed man, and I'm very proud and happy for you as well."

After chatting briefly about their parents and siblings, they both agreed to keep in touch. Savannah shared with Bryson that she had heard from Clay through Facebook and was happy that he was doing well. She also talked to him about giving her support to him as a friend. Bryson listened, but she knew that he was not in agreement with it. She assured him that he was no threat to their relationship. The two kept their promise to stay in touch with each other.

For the next few weeks, they talked about their lives, and he shared a significant and private part of his life. She did not pass judgment and said that God takes us down a path for a specific reason. She told him that it did not change the way that she felt about him. He spoke about the additional changes in his life and accepting Christ. She commended him for sharing and being transparent. True friends should always stand by one another no matter the situation. We all sometimes fall from grace, but God always has his hands upon us with his mercy. They prayed for each other and their families. He also talked to her about his current relationship, expressing that he was in love with this woman and wanted to marry her. It felt like a heavy weight had been lifted off her shoulders. She knew that he was okay and that everything was going to be all right with him.

Savannah no longer had unfinished business, and the feelings she thought were there were no more than the love of a lost friendship. Clay thanked her often for continuing to be a true supportive friend to him without judgment. There was still one more elephant in the room—his name was Colby, and it was not going away. Savannah continued to feel the emotional pull every time she patrolled the store.

One Saturday, she entered the store to find him restocking shelves. She was in the household supply aisle, searching for cleaning supplies. Savannah felt his presence as she was kneeling to reach a product from the lower shelf. When she stood up, he was there and spoke to her. She returned the courtesy of speaking back with a happy greeting and smile. The two were very cordial to each other as they caught up. He showed her pictures of his family, and she did the same. He asked about Bryson, and she told him that he was doing good and that they just lived a few blocks up the road. Colby mentioned that he and his wife had been married for twenty-five years. She was happy to say that she and Bryson had been married thirty-one years. Colby responded with "You guys have been together for a long time."

After catching up with each other, she continued her shopping and on to the next errand for the day. Savannah discovered she was in a state of conflict between what was in the past and the reality of the present. She had found herself becoming obsessed with wanting to know about the what-ifs from her past. It was evident that she had made the right choice, but her curiosity continued to burn.

Most have heard the saying "The grass is not always greener on the other side." She did believe it to be true, but something was going on with her heart. So she continued to patrol the store every weekend, and each time she and Colby talked about everything from family to sports. It felt like two old childhood friends rekindling a friendship. But then things started to get weird when she noticed that he was appearing in her dreams. One Saturday morning, she was lying in bed, asleep, and while she was in a dream state, she could sense that he was thinking about her. It was so vivid that she heard him say that he wanted to see her.

Opening her eyes, Savannah replied with no hesitation to his request, saying, "Okay." This was no surprise based on her past gifts of communicating with others supernaturally. It most likely would not be the last of these events. She rose to her feet and headed to the shower, bathed, and got dressed before making her way out to the store. When she arrived in the parking lot, there was a busy stream of people entering the store.

The day seemed to be busier than ever as she walked in to find Colby at the front of the store, grabbing a shopping cart and proceeding to peruse the floor. He approached her to say that he was hoping she would come to the store today. With curiosity written all over her face, she responded with a sarcastic reply that put him on guard. In her mind, she continued to repeat that this must come to a stop for both of their sake. Although there was no apparent violation of their friendship or individual marriages, it was a recipe for a catastrophic disaster. Savannah had to confess to herself that after all those years she was still emotionally and physically attracted to him. The prize-winning question that loomed over her head was if she had some unresolved feelings for him. The one thing she did believe was that she would never act on those feelings if it were true. Savannah had made one mistake in her marriage and was not going down that road again.

Later that week, she was downstairs exercising on her elliptical, listening to her music. She was alone in the house that night because Bryson was already on the road. As she was getting a good workout, there was a presence upon her. She could sense his thoughts, and it was so overpowering she could hardly stay on her machine. Pausing to step down onto the floor, it continued to be so tremendous she had to lean over one of the chairs to catch herself. He was in her head now; this was not the first time she had experienced someone physically as well. It was like every nerve in her body was electrified times ten and then some. Why was she feeling like this? There had to be a sensible explanation, and she did not have the answer. When she thought it would get better, she was proven wrong. She found herself at the store again later that week. Although she did not see him right away, she felt his presence as she walked behind her shopping cart. It was unbelievable that as she walked, that same strong urge was upon her greater than ever.

All she could think about was enough was enough! If she did not make a drastic change in her behavior, she felt in her soul that she was headed into a brick wall at a hundred miles per hour. Savannah was sure that she was not imagining any of this. Maybe it was all on her, but she had to stop herself. All she could figure was that something in the universe had a magnetic pull on her.

She needed to be saved from herself, and God was the answer. Savannah continued to remind herself that she was happy with her life and would not trade it for another. She did not understand why she was being tested in her relationship now. Savannah asked herself, "What is the purpose or reason?" God had wiped her slate clean. She believed that any suppressed feelings or memories from her past was just that: a memory, null and void. She honestly believed that she was being spiritually attacked from things that were not of God.

Chapter 35

Savannah understood that the choices she made under her own free will can be detrimental or can be some form of redemption. Savannah believes that God allows free will, but what one do with it determines their path. She knows that God's grace and mercy steps in to protect her from herself. Savannah believes it is necessary so that she may learn from her mistakes. Some may say that it is growth spurt in which no one is exempt. There are plenty of Savannahs, Bryson, and Colbys in the world. The fact remains the same that no one is perfect and can vouch for not walking the straight and narrow path indefinitely. Savannah had to face the music when she got home. Bryson had gotten up from his morning nap after getting in off the road the night before.

The two had their normal flirty conversations as usual, but things took a left turn. He admitted that he was not in favor of her friendships with Johnathan and Colby. She had been honest with him months ago about her and Colby prior to them meeting in high school. It was pointed out that she was in a relationship with Colby and broke it off with him to be with Bryson. Savannah tried to discount it as boyish jealousy and asked him to get over it. The sparks started flying after that statement as Bryson grew angry, and the boom in his voice accompanied his reaction. He was upset that she had reached out to them and that he did not like it. This turned into a full-blown argument where he brought up her indiscretions years ago. It felt like a sharp knife had cut her deep in the heart. The excruciating pain in his eyes caused the memories to come rushing back.

For the first time ever, he stated that they never dealt with the truth. He asked why he was not enough as he broke down in tears and sobbing uncontrollably. She had not felt pain like that come from him and found herself comforting him and promising that he was everything to her. What was swept under the rug had come out in its full rage. She could not breathe as she found herself lying on the living room floor, asking for forgiveness. Savannah later heard footsteps, and it was Bryson kneeling beside her. The two went into instant prayer, and the spirit of the Holy Ghost fell upon them. This was their spiritual cleanse and redemption of all the things in their marriage and relationship that were broken. Savannah felt his arms around her as he told her to look up and over to their family picture. The blinds and curtains were closed, and there was a bright light shining on their family. When she witnessed this event, it only pushed her over the top as she lost all control of her emotions. All had been forgiven, and at that moment, the two touched and agreed that from that day forward, it was done. When God forgives and forgets, then as children of God, they must do the same.

The unresolved issues in their relationship were complete and null and void. It does not matter how long one has been in a relationship. Whether five years or thirty-five years, it does not mean that it is perfect. The challenge is surviving those years with all the bumps and bruises that come with emotional and personal losses. Savannah prayed that God would remove the magnetic pull of things that were not of him out of her life and he did just that. All was well again, and their relationship was stronger than ever. The two began to make long-term plans for change in their relationship and future. They each were sent on a spiritual journey for approximately two years, leaving them to trust God entirely. Look at God! He blesses the imperfections of those to be gifted and chosen.

About the Author

Sonia Anderson is a native of a small metropolitan area of southwestern Virginia and married with two adult sons and firstborn grandson and the author of *Imperfections but Gifted and Chosen.* Writing this novel opened a door to an unimaginable height, which presented itself with the opportunities to inspire and mentor. She graduated from Liberty University with master's degrees in management and leadership and human services counseling: marriage and family. When she is not engrossed in her writing, Sonia loves to create mouthwatering recipes and build and repair projects with her handy power tools.

Even with all the hustle and bustle, she still finds the time to afford her attention to others, narrating stories about her life to lead the imagination of her listeners as they are captured in the moment. She honestly believes that life lessons are the greatest tools for educating and presenting opportunities for one to evaluate their current circumstance. She also believes that, in time, our efforts are proven to force our accountability in which redemption and new beginnings are eminent. Sonia defies the rumors of all work and no play when she takes these spontaneous trips to the Caribbean or deciding to throw a Hawaiian luau for her close friends and family just because.

She laughs at her own corky anecdotes and is a fool for reading a great sci-fi novel and even better taking in a movie thriller. Most of all, she enjoys the infectious laughter and smiles of her close family and friends.

CPSIA information can be obtained
at www.ICGtesting.com
Printed in the USA
LVHW051525240622
722062LV00004B/138

9 781637 105184